Problem-oriented Policing and Partnerships

Crime Science Series

Series editor: Gloria Laycock

Published titles

Superhighway Robbery, by Graeme R. Newman and Ronald V. Clarke
Crime Reduction and Problem-oriented Policing, by Karen Bullock and Nick Tilley
Crime Science: new approaches to preventing and detecting crime, edited by Melissa J. Smith and Nick Tilley
Problem-oriented Policing and Partnerships, by Karen Bullock, Rosie Erol and Nick Tilley

Problem-oriented Policing and Partnerships

Implementing an evidence-based approach to crime reduction

Karen Bullock, Rosie Erol and Nick Tilley

WILLAN
PUBLISHING

Published by

Willan Publishing
Culmcott House
Mill Street, Uffculme
Cullompton, Devon
EX15 3AT, UK
Tel: +44(0)1884 840337
Fax: +44(0)1884 840251
e-mail: info@willanpublishing.co.uk
website: www.willanpublishing.co.uk

Published simultaneously in the USA and Canada by

Willan Publishing
c/o ISBS, 920 NE 58th Ave, Suite 300,
Portland, Oregon 97213-3786, USA
Tel: +001(0)503 287 3093
Fax: +001(0)503 280 8832
e-mail: info@isbs.com
website: www.isbs.com

Hardback
ISBN-13: 978-1-84392-139-4
ISBN-10: 1-84392-139-1
British Library Cataloguing-in-Publication Data

A catalogue record for this book is available from the British Library

Project managed by Deer Park Productions, Tavistock, Devon
Typeset by GCS, Leighton Buzzard, Bedfordshire, LU7 1AR
Printed and bound by T.J. International Ltd, Padstow, Cornwall

Contents

Figures, tables and boxes

Figures

Tables

Boxes

Acknowledgements

Whilst we have to accept the blame for remaining errors, omissions and misunderstandings, we should like to thank the following people for substantially reducing the number there would otherwise be. In one or two cases they have been brutal but at the same time have saved us from major embarrassments: our private pain has been preferable to the public humiliation we would otherwise have faced for some of the errors our generous readers uncovered for us.

We are grateful to: Lesley Duff for comments on Chapters 6 and 7; Niall Hamilton-Smith for comments on Chapter 3; Barrie Irving for comments on Chapter 3; Andy Feist for comments on Chapter 3; Shane Johnson for comments on Chapter 5; Gloria Laycock for comments on Chapters 1–4; Sandra Nutley for comments on Chapter 7; Paul Quinton for comments on Chapter 6; Tim Read for comments on Chapters 1–2; Mike Scott for comments on Chapter 4; and Rachel Tuffin for comments on Chapter 6.

We are indebted to Johannes Knutsson, who kindly read and commented on the whole volume at short notice as we approached the deadline for submitting the complete manuscript. Nick's wife Jenny went way beyond what can reasonably be hoped of any spouse by also patiently reading the whole thing through and tactfully highlighting a number of weaknesses in style and continuity.

We would also like to thank the Police Standards Unit and the Government Office for the West Midlands for their support of the Jill Dando Institute Crime Science Laboratory during the preparation of part of this work.

We owe a particular debt of gratitude to the chief constables, officers and civilian staff of Hampshire and Lancashire Constabularies for facilitating this research and giving up their time to speak to us. Special thanks go to Chief Superintendent Mike Barton, Inspector Keith McGroary and Constable Steve Postlethwaite for organising the interviews and focus groups and for their generous hospitality.

Finally, research of the kind reported here depends on the willingness of those spoken to to give up their time and to talk openly and thoughtfully to curious strangers. We have benefited from the apparent candour and commitment of those we met. Without them there would have been no book to write!

Karen Bullock
Rosie Erol
Nick Tilley

Chapter 1

Introduction: problem-oriented approaches to crime reduction and policing

This book is about attempts to introduce problem-oriented policing in Britain. Its virtues as an ideal are largely taken for granted. No critique of the concept is included here. Instead, our concern is with its implementation, both organisationally and in specific local initiatives to address identified crime and other problems. In looking at the implementation of problem-oriented policing we are concerned especially with three issues.

First, we look systematically at what is regarded as amongst the best problem-oriented work in Britain in order to distil what has been learned for others who choose to introduce the approach in areas over which they have responsibility, or who wish to undertake specific problem-oriented pieces of work. In connection with this aim we also discuss methods in problem-oriented initiatives that have so far been used rather little in the UK but may be useful in making improvements on what has been achieved so far. For these purposes, we hope that the book will be used by police managers, officials with responsibility for policing, police practitioners and analysts in police services as well as other practitioners concerned with crime and disorder.

Second, we provide case studies of efforts to bring change to the style and methods of policing in the UK. This, we hope, may be of interest to students and members of the academic community concerned with policing. The police are self-evidently an important and influential social institution, responding to our problems and endowed with powers that may significantly affect our lives. The drivers of police priorities and methods are important. The hindrances and opportunities for change and innovation within policing provide, we think, some insight into the nature of contemporary policing.

Third, though the thinking behind problem-oriented policing goes back more than a quarter of a century, its emphasis on evidence-based policy and practice (EBPP) resonates with much more recent thinking in Britain about the ways in which public services should operate. This book has, we hope, something useful to say about some determined and quite sustained efforts to turn this into a reality. Academics, who as observers wish to understand attempts to undertake EBPP, and policy-makers and practitioners, who wish realistically to implement EBPP, will, we hope find material of interest here, even though some of the issues we focus on will be specific to policing and partnership work, and all the examples are police-specific.

This examination of the implementation of problem-oriented policing brings out many obstacles, disappointments and doubts about the existing achievements of and future prospects for problem-oriented, evidence-based policing and practice. Notwithstanding this we continue to think that the vision of problem-oriented policing and partnership in particular and EBPP more generally is admirable, but are left with a more jaundiced view of the practicalities.

There is a risk of naïve utopianism to which this volume should act as a corrective. This, we think, is no reason to abandon the aspiration to reform and we are left in some awe of those many individuals who have had the determination and guts to fight their way through the thickets and thickheads they have encountered as they have sought to change policing and the lives of those whose problems they have helped solve or assuage.

The concepts, relevance and implementation in the UK

Problem-oriented policing has become increasingly important in crime reduction policy and practice. The approach has been adopted explicitly in a growing number of police services and partnerships in the UK and is used in an *ad hoc* or implicit way in many more. The basic idea, *the application of scientific principles to tackling crime and disorder problems*, resonates with a range of new developments in crime reduction and policing. On a wider level it also resonates strongly with the push towards Evidence Based Policy and Practice which has become increasingly important in discussions of policy and practice. Specific key changes in policing and partnership include the increased focus on intelligence-led approaches, research and analysis and in particularly the requirements of the 1998 Crime and Disorder Act and the National Intelligence Model. The ideas also feature heavily in recent Home Office policy, and plans for the implementation of neighbourhood and community policing models (see the 2004 White Paper *Building Communities, Beating Crime* and the 2005–08 National Policing Plan).

This introductory chapter describes the basic principles of problem-oriented policing and the language that is associated with it. It examines the case for change in the police service and the rise of the problem-oriented approach. Finally, it sets out the purpose of, methodology for, and structure of, the rest of the book.

The basic principles: what is problem-oriented policing and how do you do it?

An American professor and former adviser to O.W. Wilson when he reformed Chicago's police department, Herman Goldstein, first described the principles of problem-oriented policing in a 1979 article and later in a book published in 1990. Goldstein was critical of the way that the police service concentrated on organisational efficiency to the detriment of focusing on its core outcome: reducing problems of concern to local people. Goldstein (1990) stated that a problem-oriented police service would be characterised by the following:

1 Focus on the wide range of community concerns that the public expects the police to deal with, including troublesome groups, individuals and places.

2 Concentration on effectiveness in reducing, eliminating, better handling or lessening the impact of problems.

3 Pro-activity, based on careful enquiry, both in the early identification of problems and in the formulation of suggestions as to ways in which the police, community, and other agencies, might better handle them in the future.

4 Dis-aggregation of incidents that are normally lumped together in the broad, generic crime-type categories used by criminal justice agencies, into distinctive separately identifiable problems.

5 Commitment to systematic enquiry as the first step in solving problems: grouping together incidents and probing them for

common attributes and common conditions, such as place, time, people involved, the physical environment, causes, motivations, and methods; identifying the range of interests in the problem; interrogating, documenting and critically examining existing responses; and moving beyond the pooling and analysis of information simply to improve detection.

6 A broad, uninhibited and imaginative quest for tailor-made solutions to individual police-related problems, rather than dependence solely on standard tactics of arrest and prosecution through the criminal justice system.

7 Higher levels of accountability through the use of transparent evidence-based grounds for problem-focus and response, community involvement and improved community understanding of what the police can and cannot do.

8 Acceptance by police and others that efforts to address problems involve risk-taking where standard methods are ineffective, and alternative, ethical methods are attempted in relation to hitherto intractable problems.

9 Routine, skilful, methodologically informed and, ideally, independent evaluation of the effectiveness of innovative methods of addressing problems, to avoid replacing one ineffective response with another and to learn lessons for future practice and to check that existing methods continue to be effective.

10 Encouragement of rigorous methods in making enquiries.

11 Full use of police skills and expertise.

12 Acknowledgement of the limitations of the criminal justice system in responding to problems.

13 Identification of the multiple interests in a problem and attendance to them when valuing different responses.

Problem-oriented policing in practice

Problem-oriented policing suggests four processes through which problems should be tackled: problem identification; problem understanding; the development of responses; and evaluation. These can be briefly elaborated as follows.

Problem identification and understanding

Problem identification involves the systematic grouping of recurring incidents, recognising that there are links between incidents, and an attempt to understand how and why these sets of incidents arise. A problem should involve a group or set of related incidents, not a random collection of disconnected events. Most important, they should comprise matters of concern to the public that are relevant to the police function.

A tight definition and detailed breakdown of each problem is essential for the purposes of problem-oriented policing, as broad legalistic definitions of crime can hide what could be a variety of different problems, which manifest themselves in different ways and which would ultimately require different responses to deal with them.

Goldstein pointed to the use of police recorded statistics as a starting point for analysing problems, though he acknowledges the limitations of them. Police officers should seek to understand a problem through looking at it in detail. They should be thinking about what is already known about a problem. This involves reviewing existing research and other evidence, and making an assessment about whether more needs to be learnt about the problem. Officers also need to analyse, understand and critically assess the nature of current responses to problems.

Response development and evaluation

Responses to identified problems should be tailor-made to the explanations of why that problem exists. Goldstein did not believe that effective responses necessarily have to address the 'root causes' of problems. Rather, attention should be focused on a specific aspect of the problem seemingly amenable to intervention. In particular he thought that the police service should be looking to expand its responses beyond its normal remit of law enforcement. He argued that the police service is overwhelmingly concerned with its authority to enforce the law and that this view has impacted on the way that the police operate. Policing should be about seeking the best way to develop responses to a whole range of problems and in many cases this need not be law enforcement. Police officers need to recognise their role as more than enforcement of the criminal law. Even if the police do not directly provide what may be needed to deal with a problem, for example youth diversion services, they should recognise the role that those services can play in reducing crime and hence work in partnership with other organisations. In any case, Goldstein argues, it is unlikely that an effective way of dealing with a problem will consist of a single type of response. It is more likely that a range of interventions will have the greatest impact. Attempts should also be made to review existing literature and other evidence to inform interventions.

The new response should be monitored and evaluated to ensure that one ineffective response is not merely replaced with another. This will also guard against a response simply reverting to its older form. The extent of the evaluation would have to be variable, as the size and extent of the problems varies.

So, simplifying a range of issues identified here, there are basically four main processes underpinning problem-oriented policing as shown in Figure 1.1. This figure draws on the SARA process described by Eck and Spelman (1987). SARA refers to Scanning, Analysis, Response and Assessment. It is presented here as a cycle, rather than a linear process, as it is sometimes shown, in order to convey the importance attached in problem-oriented policing to feedback and to continuous attention in order that new problems are addressed and old methods checked and modified where necessary.

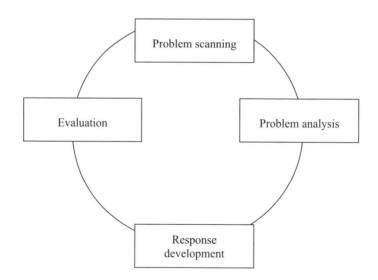

Figure 1.1 The main processes underpinning problem-oriented policing

The language of the problem-oriented approach

The language used to describe problem-oriented policing varies in ways where the significance will become increasingly clear throughout this book.

Problem-orientation and problem solving

The term 'problem solving' is widely used in UK policing, partly as a matter of taste. The link between Goldstein and problem-orientation is usually acknowledged (Read and Tilley 2000) and the models associated with the implementation of problem-oriented policing (SARA, PAT, RAT and so on: see Chapter 5 for explanations) are usually used to focus problem-solving work.

However, the difference in language is not without substantive significance. Problem-orientation, as we have described it, is about the systematic grouping of recurring incidents as problems and looking for the links between them to understand why they arise, the formulation of responses that are tailor-made to explanations of why problems recur (and which for the most part go beyond police enforcement), and evaluation of the effectiveness of the measures put in place. As we shall see in later chapters this presents a considerable challenge for the police service. In practice, much that is described as problem-oriented policing falls short of this ideal and is indeed better described as 'problem-solving' as some scholars have come to understand that term.

Clarke (1998) uses 'problem-solving' to refer to efforts to tackle fairly small-scale problems, such as the activities of one offender, noise nuisance associated with one house or late-night violence associated with a particular nightclub. Moreover, in problem-solving, as compared to problem-oriented work, there is less systematic analysis, responses are less likely to be rooted in that analysis and evaluation is either not undertaken at all or is cursory.

Problem-oriented policing and problem-oriented partnership

Goldstein used the term 'problem-oriented policing' to describe his approach to addressing problems. However, as we have already seen, Goldstein intended that problem-orientation would involve a search for the best response to a problem, whether or not the police could deliver it. For this reason there is a strong implication that the resources of other agencies will often need to be drawn in to adequately address a problem. More recently, in the UK, the term 'problem-oriented partnership' has come to be preferred by many to 'problem-oriented policing'. The change in term in part reflects the general move towards partnership begun with Home Office Circular 8/84 and now put on a statutory footing by the 1998 Crime and Disorder Act. It serves to reinforce the view that solving community problems is generally beyond the competence of the police service alone and to emphasise the importance of engaging partners. Nevertheless, in practice what is undertaken in the name of problem-oriented partnership is ordinarily led by the police and the term 'partnership' is used as a device for engaging others.

The terms 'problem-oriented policing' and 'problem-oriented partnership' are used somewhat interchangeably in practice in the UK as indeed they are in this volume.

Crime versus non-crime problems

Goldstein is clear about what types of problem should be addressed by a problem-oriented approach: *any* that is identified as a cause of community concern and leads to demand for a police response. The cover of Goldstein's book lists some of the wide range of possible examples, including: landlord-tenant disputes, intimidation by gangs, drug sales in or near schools, loud stereos, child sex abuse, residential burglary, offensive odours, hit-and-run drivers, noisy parties, spousal abuse, robbery of cab drivers, abandoned vehicles, protection of controversial speakers, shoplifting, gangland slayings, elderly abuse, fortified crack houses, graffiti, auto theft, street prostitution, muggings, barking dogs, bank hold-ups, racially motivated assaults, abandoned children, reckless driving, rowdy children hangouts, gay bashing, littering, suicides, false alarms, obscene phone calls, speeding, drug trafficking, kidnapping, witness intimidation, robberies at ATMs, bar fights, fencing stolen goods, drink-drivers, insurance fraud, fear of using parks, bomb threats, bicycle theft, drownings, terrorism, sexual assault, medical emergencies and so on. Some are crime-related, some not. Some are serious, others less so.

In a book written before he coined the term problem-oriented policing Goldstein had argued that policing should be construed as an 'agency of municipal government' in order: to indicate that policing should be seen not solely as part of the criminal justice system; to signify that the police function is to deal with what the community has defined as problems using the best means available not simply through enforcement of the law; to indicate that non-crime issues should not be seen as peripheral; and to challenge 'the widely held belief that dealing with crime is the sole function of the police' (Goldstein 1977: 33). At the same time he suggested eight main functions into which the business of policing could be put:

1 To prevent and control behaviour that threatens life and property.
2 To help people who are in danger of physical harm.
3 To protect constitutional rights and guarantees.
4 To facilitate the movement of people and traffic.
5 To help those (such as the drunk, old or mentally disturbed) not able to care for themselves.
6 To manage interpersonal and inter-group conflicts, including those with government.
7 To spot embryonic problems that may become more serious.
8 To create and maintain a feeling of security in the community.

What is significant here is that these are not framed in terms of the criminal law and that they describe the ends, not the means.

Goldstein builds on this in his later work. He stresses that the real challenge of problem-oriented policing is the search for the most effective way of dealing with an identified problem (Goldstein 1990). He makes the search for alternatives to enforcing the law an integral part of policing, and he stresses that non-crime as well as crime problems fall within the remit of the police. So, for Goldstein, a problem need not be a crime problem and an adequate response need not be delivered by the police.

The case for change in the police service and the rise of the problem-oriented approach

The case for change towards problem-orientation in the police service comes from three main sources: research evidence; frustrations within the police service; and a wider government concern with modernising public services.

Goldstein (1990) draws on a range of research to argue that the standard police responses to problems, such as motorised patrols and a fast response to incidents, have been largely ineffective. There is also evidence to suggest that problem-oriented policing can reduce specific crime problems. Reviews of what works in policing and crime reduction have concluded that problem-oriented policing generally is promising as a means of crime reduction (Sherman *et al.* 1998; Weisburd and Eck 2004). There are also many localised examples showing how problems have been reduced where problem-oriented policing principles are adopted to tackle them (see The Centre for Problem-oriented Policing, www.popcenter.org for examples).

Many practitioners are keen to provide a better service for the public. As a community-focused approach stressing effectiveness, problem-oriented policing appears attractive to them. Furthermore, there has been an explosion in calls for service from the police without corresponding increases in the number of police officers (Tilley 1999). Police services are being forced to find means of reducing demand on their resources, and problem-oriented policing appears to offer a viable means of doing so whilst still responding to legitimate public expectations (Kirby and Reed 2004).

Government has become increasingly concerned with modernising the public services. The 1999 *Modernising Government* White Paper stressed, amongst other things, 'forward-looking policy' which would include the identification and spread of best practice, more responsive public services, new targets and monitoring of performance. The White Paper highlights the importance of dealing with real problems, based on causes, not symptoms, and on the measurement of results. It emphasises outcomes, involving others in policy making and accounting for the needs and experiences of a wide variety of people. The roles of evidence, research and assessment of outcomes are all stressed. Similarly, the 2002 Office of Public Services Reform report *Reforming our Public Services: Principles into Practice*, amongst other things, stressed the importance of national standards and tough performance monitoring at the local level; devolution from Whitehall and local flexibility; and the importance of putting the customer first. The modernisation agenda, with its clear focus on evidence, implementation of what works, and evaluation, is strongly associated with Evidence Based Policy and Practice. We return to discuss this in relation to problem-oriented policing in Chapters 6–7.

There have been particular changes affecting the police service specifically, including: the development of devolved budgets and performance management for comparative purposes (Harper *et al.* 2001, 2002; Sheldon *et al.* 2002); best value reviews (Leigh *et al.* 1999); and increased interest in measuring the cost effectiveness of police activity (Stockdale *et al.* 1999; Brand and Price 2000; Stockdale and Whitehead 2003). More particularly the 'police reform' agenda being followed under the Blair government has emphasised: improving the performance of the police service; making policing more flexible through diversity and workforce modernisation; increasing capacity and reducing bureaucracy; training and development; and investing in communications, IT, forensics and best practice (www.policereform. gov.uk).

Whilst several of these developments have not been framed explicitly in terms of problem-oriented policing, they are equal to it. Moreover, there are frequent mentions of problem-orientation in the relevant policy literature, and in guidance documents arising out of the police reform agenda.

The story so far

Owing to the combination of factors described above, interest in introducing problem-oriented policing in the UK has grown rapidly since the mid-1990s and there is now a near consensus that the problem-oriented methodology is a suitable means of addressing problems (Crawford 1998; Read and Tilley 2000). Goldstein (1979) stimulated a number of experiments in police agencies which attempted to put his ideas into practice and triggered debate regarding how best to implement the strategy (Sherman 1992). There is, by now, a relatively long history of problem-oriented policing in the UK and elsewhere (see Chapter 2).

Specific developments fostering interest in problem-oriented policing in the UK have included the following:

1 HM Inspectorate of Constabulary's crime reduction thematic reports (*Beating Crime* 1998, and *Calling Time on Crime* 2000) have explicitly encouraged the adoption of a problem-oriented approach.

2 The Home Office Policing and Reducing Crime Unit report *Not Rocket Science* (2000), which was a supplementary product of the *Calling Time on Crime* HMIC inspection, provided both a review of problem-orientation at the time and some suggestions for ways to improve its implementation.

3 At the practitioner level, the former Home Office Police Research Group demonstration projects in Leicestershire and Cleveland marshalled evidence about and interest in problem-oriented policing (Leigh *et al.* 1996, 1998).

4 The substantial government-funded Crime Reduction Programme provided resources for police services and their partners to

implement problem-oriented principles (see Bullock and Tilley 2003).

5 The national annual problem-oriented partnerships conference part-funded by the Home Office and the Tilley Award scheme (which is linked with the annual problem-oriented partnerships conference) have sought to encourage and disseminate good practice in problem-oriented policing since 1999 (see Chapter 4).

Despite this, implementing problem-oriented policing has proved to be far from trouble-free: commitment is widely stated (Scott 2000; Read and Tilley 2000) but translation of the concepts into reality has proved more problematic. Research relating to problem-oriented policing so far suggests that implementation has been piecemeal, with little mainstreaming and a tendency for specialist units to be responsible for it. There have been mixed successes in terms both of implementation of the concepts and the subsequent impact on crime problems. Chapter 2 discusses this issue in some detail.

About this volume

Chapter 2 reviews efforts over 25 years to implement problem-oriented policing. During this time there have been some key changes in the context of policing and crime reduction that have facilitated interest in problem-oriented policing. Implementation problems nevertheless continue to surface. As will be seen, some are related to the nature of police services and some to more specific technical issues related to analysis and evaluation.

Chapter 3 examines how mainstreaming of problem-oriented policing has been attempted in two police services, Lancashire and Hampshire, which, whilst very different, can be considered to be amongst the UK's very best in terms of the vigour and resources that have gone into it. This chapter looks at the history of the implementation of problem-oriented policing in these forces and describes those factors that appear to support, or still to compromise, its delivery.

Chapter 4 looks at a sample of problem-oriented projects. It presents a thematic overview of a random selection of entries to the UK Tilley Award (1999–2004). As with Chapter 3 it presents what can reasonably be considered the best of UK problem-oriented policing initiatives. We discuss the strengths and weaknesses of the projects and the implications for problem-oriented policing.

Chapter 5 presents a range of tools and techniques that are available to improve the conduct of problem-oriented policing. These cover the main processes: scanning, analysis response and assessment.

Chapter 6 explores the changing context in which problem-oriented policing is being implemented in the UK. We consider the relationship between problem-oriented policing and the government's broad modernisation agenda and especially the move towards Evidence Based Policy and Practice. We also look at the links between problem-oriented policing and developments that are more specific to policing and crime reduction: inter-agency crime reduction; intelligence-led policing and the National Intelligence Model; and neighbourhood policing.

Chapter 7 concludes with a discussion of what has been learned from the best efforts to put problem-oriented policing in the UK and what this means for evidence-based policy and practice in policing.

Chapter 2

Experiences of problem-oriented policing implementation

This chapter begins with a brief history of the implementation of problem-oriented policing in the UK and US. It then describes problems that have been associated with the implementation of the main processes of problem-oriented policing and organisational and technical explanations for these problems and those explanations that are associated more generally with the nature of the police task and partnership working.

A brief history of the implementation of problem-oriented policing

Efforts to implement problem-oriented policing in the UK and elsewhere have now been on going for well over 20 years. The first efforts at police service wide implementation were made in Madison (Wisconsin, US) and Baltimore County (Maryland, US) in the early 1980s. In the UK, Surrey Constabulary (in the south-east of England) began implementing the ideas in 1982 and London's Metropolitan Police Service in 1984. One of the first and largest evaluations of implementation was undertaken in Newport News (Virginia Police Department, US) by the Police Executive Research Forum in the mid-1980s (see Eck and Spelman 1987).

Since the early 1980s, many police services in North America have implemented problem-oriented approaches, often as part of a wider community policing agenda (see Chapter 6). New York, Edmonton, Los Angeles and Houston are all early notable examples (see Goldstein 1990). During the 1990s in the UK, Northumbria, Thames Valley, West Yorkshire and Merseyside police services were all associated with efforts at implementation. The Home Office helped set up and also evaluated a demonstration project in Leicestershire, which was quickly followed by parallel efforts to do the same in Cleveland and Merseyside, building on the Leicestershire experience (see Leigh *et al.* 1996, 1998). Lancashire Constabulary, in the north-west of England, has systematically been implementing a problem-oriented philosophy for almost a decade, and is currently probably most strongly associated with the problem-oriented policing philosophy in the UK (see Chapter 3). Greater Manchester Police, Hampshire, Hertfordshire and the Police Service of Northern Ireland have been implementing the principles of problem-oriented policing with some vigour and dedicated resources over recent years. Although not quite the same, increasing numbers of police services in the UK profess to be 'intelligence-led' (see Chapter 6). Kent Constabulary (in the south-east of England) probably is most associated with this approach in the UK. But the requirements of the National Intelligence Model have led other police services into thinking much more systematically about the police use of intelligence and analysis of patterns of crime and criminality (see Chapter 6).

As well as early experiments and police service attempts at widespread implementation there have been countless examples of small-scale crime reduction projects using problem-oriented principles, which have been successful to varying degrees. These efforts have tended to be associated with particularly motivated individuals (Read and Tilley 2000). The very best ones have often involved collaboration between the police service and professional researchers (Goldstein 2003). Noteworthy published examples (shown in Boxes 2.1–2.2) include the Boston Gun Project's Operation Ceasefire, which was associated with a fall in youth homicide (NIJ 2001) and the Kirkholt burglary reduction project, where a dramatic reduction in overall levels of burglary was achieved (Forrester *et al.* 1988, 1990). The very many Tilley Award and Goldstein Award entrants give a good overview of the achievements that are possible when systematic problem-oriented policing approaches are utilised and this is explored fully in Chapter 4.

Box 2.1 The Boston Gun Project

The Boston Gun Project aimed to tackle homicide victimisation using a problem-oriented approach. Like many parts of the US, Boston experienced high levels of youth homicide in the late 1980s and 1990s: on average 44 youth homicides per year between 1991 and 1995. The Boston Gun Project involved: assembling an inter-agency working group of line-level criminal justice (and other) practitioners; applying qualitative and quantitative research techniques to assess the nature and dynamics driving youth homicide; developing and implementing interventions to impact on the problem; and evaluating the impact. The project was associated with a 63 per cent decrease in youth homicide per month.

Box 2.2 The Kirkholt burglary prevention project

This project aimed to tackle high levels of burglary on the Kirkholt estate in the Rochdale area of Greater Manchester. The rate of recorded domestic burglary on the estate was over double the rate of all burglaries, reported and unreported, characterising 'high risk' areas as reported in the 1984 British Crime Survey (Hough and Mayhew 1985). Domestic burglaries on the estate in the first five months of 1985 were equivalent to an annual rate of 24.6 per cent. By any standard Kirkholt suffered from a severe problem of domestic burglary. The Kirkholt project consisted of a number interrelated initiatives, including: upgrading of household security; property postcoding; removal of gas and electric cash pre-payment meters; cocoon neighbourhood watch; home watch; and, the establishment of a computerised monitoring and evaluation system. Dramatic reduction in overall levels of burglary was achieved, and the reduction in the rate of repeat victimisations outstripped the reduction expected on the basis of the lower rate of burglary generally.

The problems of problem-oriented policing

There is quite extensive literature describing both the broad-brush implementation of problem-oriented policing in police services and its use in smaller scale localised problem-oriented projects. There have been numerous relatively successful attempts to bring in and apply a problem-oriented approach, but this literature is littered with tales of frustrating implementation problems (see, for example, Bullock and Tilley 2003). The results of implementation problems have included delays, stalled efforts and finally reversion to traditional forms of reactive policing. The delivery of problem-oriented policing in the UK today consequently is probably best described as pockets of isolated good practice which tend to be associated with highly motivated individuals (Kirby and Reed 2004). There is clearly widespread nominal support for the principles of problem-oriented policing but successful implementation is far rarer in practice (Read and Tilley 2000; HMIC 2000). The basic finding is that processes of problem-oriented policing are seldom faithfully followed (Capowich and Roehl 1994; Gilling 1996).

The following sections will look briefly at implementation problems in terms of: identifying, analysing and understanding problems; developing and implementing responses; and evaluation and measuring outcomes.

Identifying, analysing and understanding problems

There are many individual examples of well thought out and thought through problem analyses in the police service, but it is clear that there have generally been weaknesses in analytic capacity and this has had an impact on the ability to implement problem-oriented approaches. The analysis stages in problem-oriented policing are often skipped (Capowich and Roehl 1994; Sampson and Scott 2000) or rushed, superficial or limited in scope (Cordner 1998; Clarke 1998; Scott 2000). This is important because where problems are not properly understood, the response developed will be unspecific, untailored and in all likelihood the problems will persist (Scott 2000).

It is important to group incidents and to develop a practical understanding of why they have recurred (Goldstein 1990). However, police services rarely try to do this (Scott 2000). It is not that the motivation for offending needs always to be understood. Seeking to understand the root causes of criminality – which are likely to be based in complex social, psychological and economic issues and be quite intractable in anything but the very long term – will not always be required to deal with individual crime problems. Problem-oriented policing aspires only to a form of understanding that identifies those conditions that are amenable to intervention, which enable or encourage the presenting problem (Scott 2000): it focuses on pinch-points and sets of incidents where common pinch-points are available. It is not deemed essential always to understand the root individual or social sources of criminal (or other problematic) behaviour to develop practical responses to tackle crime (or other) problems. For example, the Boston Gun Project showed counter-intuitively that it is not necessary to know the underlying causes of a problem to have an impact on it (NIJ 2001).

A range of difficulties have been associated with the conduct of analysis to inform the selection of tailored measures to deal with problems. These have included: converting raw data into a form which can be useful for problem solving; making inferences from crime (and other relevant) data; and distinguishing specific crime (or other) problems with sufficient commonality to be open to preventive intervention. There have been additional problems working out what to do once problems have been identified; developing a range of alternative responses; and working in partnership to implement them.

There have been problems associated with the data sets used for analysis, making it difficult to produce analyses of practical use (Irving and Dixon 2002). It is not clear, however, that even where high-quality data are available in the police service they have been well used (Goldstein 1990). Basically, just having data to hand does not ensure that they are used for problem-oriented policing or crime reduction purposes (Brown and Sutton 1997; Leigh *et al.* 1998). Studies have generally pointed to difficulties in utilising analysis for the purposes of crime reduction. If only descriptive statements are produced to identify crime problems, the solutions that are then generated will either be superficial or not targeted enough to be useful and will reduce crime only by chance or good fortune (Townsley and Pease 2003). Analysis for problem-oriented policing needs to make *inferences* from the data about what causes, encourages or enables problems and thereby some hooks on which to hang one or more interventions.

Commentators have noted that it is common for problems to be inadequately defined for crime reduction or problem-oriented policing purposes. It is important to break problems down into their separate components, to consider the social context, the physical setting and the sequence of events leading up to the problem behaviour and its aftermath, in order to understand the problem, and the potential scope for intervention (Eck and Spelman 1987). In particular, problems are often inadequately defined and disaggregated for the purpose of analysis (Eck 2001; Bullock and Tilley 2003; Scott 2000). Broadly defined problems have been commonly identified for problem solving, which has led to poorly focused responses that are too ambitious (Clarke 1998). The capacity to address these problems has either been beyond the competence of the police service or broad, complex, multi-component multi-agency strategies have been formulated that have been hard to manage (Scott 2000).

The tendency to look at broad problems might well be a consequence of the fact that police data are typically recorded in broad criminal categories (Eck and Spelman 1987; Scott 2000; Eck 2001; Townsley and Pease 2003). Although it is not surprising that the police service uses these categories, doing so makes it difficult to conceptualise problems narrowly enough to come up with operationally useful findings (Irving and Dixon 2002; Green Mazzerolle and Terrill 1997). A related issue is that of feasibility and targeting. Responses are likely to be more effective where they are targeted on an identified and significant aspect or attribute of a problem rather than merely on a high-crime-rate area or given crime (Bullock *et al.* 2002). But inadequate targeting of responses has been highlighted by a range of studies (Clarke 1998; Scott 2000; Bullock *et al.* 2002). Without it, an intervention is unlikely to use resources effectively.

Developing and implementing responses

Even where problems have been well defined and analysed, officers have often not been in a position to work out what to do about them. Police officers do not habitually read the crime reduction literature relating to the problems that they are expected to deal with (Clarke 1998; Tilley 1999). They do not typically have access to a body of knowledge about these problems and in these circumstances it is, perhaps, not surprising that officers resort to standard responses (Goldstein 1990). Tools for improving the development of projects are elaborated in Chapter 5.

The need to develop a range of responses that go beyond standard policing and criminal justice responses has been an important element of problem-oriented policing (Goldstein 1990). Responses might include (amongst other things): drawing in other agencies; using mediation or negotiation; conveying information; mobilising community resources; changing the physical setting and increasing regulations (see Goldstein 1990). Despite the wide range of alternatives available, studies suggest that there has still been a primary focus on conventional police activities when developing responses to identified problems (Scott 2000; Cordner 1998; Clarke 1998). It may be that police officers find it hard to conceive an approach in which law enforcement is only one of a range of responses (Brown and Sutton 1997). Whilst conventional policing approaches are not always ineffective, the police service probably over-use them because they are not clear about what alternatives might be available (Eck 2003).

Evaluation and measuring outcomes

There is general consensus that evaluation is important but rarely done well in police services (Goldstein 1990). It is commonly omitted altogether (Cordner 1998; Tilley 1999; Capowich and Roehl 1994; Read and Tilley 2000; Clarke 1998). What is included is often added as something of an afterthought and not an integral part of the problem-oriented policing process. High-quality evaluation is technically difficult. There are a range of practical problems associated with: access to data; data manipulation; understanding data; process and impact measurement; research design; and estimations of cost effectiveness (Scott 2000). The practical problems associated with making use of data are similar to those described previously. A common weakness of evaluations of policing initiatives has been lack of attention to processes through which they are implemented. Process evaluations are time-consuming and can be burdensome on practitioners who have not always understood what is required for this complex task (Bullock *et al.* 2002). Measurements of outcomes have also proved difficult, with evaluations neglecting assessments of the prevalence of the problem, assessment of net harm caused, possible displacement and unintended benefits (Scott 2000). Cost effectiveness is increasingly important in crime reduction but has rarely been done well (Scott 2000; Roman and Farrell 2002).

Explaining implementation of problem-oriented approaches in the police service

Despite 20 years or so of efforts to implement problem-oriented policing approaches, and some key developments facilitating this, there are still generic weaknesses in all stages of problem-oriented policing in the police service. But what causes these difficulties in implementing problem-oriented policing approaches and how can the problems of problem-oriented policing be explained? Many of the problems experienced implementing problem-oriented policing in the police service are not unlike problems experienced in implementing any change in any large organisation: organisations are reluctant to change and getting them to do so can be challenging (Gilling 1996; Irving and Dixon 2002; Hanmer 2003). Explanations that have so far been advanced fall into three main but interrelated categories: organisational and technical issues specific to the processes of problem-oriented policing the nature of the police service and the police task; and partnership working.

Organisational and technical explanations for the implementation of problem-oriented policing

The police service organisational structures and leadership

One style of policing cannot be replaced with another without some thought being given to the organisational processes that orient the service and its staff (Brown and Sutton 1997). Police organisations are normally bureaucratic, hierarchical and structured with formal accounting systems. This may not be well suited to problem-oriented policing styles that call for flexibility of response (Eck and Spelman 1987; Wilkinson and Rosenbaum 1994; De Paris 1998).

By all accounts leadership is crucial to the implementation of problem-oriented approaches (as well as other new programmes in the police service). Leadership is key to enlisting the support of key personnel, gaining commitment and support for getting things done, reinforcing the message that problem-oriented policing is the means through which policing is done and gaining investment for, say, analysts and analytic products (Goldstein 1990). But it is not enough just to have enlisted the support of leadership: important also is the right kind of leader (Bennett and Kemp 1994). To encourage problem-oriented policing, leaders need to have a strong commitment to the principles of problem-oriented policing, be able to articulate it as the key police task, and they need to address the key problem of the (formalised) relationship between management and rank-and-file police officers (Goldstein 1990). Again, more openness and flexibility of management style and decision making may be required to develop a problem-oriented policing organisation (Hoare *et al.* 1984; Goldstein 1990). So, in this context, leadership needs to be about being dynamic and empowering staff to undertake this kind of work. The problem has been that this kind of leadership has been unusual in the police service (Hoare *et al.* 1984; Irving and Dixon 2002; Bennett *et al.* 1994; Green *et al.* 1994).

Line-level management and performance management structures

Related to leadership is line-level management, and all that applies to leadership equally applies to line level management. If managers think that responding to calls is the most important aspect of police business, then that is what police officers will do (Wilkinson and Rosenbaum 1994). And this in turn is related to performance management of staff. Existing performance management regimes in the police service are not normally compatible with problem-oriented approaches to crime reduction. The guiding principles of policing still appear to be honesty, courage and willingness uncritically to follow orders (Bittner 1990). More in keeping with the focus of reactive policing, performance management regimes are typically based on arrests, response times and clear-ups and these are not in keeping with the focus of problem-oriented policing (Braga 2002). Performance management based on arrests is considered to be particularly inappropriate for measuring the success of problem-oriented policing (Fielding 1994; Metcalf 2001). This is a key problem. It is easier for police managers to measure arrests than it is to measure the analytic skills, creativity and flexibility associated with problem-oriented policing. Indeed, the unstructured nature of problem-oriented policing has been difficult to manage and maintain (Hoare *et al*. 1984; Metcalf 2001) and in the absence of suitable performance management, it is difficult to motivate officers to change the way that they do policing (Braga 2002).

Of course, individual police services do not put in place performance management provisions in a vacuum. External forces of various kinds – public opinion, media pressure, and central government priorities, for example – often condition what is prioritised, measured and delivered. These influences are rarely conducive to informed problem-oriented work.

Training

Training is important for officers who are expected to translate the concepts of problem-oriented policing into everyday practice. Generally, officers need to understand the concepts and benefits associated with problem-oriented policing and how they contribute towards achieving it. There may be, still, a lack of understanding of the principles of problem-oriented policing amongst many in the police service. Indeed, how to integrate this into conventional policing and police training remain key problems for implementing problem-oriented policing approaches. Important, too, is communication of the importance of problem-oriented policing to an organisation. Key is communicating to staff and to the public the role that problem-oriented policing plays in reducing crime and why handling problems is more important than handling incidents (Eck and Spelman 1987).

Efforts to implement problem-oriented policing with little or no training, are unlikely to be successful. Sustained and thorough training has been rare.

Analytic capacity

Much has been made of the need to raise the analytic capacity of the police service in terms of both the availability of good-quality data (from a range of sources) and the development of analytic skills in the police service.

Accessing data from a range of sources Good-quality data with which to measure crime problems are not always routinely available in the police service. This is at least partly because police databases tend not to have been designed with sophisticated aggregate analysis in mind. Bullock *et al.* (2002) summarised some key problems associated with utilising police databases for problem-oriented policing. Records are often not kept at all or they are not kept in disaggregated form or they are not computerised (which makes them difficult to use). Databases can contain poor-quality data. For example, fields may be left blank, data entered wrongly or entered into the wrong fields, more than one variable may be entered into the same column or there may be a lot of free text fields. This means that cleaning of the data sets is required prior to manipulation, and this is time-consuming and requires specialist skill. Changes in official recording practices have also created problems for long-term analysis of trends. For example, some crimes/problems no longer have to be recorded whilst other crimes do have to be recorded. This makes time series analysis, which is essential for problem-oriented policing, difficult. Extraction of data from police systems has not always been easy. The police service utilises very many databases that are not always compatible with one another.

Problem analysis has also tended overwhelmingly to make use of police data (Leigh et al. 1998; Scott 2000). Goldstein (and others) have made much of the potential for making use of data from a range of sources other than the police service (Goldstein 1990; Clarke 1998). Police statistics are, to a degree, an artefact of what the public report and the police record (Braga 2002). Making use of a range of data from different agencies would have the advantage of avoiding defining problems in entirely police terms and, possibly, avoiding some of the technical problems described above. The failure to use data other than police data appears to be due to two related problems with inter-agency data sharing. First, there are practical and technical problems associated with sharing data between agencies. Systems are not always compatible, areas into which records are aggregated are not coterminous, and there have been ongoing concerns about data protection in relation to point data. Bullock et al. (2002) described common practical problems of data sharing as follows:

1 Different agencies use different computer systems and these are not always compatible with one another.

2 There is a lack of geo-coding to a specific point and area coding is commonly to different organisational boundaries. For example, police data are commonly organised around Basic Command Units or beats whereas local authority data are generally organised around electoral wards.

3 General failure to collect, quality-assure and store information.

4 Failure to code and enter data in consistent ways.

Second, studies have pointed to some *cultural* obstacles to sharing data between agencies. Different agencies have different professional ideologies. One problem has been that there appear to be differences between agencies regarding conceptions of client confidentiality and this has impacted on *willingness* to share data (Pearson *et al.* 1992). The issue of client confidentiality seems to be of some concern in inter-agency work. The inter-agency approach can exercise considerable power on people's lives (Sampson *et al.* 1988; Garland 1996). Of particular importance are the implications for civil liberties arising from potentially unaccountable systems of information exchange between agencies. Much inter-agency work on crime reduction projects occurs on an informal basis and is, as such, unaccountable (Pearson *et al.* 1992).

The scanning and analysis of some problems will also require information sources that are not readily available from administrative data and this will need to be collected via standard methods from the social sciences. These methods include interviews, surveys and observations (Lamm Weisel 2003). The collection of these data does, of course, underline the necessity of skilled analysts in these methods within the police service.

Analytical skill Even where data are available, the sort of analysis required for high-quality problem-oriented policing represents a considerable intellectual and practical challenge to the police service (Irving and Dixon 2002). It is probably not reasonable to assume that police officers will have the kinds of skills required for high-quality analysis. Indeed, much has been made of the need to raise the capacity within the police service to undertake this complex task. Most studies point to the need to develop the role of the analyst within the police service (Read and Tilley 2000; HMIC 2000). Low salaries for analysts working within the police service and poor promotion prospects have resulted in shortages and high turnover of these specialist staff. These kinds of analytical skills are in high demand and can command higher salaries elsewhere (Read and Tilley 2000). Additionally, in this context, it is not enough just to have the technical skills to manipulate data and analyse them. Good-quality problem-oriented policing in the policing and crime reduction environment requires individuals with knowledge of situational crime prevention and environmental criminology as well as broader research methodology. Recruiting people with this level of specialist skill and retaining them have posed a challenge for the police service. Clearly, these skills are more likely to be found in a university department. However, although there are notable exceptions, partnerships between the police service and the academic world to conduct this kind of work are rare (Goldstein 2003; Kelling 2005). The two settings contrast in their assumptions and working methods, and there has only been a small number of academics seemingly willing to undertake this kind of work.

Perceived time for problem-oriented policing

A common problem is the time that it takes to implement problem-oriented policing approaches. Police managers have been frustrated by the time that it has taken for problem-oriented policing to become established. Change takes time and it is unrealistic to think that changing the focus of an organisation from reactive to proactive policing will be quick (Irving and Dixon 2002; Scott 2000).

The nature of the police service and the police task in explaining the implementation of problems solving

A number of specific organisational and technical issues of the kind already mentioned help to explain the problems associated with the implementation of problem-oriented policing approach. The implication is that to improve implementation, these issues have to be attended to. Much of the literature referred to has been focused on just this. Several studies have concluded with checklists designed to assist policy makers and police managers improve the implementation of problem-oriented policing.

In terms of understanding change in the police service more generally, however, much has been made of the impact of the distinctive nature of the police service and of the police task. Conditions that have been mentioned in this context have included: the fact that the police service is highly resistant to change; the high level of discretion that police officers have on the ground, which has proved difficult to control, and the highly problematic nature of inter-agency crime reduction work in practice. These issues will be discussed in the next sections.

Resistance to change

Implementing planned change in any organisation is difficult (Ekblom 2002; Gilling 1996; Irving and Dixon 2002) but, by all accounts, the police service is especially resistant to change (Green *et al.* 1994; Goldstein 1990). Change requires a new focus and role. Police officers are attached to their traditional roles, and are reluctant to change (Capowich and Roehl 1994; Green *et al.* 1994). The assumptions and constraints of policing have had a powerful impact on willingness to change (Goldstein 1970). There is strong pressure in the police service to respond to incidents in the here-and-now, and this mind set has affected the whole organisation (Townsley and Pease 2003). The demands of problem-oriented policing and of proactive policing more generally, are in conflict with the demands of an event-driven organisation (Goldstein 2003; Townsley and Pease 2003).

The broad, longer-term, reflective and analytic approach stressed in problem-oriented policing is in tension with the emphasis on action to deal with emergencies as they arise, and with the habitual use of enforcement powers as the bread-and-butter method of dealing with crime issues. It is the latter that have given police officers their identity and which have attracted many individuals into policing. Understandably, they are hard to shift.

The nature of police discretion

Police officers have a high level of discretion on the streets and the gulf between what management wants officers to do and what police officers actually *do* on the ground is fairly well documented (Reiner 1992;

Reuss-Ianni and Ianni 1983; Waddington 1999). There is something of an assumption that the police service is heavily top-down, mechanical and military-like, and therefore reforms can be imposed from the top through tightening rules and procedures (Chan 1997; Reuss-Ianni and Ianni 1984). The problem is that officers do not follow orders uncritically and they have an unusually high level of discretion that has proved difficult to control (Goldstein 1960; Waddington 1999). Basically, police management cannot always know what officers are doing because it is not routinely recorded (Goldstein 1960). There may also be differences in opinion between management and front-line officers regarding the means by which crime ought to be tackled (Reuss-Ianni and Ianni 1983). The limited management control of officers means that there is the potential for officers to behave in ways that management had not intended (Reuss-Ianni and Ianni 1983; Goldstein 1960). Because of this, attempts to reform the police service from the top down have not always succeeded. Indeed, efforts to be directive about implementing the principles of problem-oriented policing have appeared to result in officers merely paying lip service to them (Leigh *et al.* 1998).

The nature of partnership working

As indicated in Chapter 1, Goldstein (1990) stressed the need to implement the most effective ethical response, which may or may not include police enforcement. Therefore, the implementation of problem-oriented policing is reliant on drawing in the resources of other agencies and organisations that have not traditionally included the explicit crime control functions held by the police. Currently, crime reduction policy and practice in the UK are heavily underpinned by a partnership approach. (See Chapter 6 on the development of the partnership approach in the UK and its relationship with problem-oriented policing.) As Chapter 6 demonstrates, there has been a fairly long history of inter-agency working in the criminal justice field in the UK and experience suggests that it has been far from trouble-free.

In general, there have been variations in the willingness of agencies to engage in inter-agency crime prevention. The review of the provisions of the 1998 Crime and Disorder Act also noted that whilst many agencies have a role to play in community safety only a handful have actually been held responsible (Home Office 2006). The police usually have a key role in crime prevention initiatives (Liddle and Gelsthorpe 1994a, 1994b; Foster 2002). However, they do not have to take the lead for initiatives to be successful (Home Office 1993). In particular, local authorities, which manage a range of services central to crime reduction and which collect data on crime and disorder problems, have been considered to be vital to the success of inter-agency initiatives (Home Office 1993) and under the provisions of the 1998 Crime and Disorder Act both the police and the local authority are both named as responsible agencies (Home Office 1998). The extent of their involvement has, however, been variable (Home Office 1993) and others have questioned whether local authorities are the 'right' agency to share a community safety function given their failings in other areas (Foster 2002). Studies have also highlighted problems engaging other agencies. Difficulties engaging the probation service in inter-agency crime prevention work has been noted (HMIC 2000) and a number of studies have pointed to difficulties engaging the health service (for example, Philips *et al.* 2002; Irving *et al.* 2001). Indeed, the review of the 1998 Crime and Disorder Act refers to the 'challenges' of engaging health partners (Home Office 2006). This is despite the obvious impact that crime has on the health service, including, for example, the impact of drug misuse, assault and domestic violence on demand for health care, as well as the property and personal crimes that frequently occur within hospital settings.

Research has also highlighted a very wide range of practical and capacity-related issues that have had an impact on what partnerships have achieved in practice. Byrne and Pease (2003), for example, pointed to a high ratio of talk to action and lengthy delays in implementing decisions. Drawing on Phillips *et al.* (2002), Gilling (2005) summarises problems as being related to data sharing, technical capacity, expertise in crime auditing and consultation and setting targets. Bullock *et al.* (2002) also pointed to practical problems related to confused or mixed agendas in inter-agency groups, a tendency to lose sight of the project objectives, problems of ownership and direction of the projects impacting on their ability to achieve their aims.

Not all problems have been practical in nature. Partnerships draw together organisations with a range of cultures, ideologies and traditions as well as differing working routines and hence structural conflicts exist between these organisations when they come together (Crawford 1998). Early research indeed noted overt conflict between agencies in partnership settings, which was considered to be linked with power differentials between them (Blagg *et al.* 1988; Sampson *et al.* 1988; Pearson 1992). Power differentials between agencies are the result of differing professional responsibilities and ideologies and differences in access to human and material resources (Crawford 1998). More recent research has noted similar problems. Bullock and Tilley (2003), for example, noted conflict in an inter-agency setting that resulted from marked differences between agencies regarding what were thought appropriate interventions. This was linked with deeply held cultural and philosophical differences between agencies. That said, other studies have argued that *overt* conflict between agencies has been overstated (Crawford and Jones 1995). They argued that, despite these cultural differences between agencies, managers can avoid conflict through resolving problems informally or setting vague and/or multiple aims as a means of ensuring that things get done (Crawford and Jones 1995). On a more positive note, Gilling (2005) points out that there is no reason to believe that conflict between agencies will be present in the future. He argues that the growth of the partnership approach within areas of social policy, along with the general move towards managerialism, will help inter-agency working, minimising problems.

Conclusion

There has been a quarter of a century of efforts to implement problem-oriented policing approaches in the police service. During this time there have been some key changes to the context in which crime reduction and policing is conducted that have helped to facilitate interest in them. Certainly, there now seems to be a consensus that problem-oriented policing is a suitable means through which policing should be done. That said, there are clearly general weaknesses in the ability of the police service to implement these kinds of responses and to move from reactive to proactive forms of policing generally. These are related to aspects of how the police service is organised and to more specific technical problems associated especially with the analysis and evaluation stages of problem solving. In particular, the fact that police organisation, leadership and staff management still typically revolve around formal accounting structures that facilitate incident-driven policing; the fact that there are still weaknesses in the capacity to conduct high-quality analyses; and the length of time it takes to implement change have all impeded progress in turning the ideal model of problem-oriented policing into a reality. Additionally, there are more general features of the police service that make it highly resistant to change. These include the high levels of discretion employed by police officers that have been difficult to control and the investment police officers have in their traditional roles, methods and identities. Finally, there are specific difficulties associated with partnership working, which is required if responses to problems are to go beyond those traditionally used by and under the direct control of police services.

Chapter 3

Mainstreaming problem-oriented policing in the UK

Background

The previous chapter reviewed what has been previously found in relation to the implementation of problem-oriented policing. In this chapter we look specifically at attempts to mainstream it within two British forces, where relatively sustained and systematic efforts have been made to overcome implementation difficulties. The first is Lancashire Constabulary, in the north-west of England, where problem-oriented policing has been a main thrust of the policing philosophy for some eight or nine years, which makes it durable by national or international standards (Scott 2000). The second is Hampshire Constabulary, in the south of England, which embarked on an ambitious programme trying to implement problem-oriented principles, beginning in 2002. Both forces are fairly large by national standards. In March 2005, Lancashire had an establishment of some 3,600 officers and Hampshire had 3,800. Lancashire had six divisions (what are now often termed Basic Command Units or BCUs), whilst Hampshire had ten of them at the time of the fieldwork, although it was in the process of reorganising into a smaller number. Both forces include a mix of small and large towns and rural areas, with a diverse range of policing problems and of crime levels.

We selected Lancashire and Hampshire specifically because it is our impression, on the basis of past correspondence with members of the forces and past entries for the Tilley Award, that they are amongst the most advanced problem-oriented police services in the UK. We do not claim that they are representative of activity in other police services in the UK: quite the reverse. It is the distinctiveness of the experience of these two police services that we wish to capture in this chapter. We are interested both in what has been done within them to avert some of the characteristic implementation problems found elsewhere, and in what have proven persistent weaknesses.

The discussion is based primarily on interviews and focus groups with police officers from different ranks and from different specialisms, analysts and partner agencies, broken down in Table 3.1.

Table 3.1 Interviews: Lancashire and Hampshire

Lancashire 22–24 November 2004	Hampshire 3–6 May 2005
• Chief Superintendent, Blackpool • Chief Inspector, Blackpool • Nine divisional officers, Community Beat Managers and Community Support Officers, based in Blackpool • Nine divisional officers, Community Beat Managers and Community Support Officers, based in Burnley • Chief Superintendent based at force headquarters • Chief Superintendent based in Burnley • Chief Superintendent based in Blackburn • Accrington Public Protection Unit • Nine divisional officers, Community Beat Managers, Community Support Officers and analysts based in Skelmersdale • Inspector based at force headquarters • Civilian for corporate affairs based at force headquarters • Two inspectors based at force headquarters with responsibility for training • Assistant Chief Constable	• Implementation team (one constable and one inspector) • Four officers from the training school • Group of twelve police and other officers based in Southampton • Four force intelligence analysts • Chief Inspector for Community Safety • Assistant Chief Constable • One road policing officer • Two officers from CID • Group of seven officers and other staff based in the New Forest • Group of PRIME co-ordinators and analysts • Group at Portsmouth BCU

The interviewees were not selected randomly and for the most part we talked to a mix of leading lights within each force, and chosen or self-selected groups.

We also reviewed a range of documents from each of the forces to help inform our account of their implementation of problem-oriented policing. These included minutes of meetings, and policy and training documents from the past and present. As with the interviews, the documentation that we looked at was collected opportunistically rather than systematically.

Despite limitations of the data collected, which readers should bear in mind, many of our observations in Lancashire and Hampshire match those found in previous studies of the implementation of problem-oriented policing.

The chapter starts with brief overviews of developments in problem-oriented policing in Lancashire and Hampshire. It then goes on to discuss those factors that were said to have been important in the implementation of problem-oriented policing in these two police services. It finishes with our conclusions about the key challenges faced by police services seeking to mainstream problem-oriented policing, based on the material we collected.

Quotes from the officers, analysts and other civilian staff that were interviewed are provided for illustrative purposes.

An overview of Lancashire's development of problem-oriented policing

In 1997 the then Chief Constable of Lancashire, Pauline Clare, initiated involvement of the force in problem-oriented policing. The first annual Lancashire problem-solving conference, which showcased early work and attempted to stimulate grass-roots interest, took place in 1998. A BCU commanders' conference in 1999 formally endorsed problem solving as force policy. The first 'problem-oriented policing steering group' was held in late 1999, chaired by the then Deputy Chief Constable, Paul Stephenson. A good practice problem-solving database was established in 1999. At about the same time guides on problem-oriented policing were developed for each BCU and for headquarters departments. The first annual prize in Lancashire for the best problem-solving project was awarded in 2000, to recognise and stimulate problem-solving efforts. Problem-oriented policing co-ordinators were put in place in all areas in 2000, tasked with fostering and encouraging problem solving across the force.

As found in other efforts to effect substantial changes in policing practice (see, for example, Skogan and Hartnett 1997 on Chicago, Kelling and Coles 1996 on New York and Scott 2000 as well as Chapter 2 of this volume), particular individuals appear to have played critical roles, even though they can neither be credited nor blamed for all that happened. Mike Barton, then a Chief Inspector and Stuart Kirby, then a Superintendent, were universally deemed to have played key parts in introducing problem solving within the force. They took the lead in formulating implementation plans and also in encouraging individual officers in specific pieces of work. In 1999 Barton developed a presentation, entitled 'POP on a Beer Mat' that was designed to explain problem-oriented policing and persuade front-line police officers that it was a good idea (Barton 1999). Kirby worked through many of the organisational changes and developments needed to put problem solving in place.

Pauline Clare, Paul Stephenson, Mike Barton and Stuart Kirby were, by common consent, key drivers for problem solving in Lancashire. That said, success depended on others becoming convinced that problem solving was practicable and appropriate. By 2002, Pauline Clare had retired as Chief Constable. She was replaced by her Deputy, Paul Stephenson, who shared Clare's commitment to a problem-oriented approach. By 2005 Stephenson too had left to become Deputy Commissioner of the Metropolitan Police Service. We conducted our interviews at a time when successor arrangements had not yet been finalised. It is not yet clear whether changes introduced will be sustained as and when new leaders take over. Scott (2000: 38) warns that:

> Many of the problem-oriented initiatives generally associated with a particular agency prove, upon closer inspection, to be attributable to one or a few individuals. Usually these are high ranking personnel … When the high ranking champions leave the agencies, the push to engage in problem-oriented policing typically wanes, as well.

There was mixed evidence on the degree to which problem-oriented policing had taken root in Lancashire. Some officers argued that problem solving had become the way in which policing is routinely conducted in Lancashire:

> [POP] still seems to be ingrained in day-to-day work. Everything is very much intelligence based – not just seen as doing POP,

just part of the job, just part of everyday business. (Skelmersdale group)

POP within Lancashire has matured sufficiently that there is no need to keep shouting about it all the time now, you just get on with it. (Chief Superintendent)

As we shall see in due course, others were less sanguine.

Lancashire Constabulary has certainly produced a number of high-quality individual problem-oriented projects, evidenced by their history of producing successful Tilley Award entries as well as success in the American Goldstein Award (see Chapter 4 of this volume). Some of Lancashire's problem-oriented projects have been highly influential. For example, the Tower Project (which was a finalist in the 2003 Goldstein Award) started as a pilot in Blackpool and is now a force-wide multi-agency initiative that targets persistent offenders who are addicted to drugs. Efforts to repeat it have also been made in many other places. Very simply, this project works through identifying persistent offenders (whose offending is known to be linked to the use of drugs) and proactively offering them immediate drug treatment and lifestyle support, such as help with addressing housing or employment problems. Offenders who do not choose to take part in the Tower Project or who commit offences whilst receiving treatment are immediately targeted using more traditional police enforcement tactics, and it is made clear to them that this will be the case. (A summary of the project can be found on Lancashire Constabulary's website and the summary of the Goldstein Award entry on the Center for Problem-oriented Policing website: www.popcenter.org)

Lancashire's has tried formally to interpret new national policing initiatives in ways that enable a good fit with problem-oriented policing. For example, Paul Stephenson states that:

The National Intelligence Model will build on existing processes and complements the POP's philosophy. It encompasses current good practice and moves towards developing a corporate approach to intelligence.

While it will not herald a change of direction it will bring a greater degree of sophistication and professionalism to how we go about our work.
(quoted on Lancashire Constabulary website, accessed 22 December 2005: http://www.lancashire.police.uk/nimhome.php)

The National Reassurance Policing Programme has also been seen by some to be strongly rooted in problem solving (Tuffin *et al.* 2006), a view endorsed by Lancashire's officers:

> Problem solving is seen as integral to community safety and especially to community reassurance and cohesion. (Chief Superintendent)

> Big changes for us include ... the national reassurance project. That is done through a POP approach here. (Inspector)

Lancashire's Policing and Community Together (PACT) initiative in Brunswick was presented as an example. It involves meetings to provide the public with the opportunity regularly to discuss policing issues affecting the areas where they live with their Community Beat Manager. It provides information about how individuals can get in touch with their local Community Beat Manager or Community Support Officer. It offers a way in which local officers can be tasked by the public to address the public's priority problems. The initiative also involves drawing in other front line service delivery agencies where the concerns expressed by the public cannot be dealt with by the police alone.

Whilst in Lancashire there is evidence of success in implementing problem-oriented policing it would be misleading to think that the processes are seen by officers to be embedded in an unproblematic manner across the board, as a headquarters inspector told us:

> It's not really embedded in the culture of service but there are plenty of examples of it going on.

Moreover, the delivery of problem-oriented policing in Lancashire has come to be associated with the local problem-solving efforts of community beat managers, rather than involving response officers or those with other specialist functions as had originally been hoped. It is also evidently occurring patchily through the force area. The following quotations summarise the views of many of those spoken to:

> The Community Beat Officers do it [problem solving]. The response teams do less of it. It isn't their role really. (Chief Inspector)

There is a lack of integration of problem solving into the whole organisation. It's seen as a specialism of the community beat officers. (Chief Superintendent)

Community Beat Officers tend to look very locally at specific problems and decide how to deal with them. But again this depends on the area. (Blackpool group)

There are quite a lot of POPs in Burnley. But it is very variable throughout Lancashire. (Burnley group)

An overview of Hampshire's development of problem-oriented policing

In Hampshire recent efforts to implement problem-oriented policing began in 2002. A small team of officers was established in December 2001 to support its development. The team was set up and initially tasked to develop IT and training for problem-oriented policing within just three months. After various extensions the team was made permanent. Problem-oriented policing in Hampshire is officially branded as 'Problem Resolution in Multi-Agency Environments' (PRIME) in order to facilitate the engagement of non-police agencies by reducing the focus on policing, as this statement from the PRIME team demonstrates: 'we called it PRIME because we were uncomfortable with the policing association of POP and wanted to ensure that partners were on board'. Essentially, though, problem-oriented policing and PRIME are understood to be identical, just badged differently.

In the short time that Hampshire has been implementing PRIME, the Assistant Chief Constable suggests that some progress had been made:

Problem solving is applied. It's not stunning! But it is going on. Problem solving is being applied to a whole range of things – murder reduction, CID is using problem solving for rape and [other] sex crimes. Bike safe engaged the roads policing teams.

Operation Cobra was Hampshire's flagship large-scale PRIME project. From April 2002 to March 2003 vehicle crime in Portsmouth increased by 16 per cent. Most attempts to tackle vehicle crime had focused previously on the detection of offenders and the use of untargeted situational crime prevention measures, which were not thought to have been effective. An analysis of nine months' data was undertaken. This found, for example, that older cars (those manufactured between 1989 and 1998) were most at risk and that vehicle crimes were concentrated in specific locations: half of them occurred in one-tenth of Portsmouth's 1,600 streets. The initiative drew on these findings and on past research to develop a strategy. The response included maximising forensic potential and intelligence gathering, targeted situational measures, and a high-profile media campaign. Portsmouth City Council worked in partnership with the police to deliver parts of the plan, such as redesigning car park areas, supporting a media campaign, and helping with specific PRIME initiatives in hot-spot locations. Overall, Operation Cobra was credited with achieving a substantial decrease in vehicle crime over its first nine months. It won the Goldstein Award in 2004 and a full description of the project can be found on the Center for Problem-oriented Policing website (www.popcenter.org).

The Cobra project was well known amongst staff that we spoke to. It had evidently led to attempts to copy the principles and had also increased the profile of problem-oriented policing in Hampshire. An Assistant Chief Constable told us that:

> Winning the Goldstein was important for increasing the profile of PRIME amongst the officers ... Cobra methods were important. The branding of Cobra was important for getting buy in. This has been an important example of showing the impact that POP can have.

As in Lancashire, areas were said to vary in the extent of problem-oriented policing activity undertaken, and it was most associated with beat officers:

> Beat officers have tended to do PRIMEs. It's harder to get others involved. There is a tension between reactive policing and longer term problem solving and PRIME is not all that embedded in reactive policing. (Chief Inspector)

Factors that have shaped problem-oriented policing in Lancashire and Hampshire

Using the following headings, we turn now to a discussion of those factors that appear from our fieldwork to have been significant in the development and delivery of problem-oriented policing in Lancashire and Hampshire:

1 Leadership and management.
2 Practical help.
3 Analysis and evaluation.
4 Training.
5 Spreading good practice.
6 Rewards and incentives.

These are remarkably similar to the factors found by Walter *et al.* (2005) to have been important in promoting research use in practice across a variety of sectors, including health, education and social care as well as criminal justice.

Leadership and management

As we saw in Chapter 2, many studies have pointed to the importance of leadership in encouraging and enabling problem-oriented policing. It is the key to accessing resources, enlisting personnel and reinforcing the message that problem-oriented policing is a successful procedure (Goldstein 1990).

Leadership committed to the principles of problem-oriented policing was evident in both Lancashire and Hampshire. Consistent with previous research on initiatives in policing, interviews suggested that strong leadership and management had been a key factor in facilitating the implementation and continuity of problem-oriented policing in Lancashire:

> POP was developed in the force with strong leadership from the top. The chief constable was very keen on using POP and keen to see it used throughout the force. Development of POP within the force was timely as a lot of other things were going on at the time. It was at the front edge of the change programme for the force. The traditional top down approach was cleared out when Pauline Clare came in, the dinosaurs from the top were removed and younger officers were promoted. POP came on board at this time when there was a complete change of focus and has been taken up by Paul Stephenson when he took over as chief constable. (Chief Superintendent)

We found evidence of continued leadership at ACPO level in Lancashire. For example, an Assistant Chief Constable who chairs an

ACPO steering group focusing on the implementation of problem-oriented policing throughout Lancashire said:

> I initiated a new steering group to oversee all this – to look at the Lancashire POP agenda and to plan for continuation. There has been a core group established as well – to look at taking things forward.

Nevertheless, maintaining the momentum for implementation at senior level was raised as a potential problem for the future:

> Leadership is much the same as it was but there is a need for younger people to push this forward. People at the top in Lancashire are very enthusiastic – there needs to be enthusiasm at the bottom of the organisation as well. But the push to get things done has to come from the top. (Chief Superintendent)

Concerns were raised, thus, about the potential impact of turnover of key senior staff. In particular, the implementation of problem-oriented policing in Lancashire was associated particular individuals, whose departure could pose threats to its continuation:

> The POP work is fragile. It is personality based – very much encouraged by Mike [Barton] and he encourages people who are interested. (Inspector)

> It is strongly associated with Mike [Barton] and Stuart [Kirby], though at the front end there are officers who are good at it ... The challenge for me is where the next champions are going to come from – how to keep the momentum up. I have people in mind, but there need to be champions at all levels. (Assistant Chief Constable)

There was a sense amongst a minority in Lancashire that problem-oriented policing and partnership had come to be seen by some senior officers as *passé*, needing now to be superseded in view of nationally driven initiatives, notably Neighbourhood Policing, the Reassurance Agenda and the National Intelligence Model. Most of the senior officers we spoke to, though, still said they believed these developments to have complemented the overarching problem-oriented approach, for example:

There's a good fit with NIM, strategic and tactical tasking is built around the SARA principles and there are lots of examples in this division where this has happened. (Chief Superintendent)

NIM fits nicely with problem solving in Lancashire. (Chief Superintendent)

Routine overseeing of problem-oriented policing activity in Lancashire was the responsibility of co-ordinators at BCU level. These co-ordinators were also linked into BCU-level National Intelligence Model tasking. At a local level, Community Beat Managers had particular responsibility for the implementation of problem-oriented policing projects. As the 2004–05 Annual Policing Plan put it:

At a local level, Community Beat Managers, Police Community Support Officers and the Special Constabulary will continue to work with communities and our partners to identify and deal with problems ... Our problem-oriented approach to policing means that we are continually scanning to identify problems and carefully analysing them according to a tried and tested model before determining the most appropriate action to take in conjunction with our partners and local communities. (Lancashire Police Authority 2004: 13)

Though seemingly less personality-focused than Lancashire, in Hampshire officers also perceived there to be strong senior support for the adoption of problem-oriented policing:

There has been a lot of support for PRIME from the Assistant Chief Constable. (PRIME co-ordinators and analysts)

The central PRIME team were attempting to foster problem-oriented work. Having a dedicated team to provide day-to-day leadership and management and to develop the necessary support and infrastructure, has been an important aspect in establishing the development of PRIME across the police service.

In addition, as with Lancashire local co-ordinators had been put in place. PRIME was managed through a series of sergeants in all BCUs (plus one more for roads policing). These individuals had overall responsibility for promoting and managing PRIME in that BCU, for providing quality control and for supporting training. They also developed and maintained partnership links, provided advice to

National Intelligence Model Tasking and Co-ordination Groups, and attempted to mainstream PRIME.

In Hampshire there was some evidence of commitment to implementing PRIME in the CID, an area not traditionally associated with problem-oriented policing. Here, officers described the plans that have been made to apply problem-oriented principles to the problems of rape and serious sexual assault as well as murder:

> I think we can implement PRIMEs for serious crimes. We are looking at a problem-solving approach to rape and serious sexual assault and the homicide prevention strategy. (CID officers)

The issue for both Lancashire and Hampshire has been that of stimulating and then routinising problem-orientation. In Lancashire inspirational individuals seem to have played a larger part than in Hampshire in kick-starting problem-oriented work. In Hampshire the approach, with ACPO level support, has been to establish a small expert central team first and then to spread out from there.

Practical help

In both Lancashire and Hampshire practical help was provided through IT systems and through individuals whose job it was to provide advice and encouragement.

In Lancashire, the problem-oriented policing database goes back to 1999. It is both a repository of records of problem-oriented policing, and the means through which problem-oriented policing projects are managed day-to-day. The records are made available to the whole force via the force intranet. The database contains general background information about problem-oriented policing. The main part of the programme enables the user to create new records and to search records, for example by key word.

In addition to the data base practical help and advice is provided by problem-oriented policing co-ordinators in BCUs, some of whom have been in post for several years and have wide experience of problem solving. Their role was described by the Accrington Public Protection Unit.

> Our POP co-ordinator is responsible for their own area, looking at partnership working, getting others involved, tackling medium and long-term issues affecting the community, and also getting involved in tactical things. They offer advice about problem solving and help us with forms.

Hampshire Constabulary had developed a rather more elaborate IT support system, building on previous models and also trying to make good what were believed to be their shortcomings. The PRIME team's assessment of existing systems to support problem-oriented policing was that they were too police-focused:

> We saw a number of problem-solving IT systems throughout the country. But all had weaknesses – reliant on police, only police could use it, data protection issues, and there were freedom of information problems.

The system eventually developed is web facing on a secure platform, so that it can be accessed and used by other stakeholders as well as police officers in the development and storage of problem-oriented policing activities. It provides:

1 Links to resources with background information about problems and how to address them, for example the crime reduction website, the Home Office toolkits and a range of other relevant documentation and publications.

2 Links to relevant sources of (police and non-police) data to inform the analysis stages of problem-oriented policing, for example to the Office for National Statistics website for neighbourhood statistics.

3 Advice on primary data-collection tools, for example templates for designing questionnaires.

4 Records of crime reduction leaflets and advice that have previously been used in Hampshire.

5 A list of contacts in many different agencies, which is kept up to date by the PRIME co-ordinators at BCU level.

6 Guidance for analysis, response and assessment, including tips and tools for carrying out the work.

The system also incorporates a project management function for PRIME initiatives. It provides an audit trail, tasking function and project management information, referring to inputs, outputs, costs and so on. It can generate tailor-made depersonalised management summaries of projects. The system also has an inbuilt quality control function: a PRIME co-ordinator must approve each stage before the project can progress on to the next stage.

Those officers implementing PRIME projects who had actually used the system found it relatively straightforward to operate provided that they had a basic understanding of IT:

The PRIME software is a good way of recording what is going on – making project management manageable. The new IT system is usable but implies some IT awareness. (Portsmouth group)

At the time of our field work there were over 40 projects recorded on the system, the majority of which were still in the scanning and analysis stages. It was too early to tell whether the apparent promise of the system would be reflected in practice.

Personal advice in Hampshire was provided in part by the dedicated PRIME team as well as the BCU-based PRIME co-ordinators, who attended quarterly meetings for their own professional development. In practice what happened on the ground seemed to vary quite widely. In Hampshire, as in many other forces, there was a fairly high level of devolution from headquarters to the BCUs. Interviews suggested that there were differences in the understanding of PRIME and its implementation across the BCUs:

The relationship between the Crime Reduction Officers, PRIME, TCG and analysts is different in each BCU … There is a lack of consistency between BCUs in respect to community safety – it is not very corporate! (Chief Inspector)

All PRIME sergeants have the same job descriptions but what they actually do could be very different. PRIME sergeants are doing very different things and the processes could be different as well. (PRIME co-ordinators and analysts)

The variation was evidently due in part to the characteristics of some of the personnel appointed and in part to competing demands on their time: some co-ordinators were full time whilst others had to fit PRIME work around other responsibilities. As an Assistant Chief Constable told us, 'PRIME co-ordinators are often doing lots of other things – they should concentrate on PRIME.'

Analysis and evaluation

Analysis and evaluation are defining features of problem-oriented policing, notwithstanding the weaknesses often found in them (see Knutsson 2003). In relation to Lancashire and Hampshire, we discuss what has been done in relation to the supply and use of data, the provision of those with specialist analytic skills, and the conduct of evaluation.

In Lancashire, efforts have been made to increase the supply of data available for analysis. SLEUTH is the system used for marrying up data from different police systems so that that can be combined and analysed jointly. There are currently 24 analysts and numerous researchers. These are supplemented with agreements at local universities, which bring in numerous undergraduate and post graduate students who work on a variety of projects, many of which affect operational policing.

In practice, however, we were told that analysts were largely at the disposal of senior officers, and were mostly used for work on performance management and for servicing the National Intelligence Model:

Analysts get a raw deal. They tend to focus on producing performance indictor information rather than what they are trained to do. (Chief Superintendent)

There are two divisional analysts but they tend to be used for generating management information. (Burnley group)

Most of their time over the last two or three years has been spent on NIM, getting NIM compliant and getting the tasking documents right. (Skelmersdale group)

We don't have much contact with the analysts in BCUs. We can task them if they're not doing anything else but they are normally tasked by senior management. (Blackpool group)

We are not sure what the analysts do – they provide stats for the senior management team. (Skelmersdale group)

Police officers in Lancashire stated that because of the inaccessibility of analysts they would tend to undertake analyses themselves if they needed to, and they were positive about doing so:

It's easier to do it ourselves than ask the analysts to do it – we normally know the answer anyway. (Skelmersdale group)

Most officers acknowledged that the implementation of problem-oriented policing would be improved by greater use of analysts, but thought that problem-oriented policing would need the same priority as the National Intelligence Model if this were to happen. Their view, notwithstanding Paul Stephenson's comments on the complementary relationship between the National Intelligence Model and problem-oriented policing quoted earlier, was that NIM and the evidence-based problem solving in which they were engaged were in competition, at least in terms of access to analysts' time. Problem-oriented policing was not seen in practice at present to enjoy the same status:

> Analysts should be involved in POP to a greater extent and definitely before it reaches the assessment stage. For this to happen, POP needs to be given the same priority as NIM tasking and co-ordinating and needs to be done at a senior level. (Skelmersdale group)

The PRIME software developed in Hampshire and mentioned in the previous section was designed to provide access to relevant data, though in one group we heard of disappointments with available data:

> Local intelligence in Hampshire is not great and we mainly get information from the PNC [Police National Computer]. There could be more use of local information. (Southampton group)

At the time of our fieldwork, there were about 35 analysts in Hampshire. This was widely considered to be too few and limited their capacity for involvement in problem analysis, especially at the BCU level:

> There's not many analysts, not much capacity, and at BCU level not much investment. (Analysts group)

> The analytic capacity is not what it should be – both in terms of volume and focus. (Assistant Chief Constable)

As in Lancashire, analysts in Hampshire were little involved in problem-oriented work. The management and tasking arrangements steered them in a different direction. Analysts tended to be managed by police officers, sergeants or detective inspectors, which they saw as problematic:

> BCU analysts are managed by sergeants or DIs which is not ideal. They have little understanding of what the analyst role is

and little consistency of management – often five or six (different managers) a year. (Analysts group)

There's some misuse [of analysts] like asking for maps and helping out with computer packages and *ad hoc* requests. We could say no to *ad hoc* requests, but it depends on who's making the requests and sometimes we wouldn't know if they were worthless until later. (Analysts group)

Again as in Lancashire, analysts reported that a main focus of their work tended to be on informing the National Intelligence Model tasking processes and performance management, providing little access for those involved in grass-roots problem solving:

For the BCU analyst, problem solving is balanced against other roles. There's sporadic involvement in PRIME. The job consists of a range of things: mainly problem profiles and following associated changes in crime rates. (Analysts group)

The performance management regime dictates the way that BCUs use resources and hence the way that analysts are used. In Southampton, T&CG meant that analysts have greater input but consequently less time to spend on other things. (Analysts group)

There are not many analysts and it would seem that it would be hard for a beat officer to task an analyst and PRIME is not seen as a high enough priority to get analyst time. PRIME is recognised, acknowledged as important and promoted but is not seen as a priority. (Portsmouth group)

So National Intelligence Model tasking was prominent and it limited what else could be done. For the average police officer it is hard to get hold of an analyst to help with the development of problem-oriented policing in either Lancashire or Hampshire.

It is telling that the Cobra analysis in Hampshire was done by a practitioner and not by analysts, on the grounds that the police data systems were not up to it. As an Assistant Chief Constable acknowledged:

For Cobra, Alan [Edmunds] did the analysis himself because the intelligence systems were not up to it.

In Hampshire, shortcomings in analysis, including over-reliance on police data, failures to work though the implications of findings, and the development of poorly specified problems, which have been consistently identified in previous literature (for example Green Mazzerolle and Terrill 1997; Clarke 1998; Leigh *et al.* 1998; Scott 2000; Phillips *et al.* 2000; Eck 2001; Bullock and Tilley 2003; Irving and Dixon 2002; Lamm Weisel 2003) were widely recognised on the ground:

> There needs to be a lot more analysis before setting things into action, but most people don't know where to get the information from. Police figures are still the most important. (PRIME co-ordinators and analysts)

> The police often don't know how problems affect people locally. The antisocial behaviour unit at [Portsmouth] have very valuable information that the police have no idea about because no one will speak to them! Statistics from the police go some way to understanding problems but not the whole way. They don't let you understand the whole issue. (Portsmouth group)

> Analysis can be a bit shallow because you don't get the human involvement from the police stats. You need to carry out surveys to get a fuller picture. We have spent too long trying to solve problems without properly understanding the perspective of the people involved. (Southampton group)

> Analysts are not always able to make deductions from crime data and this is important – often they are not asked and they don't volunteer their deductions. (Assistant Chief Constable)

> Too broad PRIMEs are a problem. Big PRIMEs should be broken down into smaller ones. (Southampton group)

There is little to be said about assessment, because we found little evidence of it going on. The following illustrate the points made to us:

> We are typically good with ideas, structures and identifying possible solutions. Scanning and understanding is good as well. But there is less assessment. This is to do with the gung-ho element of policing. We're good at the solutions but less good at recording the work. (Chief Inspector, Lancashire)

Analysis, PAT and so on are all used. But we are less good at the assessment and evaluation stages. (Chief Inspector, Lancashire)

Evaluation is generally weak but something that is new or seems like a good idea is normally evaluated. (Chief Superintendent, Lancashire)

Problem solving is reflexive and the assessment element is often missed out because it is too hard. (Chief Superintendent, Lancashire)

The evaluation stages are not always done. (Training team, Hampshire)

Training

Training for problem-oriented policing was provided in both Lancashire and Hampshire though we were unable to observe it.

In Lancashire, formal classroom based training for probationers started in 1997. It covered the general theoretical background to problem-oriented policing, examples of problem-oriented policing in practice, and SARA and PAT as tools for undertaking it. Latterly it has also included relevant provisions of the 1998 Crime and Disorder Act.

Though some initial negative responses were acknowledged, the trainers said they generally found the police officers enthusiastic:

There was some resistance to the terms used – sometimes they thought it was management-speak … there was early resistance to the training … but they [the officers] could start to see it [POP] working and general enthusiasm rubbed off on them. Now, those who don't do this kind of thing are somewhat left behind. (Training inspectors)

In addition to classroom training probationer police officers had to look for real problems and develop solutions, and present results to senior management:

The probationers have to look for real problems, to solve them using POP principles and present them to senior management. We would contact their sergeants to make sure these things were happening. (Training sergeants, force headquarters)

Probationers were also expected to learn on the ground from other practitioners:

> Probationers learn about community policing from their time with the beat managers. There's been a greater movement from class room teaching to teaching in real life. (Training inspectors)

The officers we spoke to generally felt that whilst appropriate training was available, more was needed. In particular, there remained in their view a need for training for non-police partners:

> We do need to engage others [in training] as is fairly limited to probationers only and there is no inter-agency problem solving training. (Burnley group)

In Hampshire training for PRIME started in 2003. In contrast to Lancashire, however, training was not provided for probationer officers, although one training officer argued that 'it really ought to be a more integral part of probationer training'. Instead, a two-day course in problem-oriented policing was run twice a month for cohorts of 16 to 18 people identified by BCU PRIME coordinators. People were assigned training as they moved into relevant roles and came across problem-oriented policing as part of their job. The aim was that 50 per cent of the attendees would be non-police officers, although this does not typically appear to be achieved in practice. We were told that non-police training attendees had included officers from housing and environmental health, community safety managers, the police authority, social services, youth workers and even a forest ranger!

The content of the training as described to us broadly resembled that provided for probationer officers in Lancashire. It included problem-oriented policing exercises, processes of problem-oriented policing, relevant legislation relating to data protection issues, good and bad examples of problem-oriented policing in practice, and issues related to inter-agency working (problems with working with other agencies, barriers, stakeholder analysis and so on).

Making contact with representatives from partner agencies was viewed by trainers as a particularly useful aspect of the course, with potential benefits for future crime reduction work:

The course is of benefit to the police officers who do it as it gives them a wider perspective than usual and looks at problems from other people's point of view. (Hampshire trainers)

Reflecting the experience in Lancashire, the Hampshire trainers acknowledged that their material had been resisted by some police officers, at least to begin with:

People can be quite negative, at least to begin with. Although they get more into it as it goes on. (Hampshire trainers)

Lancashire and Hampshire have delivered training in problem-oriented policing in different ways and to different groups. In neither case, however, did it appear either to be very extensive or to have been tested for its effectiveness. There was no evidence that training specifically for problem-oriented policing was provided in either Lancashire or Hampshire for senior officers or analysts.

Spreading good practice

Before good practice can be disseminated it has to be identified. We have already noted the acknowledged weaknesses in evaluation and assessment, confirming findings of previous studies that this is the Achilles heel of much that passes as problem-oriented policing. More will be said about this in the next chapter which reviews entries to the Tilley Awards.

Making information on good practice accessible was deemed important in both Lancashire and Hampshire, though Lancashire has so far made more extensive efforts than Hampshire.

Lancashire has attempted to spread good practice by holding its own annual conference where local work is presented and national or international speakers also contribute; by sending a large delegation to the annual national problem-oriented partnerships conference (26 attended in 2005); by special meetings between the ACC and BCU commanders where initiatives are discussed and shared; and by use of the problem-oriented policing data base. Whilst overall, a range of systematic efforts were made to disseminate information about problem-oriented policing in Lancashire, there were calls for more quality controlled dissemination across the force, especially in relation to the database:

> There needs to be better control on what is recorded on the data bases. The POP co-ordinators could take responsibility for this. (Chief Superintendent)

> We don't need to record everything we do. We need to recognise a good problem-solving approach and only write it up when it is exceptionally good or innovative, especially those with good evaluation, where they can show some cause and effect. (Chief Superintendent)

In Hampshire, because of the short length of time over which PRIME has been implemented, systematic dissemination of local good practice was not considered yet to be adequate and was largely limited to word of mouth. This may well change when the problem-oriented policing data base reaches sufficient capacity. The success of Operation Cobra has, though, been widely publicised and has become influential within the force, as we have already pointed out.

Rewards and incentives

Three main incentives for participation in problem-oriented work were referred to: its use in appraisal; its use as a factor in promotion; and recognition, including prizes, for outstanding projects.

In Lancashire ability to undertake problem-oriented policing was still assessed within individual police officer's appraisals. This was believed to have helped maintain a focus on it within the force:

> At appraisal we are asked about it [POP] which keeps it on the agenda. (Burnley group)

However, it was pointed out that a few years ago problem-oriented policing was a key priority in appraisal, which it is not any more:

> Induction, reward and performance management: there is less effort in these areas now. (Chief Superintendent)

> There's been a reduced focus on POP over the past three years, partly due to the new chief constable coming in. POP used to be one of the priorities on the [appraisal]. Not any more, the focus has slipped away. (Skelmersdale group)

In Lancashire, efforts had also been made to take account of involvement in problem-oriented policing in the promotion process, though again it would appear that the focus on it had diminished over recent years:

> There is a bit in the assessment centre for promotion but it's not really encouraged that way. (Burnley group)

> There is a reduced focus on POP for promotion now – four years ago you would definitely have been asked about POP, not so much now. (Skelmersdale group)

We have seen that problem-oriented policing in Lancashire tends to be conducted by community beat officers. Officers took the view, however, that performing this role had not helped help promotion prospects:

> There is no natural progression for beat managers – they are thrown into the job with no specific training. This would not happen in most areas of policing and there is little appreciation of what the beat officers do every day. (Blackpool group)

This might be acting as a disincentive for conducting problem-oriented policing. That said, officers pointed to how the role of community beat manager was increasingly being seen as high-profile within the force and was attracting good-quality officers:

> Recently, really good officers have been becoming beat managers. Beat managers are into reassurance, crime and victims. The attitudes to being beat managers have now changed and it is a high profile role. (Chief Inspector)

> Generally beat manager is seen as a good job. It hasn't always been like this. It was seen in the past as dealing with the rubbish – not so much involvement with offenders – which is why people join the police. (Blackpool group)

As already indicated, Lancashire Constabulary has also runs a high-profile award scheme to recognise excellence in problem-oriented policing, which is linked with their annual conference. This has been vigorously competed for each year and out of this competition come the many entries for the Tilley Award. This strong internal award scheme was seen by officers to provide an incentive to conduct problem-oriented work:

There have been big wins using this approach which include the Tower Project and Atlas. These sell the message that POP approached can be successful. (Chief Superintendent)

Winning the national Tilley Award or international Goldstein Award was deemed a significant achievement by officers of all ranks:

That [Stuart Kirby] won two Tilley Awards was a source of pride and it was very helpful in implementing the approach. (Assistant Chief Constable)

In Hampshire senior police officers accepted that performance in problem-oriented policing needs to be rewarded to incentivise it, but acknowledged that at present this is not occurring systematically:

Not everyone does problem solving and it needs to fit with the performance process. There needs to be ways to reward performance. (Assistant Chief Constable)

Notwithstanding this remark, some efforts to reward problem-oriented policing were already becoming apparent. The need for evidence of involvement in the implementation of PRIMEs in Hampshire can influence officers' work programmes and hence their appraisals. In this way it may prompt problem-oriented policing work:

PRIME can influence work plans, everyone has objectives – and some kind of involvement in PRIME – not necessarily managing one. It involved thinking in a PRIME way and including PRIME methods in what they do. It should feed into all elements of work. (Chief Inspector)

Prizes were helping to incentivise problem-oriented work in Hampshire as in Lancashire. The success of Operation Cobra in winning the Goldstein Award had evidently had a wide impact throughout the force. In particular it had been influential in making officers think differently about the role of analysis and about what can be achieved through the implementation of a problem-oriented policing approach. Furthermore, an award was presented on 21 February 2006 for the best PRIME project in Hampshire at the Local Criminal Justice Board conference to fund the winner's attendance at the national Problem-oriented Partnerships conference.

The challenge of mainstreaming problem-oriented policing

Lancashire's and Hampshire's experience of trying to implement problem-oriented policing and the continued challenges each still faces provides evidence, consistent with previous research findings, of the time and effort required for achieving meaningful and sustained change within a police organisation. We have described almost a decade of fairly systematic efforts to mainstream problem-oriented policing in Lancashire and it would seem that the implementation of the processes is still patchy, at best. Officers spoken to recognised that this was the case:

> We've had this kind of approach for a while. We are now seeing the benefits. This kind of work takes a long while. (Burnley group)

> Implementation requires discipline. It takes a long time to sort things out. (Chief Superintendent)

Our interviews in Lancashire and Hampshire highlight three key challenges which are seen to be especially important for those who seek to implement problem-oriented policing: changing the dominant police culture; engaging others in problem-oriented work; and accommodating performance management regimes.

Changing police culture

Three aspects of police culture that were obstructing efforts to put in place problem-oriented policing cropped up: the value attached to quick responses to emergencies, the focus on offenders as the problem, and an aversion to bureaucratic form-filling.

The police task has come to be seen as that of providing rapid response to incidents as they arise, and changing this mindset is problematic (Townsley and Pease 2003). Some of those in Lancashire acknowledged the difficulties and the time needed in changing cultural perceptions within a police organisation:

> It's difficult to adopt POP – it takes a long time to do in a culture that works on quick fixes. People in decision making roles don't realise the time it takes to build up relationships with other agencies. It's a difficult task. (Skelmersdale group)

The same issue was recognised in Hampshire also, where concerted efforts at implementation have been more recent:

> Policing is still seen as blue-light policing. Chasing incidents and chasing excitement, not academically proven theories and methodologies. It is difficult to get the focus away from offenders. (Assistant Chief Constable)

Policing does not seem to be about rigorously applied concepts and crime reduction methods in either Hampshire or Lancashire. Rather, the pressure is still for action rather than thought, providing immediate responses to incidents as they occur:

> Lots of these issues require longer term solutions and generally the police are happier responding quickly. They don't like the time it takes to think about longer-term solutions. (Lancashire Chief Superintendent)

Even though officers noted that response teams see the futility of attending to the same locations and the same victims over and over again, they do little to address it:

> Response teams feel that they are attending the same places again and again but people don't take responsibility for sorting out their problems. (Southampton group)

Furthermore, it was evidently hard to move away from the traditional police interest in perpetrators when thinking about ways of addressing crime problems:

> It's difficult to get the focus away from offenders – Cobra was a rare example where they did lots on victims and locations, but little on offenders. (Hampshire Assistant Chief Constable)

Following the cultural preference for practical action, PRIME was resisted by some as being bureaucratic, academic, and about form-filling:

> PRIME is a more structured way of doing things. It's obvious up the chain what's been done. But this fosters the view that PRIME is bureaucratic and hard for a PC to do … There is a risk that PRIMEs are seen as a bureaucratic exercise rather

than a means of structuring the way that problems are tackled because it's a complex process to steer through. (Southampton group)

The view that problem-oriented policing is about academic form-filling was also evident in Lancashire:

[Officers] see it as filling in forms and the academic side of things. My job [the sergeant's role] is seen as the job that makes people fill in forms! (Blackpool group)

Engaging partners

Problem-oriented policing is about the implementation of the most effective ethical response and this may or may not be police enforcement of the criminal law (Goldstein 1990). A key requirement is, therefore, the ability to draw in, where appropriate, the resources and expertise of others. Chapter 2 showed, however, that engaging others in crime reduction work has not been found to be at all straightforward (see also Irving *et al.* 2001). The challenge of engaging partners, who have different agendas, performance targets and resources, in problem-oriented work was evident in both Lancashire and Hampshire:

The police drive things well but we find difficulties in getting others involved. Some of this may be to do with resources – other agencies have fewer resources and planning cycles can be quite strict. (Blackpool group)

Health is a real problem area for us, as in many places, but this could be really useful – especially in the area of alcohol and domestic violence. Social services have basically withdrawn from inter-agency work because of lack of resources. (Burnley group)

There's never been much involvement from health. (Hampshire training team)

Private shops are the worst. It's very hard to get them to make changes when they are still making money – most shops will allow a certain amount of loss. (Southampton group)

In the statutory sector youth services have been very hard to engage. There are few of them and some of them can be very negative towards the police. (Southampton group)

57

Performance indicators

The influence of police performance indicators irrelevant to problem-oriented policing was considered pervasive in both Lancashire and Hampshire. In Lancashire, officers said performance indicators were driving the majority of activity. The consequence was believed to be less scope to focus on solving local problems, less innovation and less room for the development of long-term solutions to long-term problems:

> The focus on performance indicators has made it harder to focus on problem solving because there is less room for innovation. The PIs and high demand for calls are creating a lot of work for officers and this is making it harder to look at long-term problems ... it would be hard to improve when the drive for PIs is so pervasive. (Headquarters Inspector)

Additionally, the focus on performance indicator crimes appeared to some to have moved the focus of problem-oriented policing away from issues that the community were especially concerned about:

> At the BCU level, BVPI [Best Value Performance Indicator] crimes are focused on. The Community Beat Officer focuses on quality of life issues, like litter, which are not considered to be important at the T&CG tasking level. The BVPIs are causing some problems. What the community feels is not necessarily the same as the reality of crime. (Blackpool group)

As in Lancashire, in Hampshire also there was a feeling amongst many officers that whilst problem-oriented policing was becoming more ingrained, it had to be distorted to fit into central performance indicators. Thus, local problem-oriented activity will try to respond to the needs of the performance management regime rather than the performance management regime responding to the identification of locally defined problems:

> You have to twist your problem so that it fits into the mould. You'll only get any interest if its meeting KPI's [Key Performance Indicators]. (Southampton group)

One senior officer expressed a rather different view, however, arguing that the performance management regime could facilitate problem-oriented policing:

The performance culture could be good for problem solving but short-termism is still a problem. We can't base performance on catching villains, as it doesn't engage partners. (Hampshire Assistant Chief Constable)

Overall we found that there is still some conflict between the priorities of reactive policing and longer term problem-oriented policing. It is hard to mainstream approaches when performance indicators are so pervasive, and when they point in different directions. Even in what appear to be some of our best performing problem-oriented police forces, short-termism remains a problem in terms of the pressure to respond to the here-and-now, the pressure for quick results and the temptation to respond to short-term blips in crime.

Conclusion

Lancashire and Hampshire represent examples of what we believe to be amongst the most advanced efforts to mainstream the problem-oriented approach in the UK, and they have produced some of the best problem-oriented projects.

Committed leadership and management, innovatory structural developments, and the provision of practical support for problem-oriented policing were all in evidence to support mainstreaming. Methods had been devised to disseminate successful problem-oriented policing projects. Training had been made available in both areas and officers were being rewarded for apparent successes in their problem-oriented endeavours.

Implementation has, nevertheless, been challenging and it would be a mistake to think even in Lancashire and Hampshire that problem-oriented policing has become embedded in an unproblematic manner across the board. It appears largely to be associated with certain types of officers (beat officers) and to vary in intensity by Basic Command Unit. Whilst enthusiastic leadership was present in Lancashire, it was associated with particular motivated individuals and previous experience, as discussed by Scott (2000), highlights the risk that this presents for the future health of problem-oriented work. The management structures in Hampshire appear to be quite fragile: there is little corporacy between BCUs leading to differences in what co-ordinators actually do and the time they have available for their PRIME role. Hampshire acknowledged this problem and stated that they were addressing it. Software and analysts may be present in

Hampshire and Lancashire but the role of the analysts appears to be primarily to support the National Intelligence Model and to measure performance indicators rather than to assist in the development of problem-oriented solutions. Overall there appears to be lack of relevant analytic capacity and problem-oriented work is not of high enough priority to access such that there is. Data difficulties were evident and included access to local intelligence and over-reliance on police data. Training is available, but generally there is not enough of it, in particular for police–probation officers in Hampshire and for partner agencies in Lancashire. Both forces reward and provide incentives to conduct problem-oriented work, but concerns were still raised that this area was not well reflected in officers' appraisals and promotion prospects. Dissemination of good practice was ongoing but concerns were raised about quality control, and there is very little evaluation to identify it in either force.

The experience of implementing problem-oriented policing in Lancashire and Hampshire points to some of the key challenges for mainstreaming the principles. Changing the dominant reactive police culture remains a complex problem. Partner agencies are hard to engage. The performance management regime remains pervasive, and was felt by most to distract from evidence-based problem-solving. Considerable time and systematic effort will be required by any force seriously wishing to adopt a problem-oriented approach.

The final point to be made here relates to the ways in which problem-orientation has been operationalised in Lancashire and Hampshire. From what we heard of or saw, rather a small fraction of what either force does would satisfy the strict standards of problem-oriented policing, as laid out by Goldstein. The Tower Project and Operation Cobra probably come closest to doing so. There appears instead to be rather more 'problem solving' of the sort described in Chapter 1: attention to specific local problems without necessarily conducting the kinds of background work, analysis and assessment that 'problem-oriented policing theory' requires.

The focus on problem solving is reflected in the language used by officers, who tend to refer to 'problem solving'; in the type of problem focused under the auspices of NIM; and in efforts to deliver the reassurance agenda, with its focus on what most matters to local people. The last two chapters of this volume will come back to these issues for further discussion.

Chapter 4

The implementation of problem-oriented projects in the UK

The previous chapter looked at attempts to mainstream the principles of problem-oriented policing in two police services. In addition to those police services that have adopted a problem-oriented approach widely, the majority of police forces in the UK have been involved in implementing individual problem-oriented projects to some extent over the past few years. This chapter looks initially at how the Tilley Award scheme has developed since the launch in 1999, and the forces that have participated in the scheme. We then look at these projects in more detail, and present the findings of an analysis of a sample submitted to the Tilley Awards to examine how police services and their partners have adopted problem-oriented approaches to crime reduction and other policing issues. These include how the problems were defined; the level of analysis carried out; how the responses followed from the analysis; the level of evaluation conducted. In addition to presenting some examples of success in adopting a problem oriented approach, a number of gaps are identified where further development would be of benefit to the problem-oriented process, particularly in relation to analysis and evaluation.

The Award

The Tilley Award was launched in 1999 by the (then) Home Office Policing and Reducing Crime Unit, to encourage the police service to identify and submit projects from within their force that demonstrated good practice in problem-oriented policing. Police forces and their partner organisations across the UK are invited to submit entries demonstrating good practice and effective delivery of a problem-oriented approach to crime reduction. Initially the awards focused on initiatives to reduce crime and disorder, with subsequent years introducing awards for organisational support and partnership working. More recently, this distinction between categories has been dropped in favour of considering entries covering any aspect of police or partnership work intended to support front line delivery of problem-oriented policing and partnership.

The winners of the Tilley Award are announced at the UK Problem Oriented Partnerships conference held each September, where they are presented with a certificate, and given the opportunity to present their projects during the conference workshop sessions. Coverage in the national media of the awards is an incentive for both the officers and the police service involved, demonstrating the implementation of good practice methods and a successful outcome. An additional incentive is that the winner is awarded financial assistance to attend the International Problem-oriented Policing Conference in the US, and again present the work to an international audience along with the winners of the equivalent Goldstein Awards in the US, which has been running since 1993, and is open to police forces on an international basis.

Submitting an entry to the Tilley Awards

The projects that are selected to be written up and submitted to the Tilley Awards are seen as being exemplars of how the problem-oriented approach has been adopted and implemented within each police service, although the selection process for these within the force is unclear and will undoubtedly vary across the country. Officers submitting entries are required to provide information about the project on a standard application form, and include the following sections:

1 Project details, including the title, police force, CDRP or other agency partners involved, contact details and the names of endorsing senior representatives.

2 Short summary of the project (400 words maximum) giving a description of the problem, the main interventions and outcomes.

3 A longer description of the project (4,000 words maximum).

4 A letter from the senior representative (Assistant Chief Constable or above), endorsing the project and entry to the awards.

The endorsement of a senior officer is required to indicate that the project is recognised within the force as being successful, and worthy of submission.

The guidelines for the 2005 awards described the two-stage judging process – the shortlisting process and judging. The initial sift, conducted by a small team, scores each of the entries against set criteria covering each stage of the problem-oriented process. These criteria, which are clearly spelled out in the guidelines for entrants, include the following:

1 *Project objectives* – have clear and specific objectives; clearly defined success criteria; appropriate involvement of police and partners in identifying the problem.

2 *Definition of the problem* – use of reliable data sources; analysis of appropriate information; demonstration of knowledge about the nature and extent of the problem; any gaps in information identified.

3 *Response to the problem* – clear relationship between the analysis and the design of the response; effective use of partnership working; clear planning and implementation with adequate resource allocation; problems identified and managed; any particularly innovative or creative responses; consideration of sustainability and transferability.

4 *Evaluation of the intervention* – clear use of data to provide evidence of whether the response was as intended; appropriate choice of evaluation methods; evaluation extended the knowledge and understanding about the problem, the underlying causes and potential solution.

5 *Written presentation* – well presented, using appropriate information and following a logical path.

6 *Coherence of project* – clear relationship between one stage of the project and the next, in that the response follows from the analysis, that the evaluation actually includes measures relating to the objectives, and there is some understanding of the cost effectiveness of the project.

In 2005, of the 58 entries, 11 were shortlisted for further consideration. Once a shortlist has been drawn up the entries are passed on to a judging panel for assessment and scoring. The judging panel consists of around eight to ten people, with the actual membership changing each year. This has included Home Office research and policy officials, senior police officers, academics with experience in problem-oriented policing and problem solving, and award winners from previous years. Each judge marks the shortlisted entries independently, again based on the same criteria as above. The judges can score from 'no credit' (0) to 'superior' (7), with the scores for definition of the problem and evaluation being more heavily weighted to reflect the importance of their role in problem-oriented crime reduction. The scores from each judge are collated, and the three highest scores are identified as the winners.

Which forces enter for Tilley Awards?

Since the Tilley Awards were launched there have been a total of 503 entries, as shown in Table 4.1, generating 28 winners and runners-up. The majority of police forces within the UK have submitted at least one entry at some time over the past seven years: only three forces in England and one in Scotland out of a total of 52 forces have not submitted entries. Entries have also come from the Police Service of Northern Ireland (formerly the Royal Ulster Constabulary), the States of Guernsey Police Force and the British Transport Police.

Four forces have submitted entries in each of the seven years that the award scheme has been running: Lancashire, Avon and Somerset, Greater Manchester and the Metropolitan Police Service. Cleveland, Cumbria, Northumbria and Merseyside have submitted entries in six out of seven years. Most forces have submitted multiple entries, and

Table 4.1 Tilley Award entries by year

Year	No. of entries	No. of forces submitting entries
1999	66	30
2000	56	24
2001	69	27
2002	71	22
2003	86	27
2004	98	21
2005	57	20
Total	503	171

this was seen particularly clearly in 2004, when a total of 98 entries were submitted from only 21 forces.

The number submitted by Lancashire far exceeds that of any other force: a total of 135 entries have been received from Lancashire since 1999, with at least 15 entries each year, reflecting the commitment of this force to adopt problem-oriented policing and introduce this approach into all aspects of policing. Table 4.2 shows the police forces that have entered most frequently, which includes a number of those – namely Lancashire, Surrey, the Metropolitan Police Service, Northumbria and Merseyside – which were associated with the implementation of problem-oriented policing early on, as discussed in Chapter 1.

Table 4.2 Tilley Award entries by police force between 1999 and 2005

Police force	Total submitted	% of total entries
Lancashire	135	27
Avon and Somerset	32	6
Cumbria	28	6
Northumbria	24	5
Cleveland	22	4
Greater Manchester	21	4
Merseyside	19	4
West Midlands	17	3
Metropolitan Police	14	3
South Wales	14	3
Surrey	13	3
South Yorkshire	11	2
North Wales	10	2
Devon and Cornwall	8	2

Many of the most active and successful forces in the Tilley Awards have also been proactive in submitting entries to the Goldstein Awards in the US, which follow similar judging criteria to the Tilley Awards. The number of entrants from the UK has increased over recent years, with over half the entries in 2004 coming from English police forces, primarily Cleveland and Lancashire, with the overall winner coming from Hampshire Constabulary (Operation Cobra, see Chapter 3).

Analysis of the Tilley Award entries

Copies of the Tilley Award entries, as submitted to the competition, can be found on the Center for Problem-oriented Policing website (www.popcenter.org), with summaries of them also on the Home Office website (www.homeoffice.gov.uk). For the purposes of our analysis, a total of 150 Tilley Award entries selected at random (25 from each year between 1999 and 2004) were systematically assessed in more detail how the different problem-oriented stages had been approached in each case, and to ascertain whether there were any changes over the time since the awards had been launched.

A fairly substantial coding framework was developed to undertake this descriptive analysis, which covered various aspects of the processes involved in setting up, implementing and evaluating the projects. This included the following sections:

1 *General background information on the project.* This included the name of the project, the police force involved, and when the project took place. Information about the type of initiative that took place was coded as being either crime reduction, organisational support or partnership, based on the assessment of the coders, as the categories were not distinguished in all years, and there was some debate as to whether this was always entered into the correct category.

2 *The structure of the projects.* This looked at who was accountable for the project and responsible for the day-to-day management and staffing. The resources contributed (cash, technical, staff time, etc.) and who by, were recorded. It also identified which partner agencies were involved in the project, and at what stage they became involved.

3 *Analysis and problem definition.* The level at which the problem was defined and addressed was recorded, along with information about how the problem was originally identified, where the demand for a response came from (e.g. whether it was raised by the police, public concern, CDRP audit, etc.). We looked at who was responsible for conducting the problem analysis, and the types of data that were used to inform the analysis (e.g. police-recorded crime data, calls for service, local authority data), and then went on to look at the types of analyses that had been carried out. Data difficulties identified by the project staff were recorded, along with any apparent weaknesses in the analysis. A summary of the main

findings was recorded, as was the interpretation of these findings according to the project report. Finally this section looked at the use and reference to the literature, theory and National Intelligence Model.

4 *Objectives and responses.* This looked at the stated objectives of the project and how these were set out, for example in terms of outputs, outcomes or processes. The details of the main planned interventions were recorded, with an assessment by the coders of how well the objectives and responses followed from the analysis.

5 *Outputs and outcomes of the initiative.* Information was recorded about whether the project had been monitored, what the outputs were and if there were any issues about implementation raised by the project staff. We then looked at who was responsible for conducting the evaluation, what data sets were used for evaluating the outcomes, and whether the project had successfully achieved the objectives.

6 *Sustainability and mainstreaming.* Information was recorded about whether the project would be sustained or mainstreamed, and if there was any information about replication of the project.

The projects varied greatly in terms of the scope and scale of the problem being tackled. Most were focused on crime reduction relating to specific problems in specific areas, whereas others were concerned with developing organisational structures to promote problem-oriented policing within the force, and improve partnership working. The findings of our analysis will be discussed under each of the sections in turn.

Whilst looking at these issues, it is important to reiterate a couple of caveats about the analysis. The project submissions we looked at were taken primarily from the reports that have been scanned in and stored on the Center for Problem-oriented Policing website (www.popcenter.org). In a number of cases not all of the appendices were scanned in, and so data may have been included in the original submission that were unavailable to us. However, this is a representation of what is publicly available for use by other police forces and their partners, and is a frequently used source of information about examples of problem-oriented projects. A further caveat relates to the content of the submissions. These will be restricted to some extent by the limitations put on the length of the submission, and also by the information requested for each entry to include. For example, only 30 of the projects noted difficulties they had experienced accessing and using the data. In understanding the implementation of problem-oriented policing, understanding the problems that are faced on a practical level is useful but it was not a requirement of the submission process to include this level of information.

Background information

Our analysis encompassed 150 Tilley Award entries from 39 forces in total, over a six-year period, representing one-third of the total number of entries over this period. Over one-quarter of these were from Lancashire (27 per cent), reflecting the proportion of the total number of awards that have been submitted by this force. The majority of the projects were focused on crime reduction, with 12 per cent (n = 19) looking at organisational support and two projects focused on partnership.

The projects had been running for varying lengths of time. Just over one-third (37 per cent) of the projects submitted had started in the year prior to entry for the awards; one-third had started two years before being submitted. Fifteen per cent of projects had begun three or more years before being submitted to the Tilley Awards. Only six projects had begun during the same year as being submitted for consideration. As the projects had to be submitted in April, this would leave very little time for all stages of the problem-oriented process to be addressed.

The types of problem being tackled by the projects varied, ranging from very specific crime types in carefully defined areas to overall crime over a much larger area. For example, one of the smaller initiatives looked at the problem of shoplifting in a single shopping centre, another addressed the problem of ticket touting identified at a particular Tube station, and a third project looked at reducing hoax calls to the fire brigade, which were being made primarily from a single call box. Other projects focused on all crimes and quality of life issues in a particular neighbourhood or estate. Antisocial behaviour (ASB) and general youth-related nuisance was a common theme across all the years, with one-third of all the projects submitted focusing on antisocial behaviour and disorder. Twelve per cent of the projects set out to address all crime in general in a specific area, such as a housing estate, and a further 12 per cent focused on violent crime, with an increasing number looking at violent crime connected with the night-time economy in more recent years. There were a handful of projects each year that aimed to reduce burglary and vehicle crime.

Structure of the initiatives

The implementation of the projects was strongly associated with the police service. Of the 150 projects studied, the police were wholly responsible for almost half of them (n = 73). One-quarter of the projects were carried out by partnerships between the police and one other agency, and in the majority of these the police were equally or mainly accountable. In seven of these the other agency was mainly accountable for the success of the project. The fact that the police were mainly or wholly responsible for the projects is maybe unsurprising, as the Tilley Award entries had to be submitted through the police force and so may underestimate the role of the partner agencies. In 17 per cent of the projects, the responsibility was shared throughout a multi-agency partnership. It was unclear where responsibility lay in the remainder (n = 14) of the projects.

That said, most of the projects involved more than one agency at some stage, either in identifying the problem or implementing the response to the problem. There were most commonly around three or four key partners; however, some projects were the sole responsibility of the police and involved no other agency, whilst there was one example of a project involving up to 22 partner agencies. Not surprisingly, due to the nature of the awards and the projects, the police were by far the most active key partner in the projects submitted, and participated in all the projects. Local authority partners were involved in just over half the projects (51 per cent, n = 77). Local businesses and related business organisations were also active partners in many projects (n = 34), and these were often local shops and licensed premises which were suffering as a result of local crime problems and brought in to help address these. Other statutory partners included organisations involved in education (schools, the local education authority, universities, n = 32); health-related agencies (n = 19); housing associations and landlords (n = 18) and social services (n = 14). Other partners involved to a lesser extent included residents' groups and community members (n = 10), probation (n = 9), voluntary groups (n = 9), charities (n = 8) and the fire service (n = 7). In the majority of cases where it was made clear, the project was managed by a police officer. In only eight projects was the project explicitly managed by an officer from a partner agency or a multi-agency group.

In many projects it was not clear from the submission when the different partners became involved. Only two were initiated by non-police agencies that were already participating in established partnerships. Partners were brought together at the scanning stage, when the problem was first emerging, in 36 per cent of projects, and often had a more strategic role in how the project developed. Fewer got involved at the analysis stage (16 per cent) with the majority (44 per cent) being brought in at the response stage. This generally reflects the time when partners other than the police joined the project, and were approached to help deliver a specific intervention. In a number of cases the main action in the response stage was to actually identify and engage with partners who could be brought in to help tackle specific problems: the response was to set up partnership working. Other projects involved a small number of key partners who identified the problem initially, and brought in other agencies to deliver responses as and when required.

It was not always clear from the submission what role each of the partners played, or what resources they contributed to a project. For most of the projects the resources were detailed as staff time, the provision of data and expertise in conducting analysis, and other expertise about the particular problem being addressed. In some cases, there was a financial resource generally from one of the partners to purchase particular items such as CCTV, fencing and lighting, bicycles and sports equipment. In many cases, the police contribution was of staff overtime. The amounts of money involved in funding the projects, or in-kind equivalent, were generally not provided; where this was mentioned the amounts varied from £1,000 up to £750,000, reflecting the broad range of projects being submitted.

Analysis and definition of the problem

The scale of the problem being tackled varied greatly, from force-wide projects, generally involved in organisational support and developing problem-oriented policing across the whole force, to projects that were focused down on to a specific street, building or even a single offender. Twelve per cent of the projects covered a whole force area. Almost one-third were covering a BCU level problem; this appears to have increased over time, and for more recent years just under half the projects focused on problems being identified at a BCU level. Twelve per cent of the projects were focused on a specific sector or selection of beats, and five per cent focused on problems identified in a single beat.

One-third of projects did not cover a specific 'police defined' area such as a BCU or beat area. Virtual communities, such as student populations, were included focusing on, for example, the problems faced by international students coming to study in the UK, or on the issues of student houses being burgled. Other problems were identified at specific well defined locations such as a holiday camp, university campus, a school, housing estates and a shopping mall, and became the target for the interventions. Public transport attracted some interest, with a number of projects focusing on Tube stations, an airport and taxi ranks. An increasing number of projects covered local authority defined areas, such as wards, parishes and whole CDRP areas.

One-quarter of the problems covered by the projects were originally identified by analysts working within the force. One-fifth were identified by operational officers, and the same proportion were raised through public concern and community groups. One in 20 was raised by the CDRP. Analysis by agencies other than police raised awareness of the problem in a small number of cases, the fire service, community wardens and local authorities being cited in a number of projects. In some areas a long-standing problem that had not been successfully tackled previously by conventional policing was seen to be suitable for a problem-oriented approach. For example, in a project in Cleveland submitted in 1999 there was a long-standing problem of youth disorder, increasing crime levels and diminishing public confidence. The police felt they were 'firefighting' and recognised that the only way to tackle the problem was to look longer-term and address the underlying causes of the problems, using a problem-oriented approach. Similarly, a long-standing problem of prostitution in a North London borough, submitted in 2000, was affecting the quality of life for residents, and the police response of trying to contain and manage the problem was having no discernible impact. It was recognised that a longer-term problem-oriented approach, involving partners other than the police, was more likely to eradicate prostitution and related offences. In a number of other projects, victim and fear of crime surveys brought the scale and impact of specific problems to the attention of the police, resulting in the action described in the award entry.

Once the scanning had taken place, and the general problem had been identified, the analysis stage of the process was conducted by police officers in two-thirds of the projects. Crime analysts were involved in the analysis in one-quarter of the projects. Ten per cent of the projects involved the local community in project analysis, generally through community surveys and public meetings, and for a further 10 per cent of projects officers from partner agencies participated in analysing the problem in depth. Earlier years provided examples of projects where researchers from local universities had provided assistance in conducting the analysis. The analysis for a project in

Tayside submitted in 2000 was informed by research carried out by Glasgow University, which highlighted increasing trends in the use of drugs and alcohol amongst young people, and a link between substance misuse amongst this group and antisocial behaviour, graffiti and vandalism. The submission stated that the additional research highlighted particular problems that would not have come to light through the crime pattern analysis carried out by the police. Likewise for a project submitted in 1999 based in one ward of a town in Cumbria, researchers at Lancaster University provided baseline data through an analysis of recorded crime data and interviews with residents – this was described as being the most intensive audit ever commissioned in the area. Although the university research was reported to have added value to the analysis of both these problems, in neither case was the university involved in the evaluation stage of the process.

The quality and thoroughness of the analysis varied greatly between the projects and across the years, as did the sources of data used to analyse the problem. In 22 of the 150 projects analysed (15 per cent) there was little evidence of any quantitative analysis being carried out. However, this did include seven organisational support projects, many of which did not have data, or use data analysis in the same way as the crime reduction projects to define the problems, with the focus being on the implementation of problem-oriented policing within the force. Of the 15 crime reduction projects that presented little or no quantitative data, most provided a general discussion about the area and the type of crime being faced there, or anecdotal descriptions of the problems.

Data sources used

The majority of projects made use of some form of police held data in analysing the problem. Eighty-two of the projects (55 per cent) used police-recorded crime data in the analysis of the problem, and in 23 of these (29 per cent) this was the only source of data for the analysis. Twenty-five other projects also used only a single data source for the project analysis, which for the majority of these projects ($n = 10$) was command and control data.

Thirty-nine projects used two data sources to inform the analysis, police-recorded crime data being used in 23 of these, and command and control incident data being used in 14 – four projects used both. Data held and managed by the police were used in all but one of the projects, whether it was police-recorded crime data, incident data, force intelligence, accident data or detection data.

Overall, relatively few data were presented and used in the analysis from sources other than the police, and what were used did not appear to be particularly well utilised. Relatively few data came from local authorities, health authorities or other emergency services.

Type of analysis conducted

Table 4.3 shows the mix of analysis that was carried out in the projects analysed. The type and quality of analysis carried out varied widely across the project entries. Whilst the majority of the projects did conduct at least a very basic analysis of the problem, seven projects did not present any form of analysis, and a further 20 projects did not attempt to conduct any quantitative analysis, or did not make it clear how the data had been used to conduct any sort of analysis.

Table 4.3 Types of analysis conducted

Type of analysis	% of projects using this analysis
Crime/incident/survey response counts	49
Crime, etc. rates	38
Crime, etc. trends/plots	20
Pin mapping – hotspots/other	10
Linking of crime with geodemographic data	7
No analysis done	5
Survey cross-tabs	4
GIS mapping – hotspots	3

Almost half the projects (n = 73) presented simple counts of crime, incidents or survey responses, and for 44 per cent of these (n = 32) this was the only type of analysis carried out. A further 35 projects used only a single type of analysis, most looking at crime or incident rates, with a handful analysing the trends in the data over time. One-third of the projects used more than one type of method for the analysis, most commonly combining counts of crime/incidents with crime rates, crime trends or mapping of hotspots. Hotspot mapping did not appear to be widely used, with only 19 projects producing some sort of mapping analysis using pin mapping or GIS methods. This usually involved a crime analyst or an officer from a partner agency conducting the analysis. Few projects (n = 11) linked the crime data to geodemographic data of the area, and this was only done in the projects using multiple analysis methods to attempt a more comprehensive understanding of the problem. The projects where this was done were more likely to have involved officers from partner agencies in the analysis, presumably having greater access to this type of data and being able to bring it to the analysis. This was evident for one project in 1999 submitted by Nottinghamshire Police which provided an analysis of the number of empty properties on an estate using data from the local authority.

Projects using multiple methods of data analysis all used crime counts. They were also more likely to make use of hotspot mapping, either using GIS or pin mapping, and were also more likely to bring in geodemographic data, to broaden the picture and give a wider analysis of the problem and the area which was being targeted.

Difficulties accessing and using data

Most projects did not specify that they had experienced any problems in either accessing or using the data, primarily because they were not specifically asked to provide such information in the Tilley Award submission. However, problems associated with using the data were identified by the project staff and noted in 30 of the project submissions, providing a useful insight into the sort of issues that may arise with analysis of different types of data, and in many cases details of how these were overcome. The most common data problem (mentioned in 11 projects) was that of under-reporting of incidents to the police, so that the recorded crime data were not accurately reflecting the scale of the problem under investigation. A number of examples of this were given. In one project student burglaries were thought to be under-reported, with the reason provided being that students did not have insurance, so did not have to report a burglary to the police to make a claim, although no evidence was provided to verify whether or not this was the case. A number of other projects reported that residents did not report incidents occurring to the police for fear of reprisal from the offenders. A third example was of incidents in a holiday camp which would usually be dealt with internally and not reported. In this case the records from the holiday camp were used as the basis of the analysis of the problem alongside the police-recorded crime data.

Various other types of difficulty were encountered by project staff in analysing the problems being tackled, and in some cases the project submissions included information about how solutions to these problems were found. These are summarised as follows.

Data sharing. There were problems getting hold of the data from other partners – those that got over this did so through developing information sharing protocols, or through obtaining joint funding. Analysis of these data by the partner agencies' own officers also overcame the problem of dealing with personalised data.

For a number of problems involving businesses, such as retailers, there was unwillingness to pass on data to the police that they saw as being commercially sensitive information that their competitors might see. This included details about who was losing the most stock through shoplifting, the number of customers in each store, and whether takings were suffering due to specific crime problems.

Paper-based records. When using police data other than the usual recorded crime data, such as accident data, or other incident reports, it was often found that these were not centrally collated electronically by the police but stored as paper-based records in each police station or divisional headquarters. In some cases the analysis took up a lot more time than anticipated as it involved trying to collate the information by hand from the paper records – where these could be found without too much difficulty.

Lack of historical data. For a number of the projects there were no historical data available about the problem. Often the problem had been identified through calls from the public or the media, but no data had been collected about this. Data were collected as part of the response to the project but no baseline data were available, such as a project dealing with disruptive airline passengers which received a large amount of media attention but about which the police had little data.

Lack of detail in police records. In cases where the police-recorded crime data were available, often the amount of detail contained within the existing records was insufficient to give a clear indication of the nature of the problem, to be able to tackle the causes of the problem effectively. A lack of information recorded in *modus operandi* notes in crime reports was often problematic, as was searching through large numbers of records with few analytic tools to assist. An example of this was one project looking into the problem of fraudulent claims for Giro cheques. In order to understand the extent of the problem a search of records for the word 'giro' was conducted as part of the analysis of the problem. This returned a large number of records that were actually unrelated to the problem, and therefore required further sifting to isolate the records that were specific to the problem being addressed. For a number of projects experiencing such problems the response included measures to record more detailed information in a more accessible format about the specific problem being investigated, for example making sure that the location was recorded of stolen cars within a car park that was being targeted for vehicle theft.

Using appropriate quantitative measures. Staff involved in one project, completed in 2002, realised that the data they were using to monitor the problem were not reflecting the problem as they understood it. This project was concerned with reducing the amount of graffiti in a residential area, and was using calls for service data as a measure to monitor how the problem was changed during the life of the project. Further analysis of the data revealed that that no one was actually calling in about this as a problem, and therefore the extent of the problem was not reflected in the calls for service.

Data sets using different geographical boundaries. In some projects, data sets related to different geographical areas. Analysis of incidents in an area that was covered through a Single Regeneration Budget project proved difficult using police-recorded crime data as the area was not coterminous with a police area. In one case the analysis was done by hand, and with little conviction by the project staff that they were able to do this with sufficient accuracy. In this case the analysis was conducted by a beat officer – assistance from an analyst with geo-coded data may help to overcome such problems elsewhere.

Inappropriate use of data. A project to reduce the problems associated with prostitution in one area of London that used arrest data in the analysis was concerned that changes in the numbers of arrests over time was more a reflection of changes in force policy on arrests rather than a reflection of the crime problem. Using multiple data sources, including force intelligence and environmental audits, helped to provide a more robust picture of how the problem had changed over time.

Format of the data. Data from different sources relating to the problem were collected using different data collection methods, were stored in different data formats and often did not cover the same period of time, making it difficult to draw any conclusions about the problem from the data available.

Limitations of the analysis

The previous section drew attention to a number of the problems relating to the use of data as experienced by the project staff. In addition to these difficulties, identified in the project submissions by those involved directly in the projects, the coding of the projects carried out by the authors also identified a number of weaknesses in the analysis. Many of these problems are repeated year after year, and therefore it is important to highlight these and provide some pointers to ways to avoid recurring problems in the future. For 11 projects, no comment was made about the analysis. Some weaknesses in the analysis for problem-oriented policing were found for all but 14 of the remaining 139 projects, where the analysis was considered to be reasonable, at least in relation to the data that were available to the project staff. Even so, most of these would still have benefited from a more detailed interrogation of the data.

No quantitative analysis presented. In one-quarter ($n = 31$) of the 125 projects with weaknesses identified, no quantitative analysis was presented in the analysis section of the submission. Five of these were organisational support or partnership development projects, so it may be expected to some extent that these would not necessarily use the same statistical approach in determining the nature of the problem, as would be expected for the crime reduction projects. Thirteen of these projects referred to surveys that had been carried out, or to data that had been collected and analysed, but did not actually present the findings from this analysis within the submission.

Qualitative, descriptive findings were presented in 13 projects, though there was little evidence of this being carried out systematically, and in many cases the description of the problem was purely anecdotal, based on the assumptions of project staff.

Limited use of data sources. The remaining three-quarters of the projects did present some form of quantitative analysis. However, 35 per cent of the projects made very limited use of the data sources, and said little about the analysis that had been carried out. Whether this was because the necessary data sources could not be accessed, or because the need to include it in the analysis was not anticipated at the outset of the analysis stage of the project was not clear from the submissions.

Lack of detail in the analysis. Where quantitative analysis had been carried out, often this was done on a fairly superficial level, and problems with lack of detail in the analysis were identified in 53 per cent ($n = 66$) of the projects. In 41 per cent of these projects ($n = 27$), the data were presented solely in terms of basic crime or incident counts, and did not include any rates or provide denominators which might have given a better understanding of the extent of the problem. The level of detail in the analysis was often insufficient to be able to draw any conclusions about the nature of the problem, or identify pinch points for subsequent intervention, and very broad findings were often presented. There was often little information relating to analysis about trends or patterns that emerged. For example, one project looking at theft of cars from a car park might have benefited from having further analysis about the location within the car park of the cars being stolen, to see if cars parked in particular parking spaces were more at risk than others. Identifying a pattern of cars being taken from certain spaces could help understand reasons why this might be, and then how this could be addressed.

Often the lack of detail would relate to patterns around locations, victims or offenders, making it difficult to interpret the data that were presented. Twenty-eight per cent of the projects identified the problem in terms of a specific hotspot location, or victim or offender group. However, the analysis for three such projects looking at specific locations provided no spatial analysis, and nine focusing on victims and offenders provided no further detail about these groups to justify why they were the focus of the project. For example, one project which focused on victimisation of international students in the south of England provided very limited detail in the analysis about the extent of victimisation amongst students. Another project aimed at reducing repeat victimisation for burglary victims gave little detail about the extent of repeat victimisation occurring within the estate being targeted, and no information about why these victims were being targeted more than once.

Even when a large amount of data was presented, there was not always a great deal of analysis conducted on this data. One project described as having 'masses of data' carried out very little analysis, demonstrating that simply getting hold of the data is not sufficient to understand a problem. It is the analysis of the data, that enables the problem-oriented approach to define problems and identify the best way to tackle them.

Lack of data relating to the problem locally. Ten of the projects appeared to use data that did not relate to the area in which the project was being implemented, and did not provide any analysis on a local level. For example, for one project in South Wales which was tackling problems of antisocial behaviour and problem drug and alcohol use, the analysis referred only to national-level data from the British Crime Survey and did not relate to the area where the problem existed on a local level. Another project in Devon and Cornwall aimed at improving the police response to domestic violence incidents and raising awareness of the support available to victims did not present any analysis relating to the extent of the problem within the city in which the project was being implemented. Whilst they did refer to Home Office figures, these were reported at a national level rather than locally.

A number of other occasional weaknesses were also identified.

1 *Small numbers.* In three projects the numbers used to identify the problem were too small to draw any meaningful conclusions or be able to identify any emerging crime patterns.

2 *Unclear areas being targeted/analysed.* Two projects did not specify what geographical area the analysis referred to, whether it was the target area or the wider BCU area.

3 *Poor presentation.* For three projects the data were presented poorly, making it difficult to assess whether the data actually related to the problem, or to interpret the results of the analysis.

There appear to be three levels of difficulties where improvements could be focused. Firstly many projects presented no quantitative analysis. Where no quantitative data are presented, no further statistical analysis could be carried out, although these projects often provided an anecdotal description of the problem. Secondly, where quantitative data were introduced, they were often very limited, and often provided no more than a basic description of the problem, such as basic counts of crime in one year compared with the next. Often there was insufficient information to be able to draw out patterns of offences, look at trends over time or provide any further understanding of the extent or nature of the underlying crime problems. Thirdly, where sufficient data were presented, few projects actually interrogated them, to ask why patterns were occurring, or to understand who victims or offenders were. Few explanations were given as to why the problems were occurring in a particular location or against a particular group of victims.

Understanding of the problem

Often conducting detailed analysis of a problem identified through the scanning process will change the understanding of how the problem was originally perceived. There were relatively few cases where completing the analysis stage changed the understanding of the problem being addressed – we found evidence of this in just 13 per cent of the projects. In the few cases where there was evidence that this had occurred, it often revealed that the suspected crime problem did not actually exist. One example of this was in West Mercia, which set up the Rural Safety Initiative to address problems of fear of crime and engage rural communities in problem solving. A survey of fear of crime carried out as part of the analysis showed surprising results in that crime was ranked only tenth in the list of issues concerning local residents – they were more concerned with speeding traffic, lack of activities for young people and lack of affordable housing than crime.

In another project the analysis was able to provide a better understanding of the nature of the problem, and identify the main offenders causing the majority of the problems. This project in Lancashire focused on reducing youth nuisance, and the analysis showed that, of the large group of youths congregating in one place, it was actually just two or three key young people that were the ringleaders who instigated the trouble. One of the interventions subsequently planned was then focused on dealing with these key people and their families, alongside more general high-visibility policing interventions aimed at the group as a whole.

In a couple of other cases, the analysis provided the evidence needed to raise awareness of the problem amongst partners who had previously been unaware that the problem existed. For example, the problem of hoax calls about deliberate fires was a major problem for the fire brigade in Cleveland (in 2000). In order to tackle the problem, their analysis was shared with the police, who had not known that the problem existed. A joint response was then developed.

References to research/literature

The analysis of these projects indicated that relatively poor use of the existing literature was made by the projects. It may, of course, be the case that projects had referred to the literature when searching for appropriate solutions to the problem identified, but did not reference it in the project submission.

In total, 41 projects (28 per cent) referred to research or literature to provide additional information in their project reports, with a small number ($n = 8$) referring to multiple sources. The sources of information used to inform the projects included the following:

17 projects referred to Home Office research reports.

14 projects made reference to published statistics, such as the British Crime Survey, the Youth Offending Survey, deprivation indices, and population statistics.

Seven projects referred to published problem-oriented literature, with a further seven projects referring to problem-oriented projects that had taken place previously within either their own, or other police forces.

Three projects referred to guidance literature, such as toolkits.

Three projects referenced HMIC reports.

A couple of projects made reference to academic literature and other government reports, including Audit Commission reports and reports from the Transport Laboratory. There were also a couple of projects that referred generally to academic and other literature, but did not provide references to what these were.

Setting project objectives

The majority of projects did clearly set out the objectives they were trying to achieve through the problem oriented approach. However, there were still 24 projects (16 per cent) that did not state objectives, making it difficult to assess the success of the project when it came to the evaluation stage of the problem-oriented process.

The objectives set out in the projects varied from being specific and output focused in scope to very broad and general in scope. The projects were set out as follows:

88 projects set out objectives in terms of outcomes (usually crime reduction).

68 projects set out objectives in terms of processes.

24 projects did not specify any objectives.

16 had outputs specified.

11 had outcomes with targets.

One project had outputs with targets.

Many projects had a mix of objectives in terms of outcomes, outputs and processes. Projects on average tended to set between two and three objectives. One-quarter of the projects set out only one objective to be attained through the project, with four projects having more than six separate objectives.

The objectives varied for both crime reduction projects and organisational support. For a number of organisational support projects (for example the Sudbury Sector COPS project in Suffolk, Project Management Methodology in Lancashire and problem-oriented policing across the Metropolitan Police Service in London), the objectives were set out as being simply 'to implement problem-oriented policing' within the force or sector. This was in contrast to a project in Hampshire which was also looking to promote problem-oriented policing within the force, and set much longer, more specific objectives (see Box 4.1). This project clearly relates to one of the case studies previously discussed in Chapter 3.

There was a similar variation in the amount of detail provided in the objectives laid out for the crime reduction projects, some focusing on crime in general, some on specific crimes, and some on quality of life issues. Others again focused on specific groups of offenders, and offending behaviour, such as street begging or prostitution, whereas other projects were established primarily to reduce calls for service. There was variation in the length of time over which the objectives were set – whilst most of the objectives were not set within a time frame, others were very specific. One project in Surrey set out the objective of arresting at least 15 Class A drug dealers every day, although it did not specify how long the project would last for with this objective. Another project aimed at reducing traffic accidents in Nottinghamshire set the target of reducing casualties by one-third

Box 4.1 Pocket book, Hampshire Police

This project in Hampshire was developed as part of the work to mainstream problem solving in the force, and promote the use of problem-solving techniques in the everyday work of police officers. The problem analysis had shown that the police service was not dealing effectively with the symptoms of problems, and that fear of crime was still a major problem. Also it was felt that police were not recording information accurately in a way that would help to overcome these problems. The PRIME team in Hampshire set the objectives for introducing a problem solving approach into the force to include the following:

- To immediately reinforce the strategic direction of the force as a problem-solving organisation.

- To integrate problem solving with the National Intelligence Model, allowing both techniques to be joined up, particularly at grass-roots level.

- To enhance the quality of community intelligence and the intelligence requirements of the Tasking and Co-ordination Group, including prominent nominals and repeat offenders, hotspot locations and repeat victims.

- To market the problem-solving philosophy aggressively, so that all officers will be aware of the introduction of problem solving and the general principles of the process of SARA and PAT.

- To lay the foundations on top of which problem solving can flourish and be sustainable; this also included other areas outside the scope of the submission such as training and IT.

To set out to achieve the objectives a new pocket book was developed to help recording of information, along with guidance about problem-oriented policing and how to use the new pocket book. The project reported that the objectives were partially achieved, with officers saying they felt better equipped to do their job, and more confident about problem-oriented policing and how this fitted with the National Intelligence Model.

---

over two years, making clear the target to be met, and the time frame in which this was to be achieved.

Projects addressing similar wishes often set out their objectives in very different ways. The analysis for one project in Leicestershire showed there was a particularly high crime rate across two police beats, accounting for a large proportion of crime in the Basic Command Unit, and that there was a high burglary rate and high turnover of tenants in one estate. The project objective was simply to reduce crime in the area by 30 per cent. Another project, this time in Lancashire, provided a similar problem analysis which showed that one-third of the properties were empty at any one time, with the estate showing high levels of recorded crime and being overrepresented for calls for service. This project set 13 individual objectives, most of which followed on fairly well from the analysis. These included: a reduction in crime with particular emphasis on property crime; eradicating street prostitution in the area; a reduction in police calls for service; securing and reducing points of access; improved lighting; landscaping the estate being targeted to improve natural surveillance; setting up Neighbourhood Watch and residents' associations and securing 100 per cent occupancy of available housing, with eviction of problem tenants and vetting of potential tenants. Both these projects did manage to at least partially achieve their objectives, through a combination of various interventions. The first project reported that it had achieved a 31 per cent reduction in crime in the area being targeted. In the second project, many of the objectives were also reported to have been achieved, including managing to increase the number of tenancies, towards the aim of 100 per cent occupancy, increasing the number of arrests, reducing repeat victimisation, reducing calls for service from the police, and reducing the number of recorded incidents of key crime types. An additional benefit of the project was a reported improvement in community reassurance.

Responses and interventions planned

Following on from setting the objectives, the projects provided details about the interventions planned to reach these objectives and tackle the problem identified. We assessed each of the projects in terms of how well the objectives and planned responses followed from the analysis conducted, as presented in the project submission. For almost one-quarter (23 per cent), the objectives were considered to follow on well from the analysis with a clear, logical route from the analysis to the response. For just over half the projects the objectives and responses followed on fairly well, with a reasonable link between the analysis and the objectives, or a good fit for at least part of the project. In 8 per cent of the projects we considered that there was a poor link between the analysis and the objectives and responses of the project. However, for a further 19 per cent of the projects this assessment about the analysis and response could not be made, due to the weaknesses and limitations of the data analysis.

The mix of planned interventions varied widely across all the projects that we examined. The interventions were recoded into 65 specific measures, and classified under one of eight categories. Table 4.4 shows the categories and number of projects in each category. The majority of projects stated that more than one intervention had been planned, generally cutting across category types.

The majority of projects (57 per cent) implemented some sort of enforcement intervention, most commonly deploying high visibility police patrols ($n = 31$), other forms of enforcement ($n = 27$), improved intelligence and evidence gathering ($n = 24$) or implementing Antisocial Behaviour Orders or Acceptable Behaviour Contracts ($n = 18$). Situational measures were implemented in 38 per cent of the projects, the main focus being on environmental improvements ($n = 29$). Publicity through local media was also frequently tried, with 35 projects identifying this as part of their crime reduction response. In total, 125 projects had implemented some aspect of enforcement, situational or publicity based initiative as a response to the problem

Table 4.4 Responses used in projects

Intervention category	Type of intervention covered	No. of projects
Enforcement	High-visibility policing, improved intelligence gathering, covert operations, Antisocial Behaviour Orders and Acceptable Behaviour Contracts, bail condition enforcement, wardens, exclusion orders, test purchases, doorman registration schemes	85
Situational	Environmental improvements, target hardening, security surveys, redesign of pubs, changing the layout of car parks, lighting, CCTV	57
Organisational development	Developing partnership work with other agencies, such as information-sharing protocols, including problem-oriented policing in the policing plan, development of IT systems for problem-oriented policing, and incentives for officers to adopt problem-oriented policing	53
Publicity	Media coverage of activity, poster campaigns, general or targeted awareness raising of crime prevention – leaflets drops, letters, student fresher packs, videos, education packages to schools	53
Stakeholding	Community engagement through consultation and public meetings, radio link schemes, Pub Watch, Neighbourhood Watch, landlord accreditation schemes, victim support, road safety and first aid training	50
Offender-focused	Identifying and targeting prolific offenders, drug treatment programmes, engagement with problem families, truancy programmes, mediation	41
Diversion	Primarily activities for young people, including sports clubs, art activities, youth clubs, discos, youth shelters, BMX/roller-blade facilities, football training	26
Training	Training and awareness raising related to problem-oriented policing within police forces, police induction, training of staff from local shops and businesses	20

identified. Table 4.5 shows the most common types of intervention implemented in the Tilley Awards.

Table 4.5 Types of interventions used

Type of intervention used	% of projects adopting the intervention
Media-based publicity	23
High-visibility policing	21
Environmental improvements	19
Enforcement initiatives	18
Developing better partnership working	17
Evidence and intelligence gathering	16
Crime prevention/raising awareness	15
Diversionary activities for young people	15
Identifying and targeting prolific or persistent offenders	13

The extent to which the planned interventions were actually implemented also showed some degree of variation, both in what was done and in the amount of detail recorded about these in the submission. In some cases detailed numbers were provided about how many hours' overtime had been spent on high-visibility policing (HVP), or how many properties had been target hardened following security surveys. Other projects gave very broad outlines of the type of activity that had occurred, simply noting that properties had been target hardened as indicated in the response section, without providing any indication of how many properties had been secured, or what proportion of vulnerable properties in the area had been covered by the intervention. The types of interventions implemented are shown in the boxed examples, with projects covering youth nuisance in Lancashire (Box 4.2) and burglary in Leicestershire (Box 4.3). A third example is given of a project, the Nook scrapyard (Box 4.4), that demonstrated how thinking around the problem enabled the development of a solution relying on other partners to get rid of a problem that could not be solved through conventional policing.

Outcomes and evaluation

We looked at the outcomes of each of the projects, and at how these had been evaluated. This included noting who had conducted the evaluation, what data sources had been accessed to assess this, what

Box 4.2   Operation Acne, Lancashire Constabulary

This project in Blackpool set out to reduce youth nuisance, which was especially problematic on Friday and Saturday evenings. It reported that the police had implemented a number of short, medium and long-term interventions to address the problem. In the short-term, high-visibility patrols, each involving six police officers, were carried out over three weekends, using a budget for 20 hours of overtime that had been made available for this project. In the medium term an increased uniformed presence was implemented, with special constables taking responsibility for the area at weekends, and a police surgery being established to provide reassurance to local residents. The longer-term plan was to provide a place that youngsters could congregate in, and whilst the options for this were being considered a temporary café was provided in a bus. In addition to these interventions, the project also planned an education and awareness-raising campaign amongst the young people in the area and their parents, and around 150 letters were sent out to the parents of those young people who had been spoken to by the police about their behaviour.

Box 4.3   'Reducing burglary – reducing the fear of crime', Leicestershire Constabulary

The analysis for this project had identified one beat with the highest rate of burglary including many distraction burglaries, and noted that older residents felt vulnerable in their properties. The objectives were set out in terms of outcomes, to contribute to a three per cent reduction in burglary in the area, and to reduce fear of crime amongst older people living in the area. The planned interventions were mainly focused around the use of media-based and targeted publicity, and awareness raising, both targeting those who had been the victim of a burglary and those who were considered to be most vulnerable. The police reported that they had successfully distributed crime prevention advice packs to 280 houses in the area, containing information about preventing burglary, theft from the garden and property marking, with a UV pen provided for this. They were involved in the production of a video raising awareness of bogus callers, which was distributed to 250 voluntary groups to be shown to older people. A media strategy involved briefing the local press about the project, and also conducting a series of radio interviews. Finally, the project linked the local work with a wider national strategy to reduce distraction burglary.

Box 4.4 The Nook scrapyard, Lancashire Constabulary

Problems around the Nook scrapyard, situated next to a rural village in Lancashire, appeared to be numerous: stolen cars being traded from the yard, and stripped down for spare parts; disputes leading to fights between staff and customers; theft and damage; suspicious characters in the area after dark; prolific offenders coming to the area to visit the yard; and speeding vehicles and a high crime rate along the access road to the Nook. Previous attempts by the police to deal with the problem had focused on highly visible foot patrols, detections and arrests. Having explored options for further intervention, the only course of action appeared to be to close the yard down. The police were not able to do this on their own, and implemented the following interventions:

- The formation of a Neighbourhood Watch scheme.
- A detailed look at how the Nook affected the local environment.
- Liaison with other agencies, including Environmental Health, the Health and Safety Executive and the Environment Agency.
- A community representative to write to the local MP.

It transpired that the Nook was also causing environmental pollution, and a visit to the site by the Environment Agency resulted in various demands that had to be met for the yard to continue to operate. The yard closed down soon after these demands were made. The closure of the yard resulted in a decrease in crime in the area, and an improvement in quality of life for residents living nearby.

evaluation methods had been used, and whether the conclusions of the evaluation were plausible.

In less than half the projects (45 per cent) was there evidence that the project had been monitored during its implementation, although for many (37 per cent) it was not clear what monitoring had taken place, if any. In two-thirds of the projects, the evaluation was conducted by staff working on the project. No formal evaluation was conducted in 13 per cent of projects. A small number of projects acknowledged that no evaluation had been carried out as it was still too early to be able to judge the impact of the project. Only three projects that we examined were evaluated independently by an external evaluator; for example the Young Citizens programme in Hertfordshire was evaluated by researchers in the Department of Health, which part funded the project. The Tower project in Lancashire was also evaluated independently by researchers at Huddersfield University.

In order to assess the outcomes of the projects, the majority (56 per cent) used police-recorded crime data as a measure of the success of the project, with a further 21 projects (14 per cent) using some other form of police managed data instead (such as command and control, force intelligence, arrest or detection data). Nineteen per cent of the projects used measures specific to the project being implemented, such as attendance of young people at an activity centre, or the number of accidents over the time the project was running, or information from a survey of users or residents. Eleven per cent of the projects used data from partner agencies such as the fire service, local authority or local businesses in the evaluation. For 18 per cent of the projects it was either unclear what data had been used in the evaluation or apparent that no data had been used. Often the sources of data and precise numbers used to assess the outcomes were vague – the projects often referred to success due to the numbers of incidents or complaints or calls for service going down, but provided no hard data to back this up. There appeared to be very little use of cost data in the evaluation of the projects.

Overall, more effort appears to have gone into obtaining data from a variety of sources and using data for the analysis of the problem than for assessing the outcomes, and certainly the amount of space taken up by the analysis in each of the submissions is far longer than that allowed for the assessment stage of the process. Data for assessment generally come from the police. This could have been because a large proportion of the objectives are laid out in terms of outcomes to do with crime reduction or reduction in calls for service. Even for the projects which had used data from non-police sources in the analysis of the problem, this was rarely followed up as part of the evaluation.

Where an evaluation was carried out, in around two-thirds of the projects, this was done by comparing data from before the initiative had been implemented with the period when the initiative was under way. In five cases the impact of the project was measured through a survey administered only after the project, to gauge residents' views since the project had been implemented. In 28 projects (19 per cent) it was unclear what evaluation methods had been used to assess the outcomes of the initiative. In almost half of the projects ($n = 71$) it was not clear what before and after periods were being used in the evaluation. For the projects where before and after periods were stated, the length of these time periods varied from project to project. Most commonly, in 35 per cent of the projects where the time periods were stated, the evaluation was conducted by comparing the data from one whole calendar or financial year prior to the start of the project to the data from the year after implementation. In 28 per cent of the projects a comparison was made between a specified time period given for one year (e.g. January to March) and the same time period the following year. Twenty-five projects used non-equivalent before and after periods, for example one project implemented by a force in the north of England to reduce antisocial behaviour compared data from the before period in March and April 2000 with the after period which they defined as November and December in the same year, with no account taken of possible seasonal changes. In another case from 2001, the before period ran for 7 months from January 2000 until July 2000, and this was compared with the 5 months from August 2000 until December 2000, so there was no account of seasonal changes or even variation in the time scales that were being compared. Examples of very short before and after periods were also evident – one project compared just one month's worth of data before the project to one month after implementation.

Based on assessment of the evaluators in the project submissions, over three-quarters of the projects felt they had achieved or partially achieved their objectives through the project, although evidence to demonstrate this was sometimes lacking. The majority felt they had at least partially achieved their objectives, or the extent to which they had achieved their objectives was unclear. The objectives were not achieved at all in nine cases – this was largely due to it being too soon after implementation to be able to tell if the project had worked or not, or because no objectives had been established at the outset of the project.

The authors also made an assessment as to whether or not the conclusions drawn through the evaluation were convincing. Although this is obviously a subjective measure, it was assessed on the extent of the data provided, whether the claimed effects seemed reasonable in terms of the extent of the action taken during the project, and other contextual factors. One-third of the projects were thought to be convincing in the arguments presented in the project submission; 44 per cent of the projects were not convincing at all; 13 per cent were partially convincing – we thought that either some aspect of the project's apparent results could reasonably be attributed to the action taken or the data supported some form of effect from the project. In 10 per cent of the projects there were no discernible data or evaluation presented, and no further assessment could be made.

There were several weaknesses in the evaluation that applied to virtually every project submitted, and provides an indicator for where future work is needed to improve the standard of evaluation for projects using problem-oriented approaches.

A major problem with the assessment was lack of data, and this was highlighted for half the projects we looked at. Whereas the use of a variety of data sources had been evident in the analysis of the problem, data for evaluation came largely from a single source, which was invariably police-recorded crime or command and control data. The lack of data clearly led to limitations of statistical analysis. Other common problems with the evaluation were a failure to make measurements related to specific outcomes, again seen in half the projects, and a failure to work out expected outcome patterns (in 40 per cent of the projects). For example one project which aimed to reduce repeat victimisation failed to provide any data relating to repeat incidents.

Another common weakness with the evaluations examined was a failure to take account of other explanations for the effects seen, with this being highlighted in just under half the projects. Whilst crime might have gone down with the introduction of the project, few details were provided about whether or not there were other initiatives ongoing within the area which might also have contributed to the measured reduction in crime. Related to this is the lack of information about the context within which the project was taking place, and lack of a comparison area.

One of the weaknesses we came across regularly in the evaluation was lack of clarity about when the interventions were actually implemented. This should be relatively straightforward to include, and is important to understand when the effects of the project might be expected.

In addition to the projects stating that they had been successful in meeting the specified objectives, almost half the projects claimed that there were additional benefits resulting from the project implementation. In most cases these related to improved partnership working with other agencies, improvements to the environment, and better community engagement, although few data were provided to demonstrate these outcomes.

Implementation issues

Sixty-two of the projects (41 per cent) mentioned problems they had experienced with implementation of the initiatives, and provide some valuable lessons for avoiding similar potential problems in other projects at the development and implementation stages. Several projects mentioned problems with abstraction of police officers to other duties, whereas in other places projects took precedence over normal beat duties, which suffered as a result of officers having to focus on project activities in addition to their normal duties. Several projects mentioned problems with having to overcome scepticism from police officers in adopting a problem-oriented approach to policing, seeing it as something additional to 'normal' policing, an issue discussed further in Chapters 2–3. Another common problem was maintaining the motivation for the project, from the police, other partners and the public, especially when the project was not designed to produce instant results. Securing funding for projects was also problematic for a number of them. Several projects made application to the lottery. Others tried to raise funds from local businesses or the community.

Some of the problems were specific to the particular time or place in which the project was being implemented, and would probably not be relevant to other projects. Although relatively rare, some unexpected events can occur which are almost impossible to plan for. For example, one project in Cheshire set out to reduce response times to emergency 999 calls and improve public reassurance, with one of the main ways of communicating the messages of the project to the public being though stalls at rural country shows. The unforeseen outbreak of foot-and-mouth disease meant that many of the shows were cancelled, and much of the work had to be postponed until the outbreak had been brought under control!

Other problems encountered in setting up and running projects were successfully overcome. One project in Cumbria planned to run a breakfast club for young children on the estate being targeted. Having it on the estate would have led to the logistical problem of project staff then having the responsibility of transporting the children to the local primary school. This was overcome by negotiating with the school to hold the breakfast club on school premises but for it to be staffed by the project with assistance from staff at a children's charity. Another problem arose when partner agencies came up against conflicting priorities. In Plymouth, a project to reduce fraudulent claims for Jobseekers' Allowance developed a protocol that required all claimants to make visits to the Job Centre in person to report the loss or theft of a Giro cheque, to demonstrate that each claim would be investigated fully in an effort to discourage false reporting. This conflicted with the Job Centre objective of reducing the number of personal visits made to the centre, which was thought to add to the administrative burden for staff. During the pilot scheme it was possible to demonstrate that despite the increase in personal visits, this actually led to a reduction in administration, as the measures implemented to discourage false claimants meant that fewer cases arose.

Sustainability of the projects

Just under half of the projects (47 per cent) stated that they planned to continue with the initiative following the submission of the project to the Tilley Awards. Eleven per cent of the projects did not plan to continue, or were designed as one-off projects that had met the objectives and would be self-sustaining, such as the redesign of a car park in a project to reduce vehicle theft. It is not known from the project submission whether the remainder of the projects planned to continue with the implementation of the project. Of the projects that were to continue, the main source of funding for the majority of these (60 per cent) was through mainstream police funding. Around 18 per cent of the projects set to continue were planning to do so through mainstream funding from a partner agency other than the police.

In many forces there were plans to roll out successful initiatives in neighbouring beats or Basic Command Units. In doing this, it may be necessary to adapt the initiative and protocols developed to suit the local context in other beats and BCUs which may differ substantially from the area in which the project was implemented. For example, in Blackpool in 1999 bike patrols had been used along the seafront, and plans were suggested in the project report for rolling this out across the whole force area. However, the distinctive conditions of the Golden Mile in Blackpool may not be found elsewhere in the county, meaning there may be problems with replication of the project. Projects which were seen as being examples of good practice were being included as part of officers' training in problem-oriented approaches in Sussex. Partnership working and protocols set up around these were extended to other problems. British Transport Police developed good working relationship with London Underground workers to tackle ticket touts in one Tube station – it was envisaged that the joint approach could be extended to other problem offences experienced within the Underground system.

There is evidence of projects being sustained after the end of the initial project life, and of good practice lessons taken from these projects being disseminated both within the individual police force and more widely. Hobbs (2004) reported that two-thirds of the 23 winning projects from 1999 to 2003 were still running, half of these as originally planned, or with only slight modifications, and the other half having been developed further, beyond the original brief. Nineteen of these projects had been adopted more widely throughout the police force in which it originated, and in the majority of cases were promoted as good practice. Where projects were not replicated, officers believed that the knowledge of implementing the project had helped in the development of subsequent problem-oriented work.

Conclusion

The analysis of projects helps us to understand the state of problem-oriented policing in the UK, and how this has changed over the past six or seven years. A number of clear trends have been identified:

1 Problem-oriented projects have covered a very wide range of problem types.

2 Projects have tended to be police-led though mostly involve at least one partner agency at some stage.

3 The scale of the problems being addressed varied greatly.

4 There was wide variety in the quality and quantity of analysis presented.

5 Analysis tended to be based on police data and limited to broad counts.

6 A range of problems accessing and utilising data were noted. These included problems with data sharing between partners, having to trawl through paper-based records, lack of detail in recorded crime data and working with data sets without coterminous geographical boundaries.

7 Relatively poor use of existing literature to help understand problems was made.

8 Projects tended to have fairly well specified objectives.

9 Most responses followed on well or fairly well from analysis.

10 The majority of projects tended to involve some kind of enforcement.

11 Implementation was monitored in less than half the projects.

12 Evaluation was generally weak overall.

13 Implementation problems were identified by around half the projects and these included scepticism from the police service, difficulties maintaining project momentum, difficulties securing additional funds, and the impact of unexpected events.

14 At least half the projects planned to continue.

The efforts and enthusiasm of individual officers in developing and implementing projects dealing with a wide array of problem types was evident. Also evident were some excellent examples of problem-oriented policing in practice, such as the Nook scrapyard and Tower projects from Lancashire, mentioned earlier, Operation Cobra from Hampshire and Safe and Secure Twenty-four- seven from Staffordshire, the winner in 2004.

However, we also identified problems in the implementation of projects. Implementation of the processes of problem-orientation was patchy. For example, we came across examples of projects where clearly much time and effort had been spent in researching the problem and producing a comprehensive analysis that led on to realistic objectives and a sensible response. In many cases this was not carried through to the assessment stage, and the evaluation was not completed with the same thoroughness. In many projects that we examined, more sophisticated analysis of the data was required. This problem is consistently found (see Chapter 2). These projects also demonstrated problems with the evaluation stage of the problem-oriented process. It was clear that far less effort was being put into assessing whether a project had been successfully implemented, and whether the project objectives had been achieved. Indeed, with some projects the evaluation was not completed at all, as the project was submitted to the awards without sufficient time after the interventions to be able to assess its success. Problems with evaluation may in part be due to projects not setting realistic (or any) objectives, or being vague about what the aims and objectives are. Also it is not always clear how the project staff envisaged that the interventions planned will actually bring about the expected outcomes.

On the whole the problems outlined seemed to apply equally to all the years that we looked at, with little obvious change over time, despite an increasing supply of examples of projects to build on and tools for improving implementation. However, there was some evidence that individual projects had improved over time, possibly as a result of understanding the problem better, or becoming more familiar with the problem-oriented process, as well as the requirements of the Tilley Award (possibly aided by the feedback provided each year by the judging panel). One example of this was Operation Aslan, which was originally set up in by Lancashire Constabulary in Blackpool in March 1999 to reduce disorder in the centre of the town, particularly associated with the night-time economy. The project was submitted in 1999, and again in each of the following two years. In the first year, the project submission gave a brief overview of the problems faced. The only quantitative data referred to showed that 82 per cent of offenders arrested for disorder had been drinking. The description of the area suggested that there were a number of problems on which to focus:

1 Repeat incidents in and around licensed premises, under-age drinking, premises that contravene licensing laws, and problems with door staff.

2 Problems with lack of transport late at night, management of taxi ranks and traffic congestion.

3 Problems of litter, urinating and vomiting.

4 Problems around restaurants and fast-food take-aways.

The planned ways of dealing with these issues, which had not been implemented when the project was first submitted, included high-visibility policing, and action around licensed premises. Despite the fact that little had been implemented at this stage, the project claimed to have produced a significant reduction in violent crime and incidents of antisocial behaviour. The analysis stage the following year included much more information about the characteristics of the victims and the offenders, the majority of whom lived locally, and also identified four hotspots where most of the problems were occurring. The analysis also looked at rates of offending – premises that had a higher volume of violent incidents also had larger capacities, meaning in terms of rates of offending none was identified as contributing disproportionately to the level of violent crime. Similarly, fast-food take-aways that were thought to be crime generators were situated close to taxi ranks, and the revised analysis pointed to the problem having a greater association with taxi ranks. The focus of the operation shifted from the licensed premises to dealing with the problems of lack of transport at the end of the night, and dispersal of crowds. Medium to long-term measures around setting up a local partnership and changing transport arrangements were starting to be introduced.

In the third year the project reported on the longer-term responses that had started to take shape, including better management of the taxi rank and encouragement of local pubs to take greater responsibility. One taxi rank was closed, and barriers were used to create a more formal queuing system for taxis between midnight and 3.00 a.m.; door staff from licensed premises wearing high visibility jackets acted as marshals for the taxi queue; additional publicity was sponsored by local businesses; and exclusion orders were used to ban persistent offenders from all licensed premises in the area. The assessment gave a different picture to that from the first year, and showed that there had actually been an increase in the number of disorder incidents being dealt with by the police over this period, although the number of recorded violent crimes had decreased across the town centre. Greater reductions in incidents were reported around the taxi ranks, where specific measures had been concentrated.

This example demonstrates how projects can change over time, and how the understanding of a problem can alter as a more in depth analysis is carried out. It shows the importance of making sure the analysis is representative of the true problem before the response stage is reached – but also that short-term measures can be implemented whilst the longer-term measures are developed. It showed the value in constantly reviewing the project, to ensure the real problem is identified and addressed.

To conclude, this chapter has looked in detail at the range and scope of the implementation of the processes of problem-oriented policing in individual projects. Whilst without doubt there are some excellent examples of problem-orientation in practice, there are still difficulties with the implementation of the main processes. One way this can be addressed is through having support within police forces from analysts who have been properly trained in the skills required to apply a problem-oriented approach effectively. These analysts need to be aware of, and be able to implement, the full range of tools available to assist with the process. Many of the tools that are available to enhance the effectiveness of each stage of the problem-oriented process are discussed in more detail in the following chapter.

Chapter 5

Resources for improving problem-oriented policing and partnership

The basic ideas behind problem-oriented policing, as conceived by Herman Goldstein, were laid out in Chapter 1. Chapters 3 and 4 showed what had been developed and delivered in practice in what is considered the best of problem-oriented policing in the UK. Chapter 4 looked at specific examples of award-entered problem-oriented projects; it was shown that there were substantial weaknesses in many of these. The shortcomings found in even the best of British problem-oriented policing are akin to those that have been found when entries to the Goldstein Award have been reviewed (Clarke 1998).

These findings reinforce those of two HMIC inspections, conducted in 1998 and 2000, that asked each police service to nominate four successful and four unsuccessful problem-solving crime reduction initiatives. In 1998, of 234 initiatives that were presented as successes, the inspection found that there was evidence of an actual problem in 68 per cent of them, 'proper analysis' in 27 per cent, monitoring in 20 per cent and evidence of effectiveness in 7 per cent. In 2000 the figures were slightly better: of 146 problem-solving initiatives deemed to have been successful 32 per cent incorporated proper analysis, there was monitoring in 29 per cent and evidence of success in 24 per cent (HMIC 1998, 2000; Read and Tilley 2000).

From all accounts there are weaknesses in the implementation of problem-oriented policing. But much has been done to try to improve this situation. The purpose of the current chapter is to corral together resources that have been developed over the past few years to inform improvements in the practice of problem-oriented policing and partnership. Some of these have been devised specifically to underpin problem-oriented work. Others have been developed with other purposes in mind, but nevertheless have a useful role to play. Further details of many are freely available at www.popcenter.org, whose specific purpose is to inform improvements in the practice of problem-oriented policing.

As shown in Chapter 1, the acronym SARA is widely used in problem-solving to capture the processes involved. SARA refers to Scanning, Analysis, Response and Assessment. It was developed and first described in the influential report of the Newport News demonstration project implementing problem-oriented policing (Eck and Spelman 1987). It will be clear that, though it is useful to distinguish these elements and their overall sequence, in practice there need to be overlaps and feedbacks between them. The SARA process is an iterative one (Laycock 2005). Scanning suggests problems for analysis though the analysis may redefine the problems. The analysis will inform choice of responses though discussions about possible responses may in turn provoke further analysis. Assessment will take its lead from the scanning, analysis and analysis-informed response, but may also prompt revisions to and fresh thoughts about problems and their analysis as well as the responses put in train.

What is described below are tools and techniques that have been devised to improve the individual stages of the SARA process and the process overall.

Scanning

The purpose of scanning is to identify problems and specify them adequately for problem solving. Clarke (1998) emphasises the need to go beyond particular individual, local issues but without using such broad categories that no effective solutions can realistically be sought. 'Violent crime', for example, would comprise a category that is too broad from which to develop problem oriented interventions. Violence within one family or around one club would comprise too narrow an issue to warrant problem-oriented intervention. Clarke refers to efforts to deal with the latter as more narrow 'problem-solving' rather than 'problem-oriented' work which is concerned with recurrent patterns of broader scope. Both are valid and useful and both might be expected in an effective police service or partnership, but problem solving does not require the effort or resource that goes into problem oriented work and the investment called for by the whole SARA process.

Scanning in the context of problem-oriented work is concerned with identifying and homing in on patterned incidents that are open to realistic solution. This needs to be stressed where much that is done in the name of problem-oriented policing takes issues that are either too specific, part of Clarke's problem solving, or too broad to be open to a well targeted set of interventions.

The following takes the reader through techniques and tools that have been devised to reach a well specified problem. We begin, though, with a few remarks on data sources that can be used for this purpose.

Data sources

Information for scanning may, in principle, derive from a variety of sources, though as Chapter 4 showed police data are most often used, with recorded crime playing the largest part. Other data sources that might be drawn on for identifying problems might include those collected by the local authority (for example on many types of disorder, fly-tipping, fly-posting, sharps collected, public surveys and noise nuisance), the health service (for example unreported woundings, domestic violence and drug abuse), the fire service (for example suspicious fires of various sorts), transport providers (for example damage to vehicles, assaults on and abuse of staff), car park proprietors (for example numbers of incidents by type and distribution within facilities) as well as police data over and above those related to recorded crimes (for example calls for service, letters from the public and 'community intelligence').

In order to identify rates of incident, the postcode address file gives information on domestic and non-domestic postal points, the census gives local information on numbers of individuals and households and their broad demographic attributes; the local authority may provide information on land use, footfall, geographical mobility, and numbers of new houses built or being constructed, and transport providers may have information on rates of travel to and from destinations and times of travel.

There may sometimes be scope for dedicated data collection exercises, including making observations in areas that are thought to present problems that are not otherwise recorded (see Shapland *et al.* 1994 for useful guidance on this), as well as arrangements for more detailed record keeping for a period, interviews of offenders, victims and other stakeholders in the problem, victimisation surveys of various kinds, and public consultation exercises (see Lamm Weisel 2003).

Each data source has more or less serious shortcomings. For example, recorded crime data miss crimes that are not reported and of those reported also those that are not recorded. They also omit those many issues that make calls on police and their partners that are not recorded as crimes. It is notable that up to 80 per cent of calls to the police relate to incidents that are not directly crime-related (Read *et al.* 1999). Calls for service data are technically difficult to analyse, often poorly coded because the nature of the incident is unclear to the call taker, with duplicates in many cases, and often reflect the prejudices of the caller as much as the nature of the incident being reported (Read and Oldfield 1995). Letters from the public reflect the views of the literate with the time and skill to write. As with public meetings they will tend to reflect the interests of those (normally though of course not invariably white, middle-class and older) people who most commonly show up and speak. Surveys are expensive if done well and at best can only capture periodic snapshots of samples. Consultation exercises mostly tap the views of self-selected consultees, even when targeting the 'hard to reach'. And observations are again expensive and can easily be misled by surface appearance.

Clearly what will be most useful will vary by problem. All sources need to be treated with some caution. And, where possible, use of more than one source can help check that misleading impressions that may derive from a single one are less likely. However, there is always a risk that rather than collect complementary information to check alternative sources the same information is simply collected from different places.

Improved problem solving will follow from more critical use of police data and greater efforts to make use of sources beyond recorded crime, whilst acknowledging their weaknesses. This should not be read as suggesting that more is unequivocally better in data use. There have been some exceptionally informative analyses using one data source and a few fields from it. The work on repeat victimisation that will be discussed later in this chapter is an example. The point being made here is that there are a host of data sources that can be used and created, that few are being used (and are often used uncritically) and that what is needed is a reflective and imaginative use of those data sources that are relevant to the issues being addressed. A sensible general principle would be, case by case, to use those requiring minimum effort to obtain robust enough results for the purpose at hand.

The discussion turns now to data use and to processes through which problems can be adequately specified for problem-oriented purposes. We begin with tools for prioritising issues.

Tools for problem prioritisation

Alex Hirschfield (2005) shows how a variety of data systems can be brought together and the data interrogated to create quite a simple chart to help inform decisions over priorities by place and crime type. In contrast to that section that follows on repeat victimisation, the focus here is on how crime is concentrated at the area rather than victim level. In relation to specific crime types in each sub-area, Hirschfield includes 'prevalence' (proportion of the relevant population affected within each sub-area), 'concentration' (proportion of all crimes of that type across the whole area that occurred within each sub-area) and 'prominence' (proportion of all crime in each area represented by the specific type). These can then be ranked as a means of informing decisions about where problem-solving efforts are to be directed. Table 5.1 reproduces the first few rows of an example given by Hirschfield where he takes wards and shows the prevalence, concentration and prominence of burglary in 'Barchester', alongside the ranks for each. There are 22 wards in all. Ward 17 comes top for prevalence: in it the highest proportion of households are suffer burglary. It comes second for concentration: only Ward 21 has a higher proportion of all burglaries in Barchester. It also comes first for prominence: in Ward 17 burglary comprised a higher share of all crimes than in any other ward. No other ward scores highly so consistently in terms of these bases for prioritisation. It would make sense to focus burglary-reduction problem-oriented work here. It might be difficult for those in other wards to argue otherwise. The analysis thus not only provides grounds for the partnership to focus there. It also comprises defensible grounds for those living in areas not prioritised (see Hirschfield and Bowers 2000).

Table 5.1 The prevalence, concentration and prominence of burglary in Barchester (from Hirschfield 2005: 658)

Ward No.	Prevalence	R	Concentration	R	Prominence	R
17	52.10	(1)	8.8	(2)	20.34	(1)
21	47.29	(2)	10.0	(1)	11.67	(14)
1	42.29	(3)	7.3	(4)	12.07	(12)
8	35.64	(4)	6.5	(7)	13.64	(8)
13	35.61	(5)	7.2	(5)	14.45	(7)

Paul and Patricia Brantingham (1997) describe the use of 'location quotients'. These compare the rate of crime in a sub-area to the rate of crime in the whole area. Formally, this amounts to:

$$\frac{\text{Number of local crimes/local area}}{\text{All crimes/total area}}$$

A list can then be created which compares different local area rates to help prioritise areas for attention. A variety of distribution quotients (other than location) can be created with different denominators (for example age of victim, gender, ethnicity, housing tenure, time of residence, etc.) comparing local sub-groups with a whole population. Table 5.2 shows calculations of the household rate quotient, alongside Hirschfield's prevalence, concentration and prominence for Hirschfield's Barchester data. In Barchester there were 51,321 households and 1,356 burglaries. The figures in Table 5.2 show the degree to which each area experiences burglary rates over and above the rate for the area as a whole. Hence Ward 17 has almost twice the prevailing rate, whilst Ward 13's rate is about a third higher than that for the area as a whole

Though useful in giving some data with which to work to establish priorities, the techniques described by Hirschfield and by the Brantinghams will never be sufficient. The seriousness of the problem is also a factor, where there are choices between problems to focus on (and views between sub-groups may well differ on this). Furthermore some problems may be more open to effective solutions than others. Devoting problem-solving efforts to the very serious or the very common when there are good reasons to believe that the problem cannot be effectively and/or ethically addressed would be a waste of resources. Finally, if the only effective response to a problem would involve unrealistically high levels of expenditure focusing

Table 5.2 Selected Barchester location quotients

Ward No.	Households (a)	Burglaries (b)	Location quotient (b/a)/(1,356/51,321)
17	2,284	119	1.97
21	2,876	136	1.79
1	2,341	99	1.60
8	2,469	88	1.35
13	2,752	98	1.35

on it would not be sensible. Now, some of this would be hard to determine in advance of analysis. Indeed, in many cases what is open to problem-orientation may be some sub-set of the total population of the original problem, that is sufficiently widespread, serious, tractable and open to interventions that are ethical and economic.

Table 5.3 combines the factors relevant to prioritisation that have been outlined here. It provides for the presentation of evidence of various sorts relating to them, to inform decisions about the direction of problem-solving resources.

Tools for specifying problems

The processes of prioritisation described so far need to be followed by further work to identify specific problems that are open to practical solution. A starting point has been provided by Eck and Clarke, who have developed a classification of problems.

A typology of problems

Eck and Clarke (Eck and Clarke 2003; Clarke and Eck 2003; Eck 2003) have proposed a classification of 66 different types of problem that may be identified. They stress that problems comprise sets of events that are linked in some way. Problems, they argue, have two major dimensions: behaviour and environment. They identify six types of behaviour and 11 environments, as shown in Table 5.4. The behaviours are not defined by crime types. Instead, the classification refers to:

1 Predatory actions, comprising criminal offences of one person or group against another.

2 Consensual behaviours that are often criminal but do not involve predation, for example drugs trafficking or prostitution.

3 Interpersonal conflicts which may or may not involve crime, for example neighbour disputes.

4 Incivilities which again may or may not be criminal but annoy, for instance 'annoying, unsightly or disruptive behaviours', 'threatening behaviours', and 'non-violent conflicts over the use of space'.

5 Endangerment behaviours when someone puts themselves or another at risk.

6 Misuse of police (or it could be another cognate agency) where demands are unreasonable or inappropriate.

Table 5.3 Scanning for priority problem

	Recorded crime	Command and control	Survey/s	Public meeting/s	Other (specify)
Evidence of rate of problem (for example domestic burglaries in specified area per 1,000 households)					
Evidence of extent of problem (for example, number of households within which the problem level is experienced, be this defined by geography or by some other means of aggregating the at-risk population)					
Evidence of period problem has been taking place (for example, at least twice the national/CDRP rate over the last three years)					
Evidence of seriousness of problem (for example, losses experienced, or public priorities, or effect on quality of life)					
Evidence of problem solvability (for example, studies showing how domestic burglary problems have previously been addressed)					
Evidence of likely cost of intervening in relation to likely benefits (for example, total pounds spent per burglary prevented)					
Evidence that the likely resources needed are likely to be available (for example, sources of financial and/or other support)					

Table 5.4 Eck and Clarke's problem classification

Environments	Behaviours					
	Predatory	Con-sensual	Con-flicts	In-civilities	Endanger-ment	Misuse of police
Residential						
Recreational						
Offices						
Retail						
Industrial						
Agricultural						
Educational						
Human services						
Public ways						
Transport						
Open/ transitional						

'Environments' help identify who may have some role and responsibility in relation to regulating the problem behaviours. Problems may thus occur within the sphere of influence or control of different constituencies who may act as 'guardians' or 'place managers' in relation to the problematic behaviour taking place. The meaning of all but the last of these should be fairly obvious. The last, 'open/transitional', refers to areas 'without consistent or designated uses' (Eck and Clarke 2003: 18), such as abandoned buildings and building sites.

Eck and Clarke acknowledge that some problems may not easily fit into a single cell in this classification matrix. For example vandalism may be predatory or a form of interpersonal conflict. They also acknowledge that environments may be 'nested' in that some may include sub-parts that comprise another, for example universities that include car parks, streets and paths. In these circumstances, though the less embedded environment may be important (for example the university) the most embedded is likely to be most significant for categorising the problem (for example the car park).

Eck and Clarke's classification system offers help in better specifying problems for further work and in distinguishing issues that do not comprise suitable problems for attention. For example, they suggest that 'bored youth' does not constitute a problem since there is no specific action that defines it. They argue that the spatial environmental reference is important since this indicates where police may be able to operate and exert influence (and the main focus of their paper is on police-related problems). They speculate that there may be generic methods of understanding and addressing categories of problems specified within their schema, and that it will in this way help inform analysis and the formulation of responses.

A typology of hotspots

It is normal to look at the distribution of an identified problem across space and time. Jerry Ratcliffe (2004) has developed a useful *hotspots matrix*, as shown in Figure 5.1, for specifying different spatio-temporal patterns. The intersection of the distributions by space and time yields nine cells, suggesting the different intervention strategies as indicated in the figure. The framework is intended to help think through analysis and possible responses, and we shall see the potential pay-off later.

Townsley and Pease (2002) help further specify the nature of hotspots. They point out that they may be defined in relative or absolute terms. Relative hotspots are defined in terms of the normal rates in those areas. That is, if there is an increase in that area, it becomes hot relative to itself. Absolute hotspots are those that are chronically high by normal standards. A major difficulty with relative hot spots is that small area crime rates are highly volatile, with short-term pseudo-random lurches in rates. Many relative hotspots will revert to normal rates through 'regression to the mean' processes independently of interventions. Absolute hotspots are more useful for problem solving. A great deal of energy can be wasted following blips and assuming that responses have been effective where falls would have occurred anyway from abnormally high short-term rates.

Incidence, prevalence and concentration

The most developed means better to specify the nature of the problem probably relates to repeat victimisation. A key distinction is made between measurements of 'prevalence', 'incidence' and 'concentration', though rather confusingly these terms are given meanings rather different from those used by Hirschfield whose ideas were discussed earlier. In the context of writings about repeat victimisation 'prevalence' refers to the number of potential victims

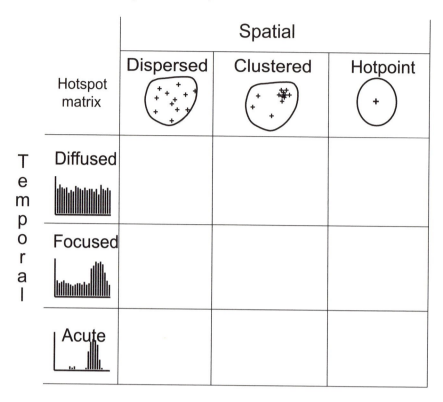

Figure 5.1 A hotspots classification matrix

experiencing a crime within a specified time period; 'incidence' refers to the total number of incidents of that crime within the given time period and 'concentration' refers to the number of incidents per victim over that time period. The relationship between these can be expressed as:

$$C \text{ (concentration)} = \frac{I \text{ (Incidence)}}{P \text{ (Prevalence)}}$$

Incidence and prevalence can be given either as absolute numbers or rates. For most predatory crimes concentration will always be 1 or more since victims may experience more than one crime but there will seldom be more victims than crimes. Crime surveys are especially useful in measuring repeat victimisation, since they do not suffer from under-reporting and under-recording and do not lack the consistent unique victim identifiers that are often missing in recorded crime data. Crime surveys have limitations however, including their rarity at very local levels, the scarcity of studies looking at patterns of victimisation where neither individuals nor households are the victims (for example businesses of various sorts, schools, hospitals, etc.), and problems of respondent memory. In practice, with some care it is often possible to obtain a rough measure from police incident and recorded crime data (Read and Oldfield 1995; Read *et al.* 1999). The concentration level tells us immediately what percentage reduction of a given crime could be achieved by eliminating repeats. If the concentration is 1.5, then a 33.3 per cent reduction would be achieved by eliminating repeats (0.5/1.5 × 100). If the concentration level was 1.15, a 13 per cent reduction would be achieved by eliminating repeats (0.15/1.15 × 100).

Table 5.5, taken from Bridgeman and Hobbs (1997), illustrates how more detailed patterns of repeat can be presented to show how far an identified problem might be ameliorated by focusing on repeat incidents. Table 5.5, which relates to commercial burglaries, allows us to make some interesting calculations. For example, the total number of businesses experiencing repeat incidents is 97 (250–153). The concentration level is 1.84 (459/250). The total number of crimes that could be prevented by eliminating repeats is 209 (459–250). That amounts to some 46 per cent of the total (209/459 × 100, or (0.84/1.84 × 100 = 45.53). Halve the number of repeats and the fall in total amounts therefore to almost a quarter, or 23 per cent. Determining how a crime problem is patterned in this way does not tell the police or partnership what to do. It does, however,

Table 5.5 Repeat victimisation calculations: an example from commercial burglary

No. of victimisations (a)	No. of businesses (b)	No. of burglaries (a × b) = (c)	No. of repeats (c − b) = (d)
1	153	153	0
2	50	100	50
3	20	60	40
4	10	40	30
5	8	40	32
6	5	30	25
9	4	36	32
Total	250	459	209

help more precisely to specify the problem and focus analysis and intervention.

Research (Johnson and Bowers 2004; Townsley *et al.* 2003) extends the concept of repeat victimisation, showing how the risk of burglary appears to spread to nearby homes, mimicking the communication of a disease. Thus, following a burglary at one household those nearest appear to be at an elevated risk of burglary for the next month or so, and this appears to be particularly the case for those on the same side of the street as the burgled home (Bowers and Johnson 2005). Such findings have inspired a form of predictive crime mapping (Bowers *et al.* 2004) which is under development and testing. They also have immediate implications for crime prevention, suggesting that where reductive effort is directed towards victimised homes it may be prudent to extend coverage to those near by, particularly where such homes are vulnerable in ways that have previously been exploited.

CHEERS

Clarke and Eck (2003, 2005) suggest a CHEERS test when defining problems. There are six required elements: Community (some section suffering from the behaviour), Harm (some form of specific harm experienced), Expectation (some members of the community expecting the police or partnership to deal with the causes of the harm), Events (the type of event constituting the problem), Recurrence (not a one-off or very short-term issue) and Similarity (some salient commonality by virtue of victim, place, circumstance, weapon, etc.). When a putative problem is being considered it is worth checking that it sufficiently specified in these terms.

The resources for scanning described here can help systematically to specify the nature of the problem to be targeted. They help answer what, where, when and who (victim) questions: what the problem is, where and when it is found, and who is experiencing it. The next section turns to the analysis of the problem. This focuses on the who (offender), why and how of the specified problems, to inform decisions about responses.

Analysis

The purpose of analysis in the context of problem-orientation is to find 'pinch points' (Tilley 2002). That is, it is to identify practical interventions that have a real chance of reducing, removing or ameliorating the identified problem. In general the everyday, commonsense language of 'root causes' is avoided. This is first because we know rather little with confidence about root causes; second because what many suspect to be root causes (such as inequitable social conditions, moral weakness and individual and family pathology) are tricky to change and we do not have a robust, established technology for making those changes; third because the 'proximal' (or near) causes (Ekblom 1994, 2002) appear to be more open to intervention and we now have substantial volumes of evidence that they can be effective; and fourth because most putative root causes require long-term interventions and are likely to have their effects only in the relatively distant future whereas those suffering problems generally want them dealt with effectively and quickly, wherever this is possible. The task, therefore, is to find modifiable conditions that encourage, enable or help reproduce patterns of specific problem behaviour. In analysis, why and how questions are asked, with the specific aim of identifying causes that can be modified or offending methods that can be disabled.

PAT and RAT: generic resources for analysis

The best-known generic analytic tool for problem-solving is the 'Problem-Analysis Triangle' (PAT). PAT identifies three aspects that are found for all problems: the location or type of location where the problem behaviour is happening, the offender or type of offender (or person/s behaving in ways creating a problem for others) and the victim or type of victim (or person/s who is experiencing others' behaviour as problematic). Figure 5.2 shows the way in which the basic Problem Analysis Triangle is often represented. Analysis can in practice often amount to no more than a catalogue of attributes or suspected attributes of the problem under these three headings, without focusing on what it is about those attributes which is crucial to the production of the problem and by implication what might be done to remove or reduce it. One simple use of PAT, however, can be to help work through whether the problem is mainly one of specific offenders or types of offender, or of specific locations or types of location or of specific victims or types of victim, and by implication which needs to be the key focus of attention in working out responses.

Routine Activity Theory (RAT) helps make much more constructive use of PAT for problem-solving purposes. According to RAT, for a direct contact predatory crime to occur three conditions must converge

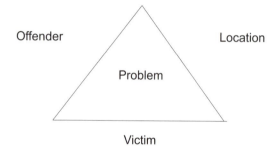

Figure 5.2   PAT 1: The basic problem analysis triangle

in time and space (Cohen and Felson 1979; Felson 2002). There must be: (1) a likely offender and (2) a suitable target, (3) in the absence of a capable guardian. Crime rate variations and changes, in the US in particular, have been explained making use of information on the supply, distribution and movement of these three and of changes in them (Cohen and Felson 1979). Once stated, this theory can seem rather obvious at first sight. Yet it has proved remarkably fertile in explaining crime patterns. Moreover, one significant implication is that once any one of the three essential conditions for producing a crime incident has been removed, that specific crime cannot take place. The victim and offender elements of RAT obviously map across to PAT easily. What of location and capable guardians? Locations are problematic not just because they describe places where likely offenders and suitable targets converge, but also because they lack sufficient guardianship to inhibit the likely offender from offending against the suitable target. The importance of RAT is that it shows why the removal of any one of the conditions for criminal behaviour will, in principle, be enough to prevent it, though in practice matters are seldom quite that simple.

The simple Problem Analysis Triangle has subsequently been elaborated. A second triangle is drawn round the first, as shown in Figure 5.3 (see Eck 2003). This brings out the practical potential from analysing problems, by specifying how the crucial situations for crime events can be undermined by the introduction of a place manager to make a location safer, or a 'handler' who is capable of inhibiting the behaviour of a likely offender, or a capable guardian who can protect a prospective victim. Which is most appropriate or has the greatest preventive potential will vary by specific problem. The issue is returned to below in a discussion of response selection.

Figure 5.3 RAT: Routine activity theory's double triangle. *Source* Eck (2003)

Hotspots: crime generators and crime attractors

Paul and Patricia Brantingham (1995) developed the concepts of *crime attractor* and *crime generator*, to describe two different mechanisms through which high crime locations (hotspots) can be created. Crime generators comprise places that have a plentiful supply of suitable targets for crime and also a large throughput of people, a proportion of whom may be tempted to take advantage of the opportunities that are available. Crime attractors comprise places that attract offenders specifically because of the opportunities available there, which they wish to exploit. Many hotspots, such as shopping malls, are both attractors and generators of crime. In other cases, it appears that places act mainly as attractors. For example Tilley (2005) found that the quiet time (night) and distinctive *modus operandi* (slit curtains) of thefts from lorries in lorry parks at motorway service areas suggested that they were mainly crime attractors, on account of the available rich pickings that could be obtained only with the right tools and at unguarded times. Rock concerts, entry to which must be paid, may comprise generators but not attractors.

If a hotspot is mainly a crime attractor then the response will try to find methods of stopping offenders from coming. If it is mainly a crime generator, the issue is that of providing protection for the targets of the criminal behaviour from those who are open to temptation once there. In some cases, of course, mixed strategies will be needed.

Understanding groups of incidents: crime sets

Poyner (1986) shows how we can analyse problems for potential points of intervention through constructing 'crime sets' that comprise suites of offences that belong together because of their close similarities. He acknowledges that these sets are often constructed from the partial information recorded by the police. Poyner likens the process of creating crime sets to archaeology, where what is available to reconstruct an account of what happened is rather limited, often only to fragments. However, thought and imagination can be used to build up a rich picture that is plausible and consistent with the fragmentary evidence that is to hand. One example, shown in Figure 5.4, relates to theft from the person at bus stops in central Coventry. Poyner builds a crime set, made up of offences committed in basically the same way, taking advantage of the environment in which a suitable target presents itself to the artful offenders. The specific crime is that of stealing men's wallets from their back pockets whilst they are jostled as they mount buses in the rush hour. Figure 5.4 shows how the offence unfolds. It suggests to Poyner some design modifications to the provisions for queuing for the buses which remove the opportunity for the thieves to disturb the target passenger and take his wallet at the same time.

Understanding how sets of crimes are committed: crime scripts

Cornish (1994) has developed the notion of *crime scripts* to capture the routinised procedural sequences through which crime events unfold. He identifies series of 'scrip scenes/functions' through which patterns of crime event may take place. He also indicates how potential crime events may be inhibited by failures at any of the sequence of stages in the script. Table 5.6 reproduces an example given by Cornish (1994: 164). It relates to a specific offence type. It is important to realise that this is not for all theft of motor vehicles or theft of a specific model or type for short-term use for fun. The scene/ function categories – preparation, entry, pre-condition, instrumental pre-condition, instrumental initiation, instrumental actualisation, doing, post-condition, and exit – are quite generic. The script actions are specific to the particular class of problem behaviours at issue. The failure explanations show how potential offence events may

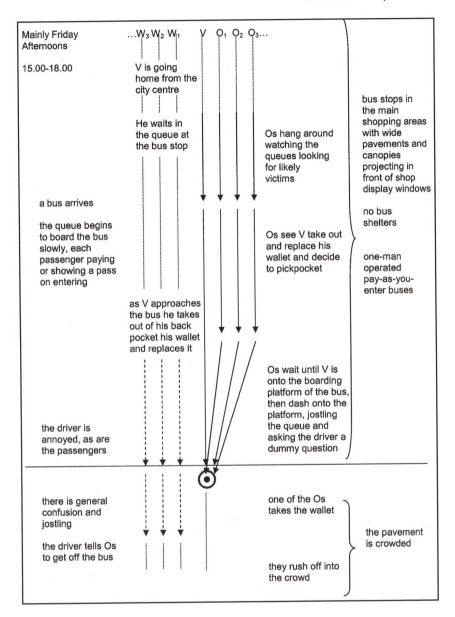

Mainly Friday Afternoons	...W_3 W_2 W_1 V O_1 O_2 O_3...		
15.00–18.00	V is going home from the city centre		bus stops in the main shopping areas with wide pavements and canopies projecting in front of shop display windows
	He waits in the queue at the bus stop	Os hang around watching the queues looking for likely victims	
a bus arrives			no bus shelters
the queue begins to board the bus slowly, each passenger paying or showing a pass on entering		Os see V take out and replace his wallet and decide to pickpocket	one-man operated pay-as-you-enter buses
	as V approaches the bus he takes out of his back pocket his wallet and replaces it		
the driver is annoyed, as are the passengers		Os wait until V is onto the boarding platform of the bus, then dash onto the platform, jostling the queue and asking the driver a dummy question	
there is general confusion and jostling		one of the Os takes the wallet	the pavement is crowded
the driver tells Os to get off the bus		they rush off into the crowd	

Figure 5.4 Pickpocketing crime set. *V* midlife and older men wearing trousers in which they keep their wallets O_1–, O_2–, O_3– ... small group of white youths; W_1 bus driver; W_2–, W_3– ... other passengers in the queue. *Source* Poyner (1986)

Table 5.6 Script for temporary use of stolen vehicle for driving fast for fun (from Cornish 1994: 164)

Scene/Function	Script action	Failure explanation
Preparation	Gather tools	Forgo scaffold tube
Entry	Enter car park	Car park closed
Pre-condition	Loiter unobtrusively	Noticed by security
Instrumental pre-condition	Select vehicle	No Vauxhall Astra GTEs
Instrumental initiation	Approach vehicle	Driver returns
Instrumental actualisation	Break into vehicle	Vehicle impregnable
Doing	Take vehicle	Vehicle immobilised
Post-condition	Reverse out of bay	Crash into wall
Exit	Leave car park	Gates closed for night

be disrupted in practice, and clearly implicitly suggest what may happen to create the counterfactual – the non-occurrence of an event that would otherwise have happened.

The script shown in Table 5.6 all takes place as the car is acquired. This, of course, does not exhaust the *scenes* for the crime. These will include also the use of the vehicle, its disposal and the withdrawal of the offender from the site of the disposal, all again with their own scripts. Whilst much will be undertaken in relatively routinised ways, this is not to say that offenders are incapable of some flexibility or innovation which may need to be anticipated as preventive strategies are developed. Cornish suggests that offenders comprise rich potential sources of information in crime scripts, and that their generation can help pinpoint proximal causes that may be open to intervention. One scene for the overall script for many property crimes relates to the disposal of stolen goods and their conversion into cash or consumable utilities. It will often be useful to elicit information on this, since the disruption of opportunities to convert stolen items into rewards for the offender comprises, at least in theory, one route to prevention (Sutton 1998).

Understanding the evolution of crime: 'arms races'

Ekblom (1997) has developed the idea of an arms race between those who aim to commit crimes and those who aim to prevent them. Each innovates in response to the others' moves and each is apt to take advantage of new resources (opportunities and tools) as they become available to pursue their objectives. The ideas are borrowed from evolutionary theory. There can be 'end points' of course, when adaptation seems no longer possible. Following a period during which safe designs and materials and means to break them evolved with mutual adaptation between relevant preventers and offenders, safes have evidently - at least for the moment - reached a stage where the offenders' attempts at adaptation have failed. Recognition of an arms race should help those attempting to prevent crime to anticipate and forestall likely countermoves. It also suggests risk-spreading in developing responses, whereby too much store is not put in a single solution lest a way round it be found and all using the crime prevention method then become vulnerable. Double glazed windows whose panes were eventually found to be unclipped by a particular technique comprise one example where they were fitted to all houses on a particular estate. Once the technique was learned all were vulnerable. New scripts were developed.

Understanding the real time business of crime: intelligence analysis

Much *intelligence analysis* undertaken in police (and to some degree also other enforcement agencies) services relates to offenders and networks of offenders, whose criminal activity may be disrupted through targeted police operations. The National Intelligence Model puts this work centre stage (though it also makes space for other forms of analysis). The analyses undertaken here identify series of offenders, prolific offenders, markets for drugs and stolen goods, organisational linkages joining together individuals and groups, co-offending and offender recruitment patterns, criminal families, and so on. Much of this is the stock-in-trade of intelligence-led policing and may contribute to crime control. It had emerged independently of problem-oriented policing, though it may have a role to play in it, especially when not undertaken to the exclusion of other forms of analysis and when not aimed only at very recent, short-term patterns of behaviour which tend not to be the focus of those committed to problem-oriented policing (see NCIS 2000)

Statistical associations: correlations between crime and social conditions

In addition to the analyses of patterns of problem behaviour outlined here, efforts are sometimes made to establish correlations between socio-economic conditions and crime. It is generally found that, apart from city centres, crime tends to be concentrated most heavily in relatively poorer, inner city areas. Some caution is needed here to avoid the *ecological fallacy*: the assumption that area level indicators are also applicable to sub-groups and individuals. Just because crime is concentrated in generally poorer areas does not entail that generally poorer households and individuals are at higher risk of crime. Indeed, in this case it appears not to be the case. Those living in detached houses in poorer areas have been found to be at higher risk than those living in other (cheaper) forms of housing (Bowers *et al.* 2005).

An overall view: the conjunction of criminal opportunity

Finally, as an overarching heuristic device Ekblom (1994, 2002) has developed the *conjunction of criminal opportunity* (CCO), whose aim is comprehensively to be able to map the causes of crime events, both proximal and distal. Figure 5.5 shows these diagramatically. Ekblom presents an array of causal conditions ranging from on the one side those associated with the situation for the offence to those on the other associated with the offender. Hence he includes crime promoters (those people or objects that may encourage or enable crime); absence of preventers (person or thing that may inhibit offending); wider environment (general circumstances favourable or unfavourable for offending); target enclosure (for example building,

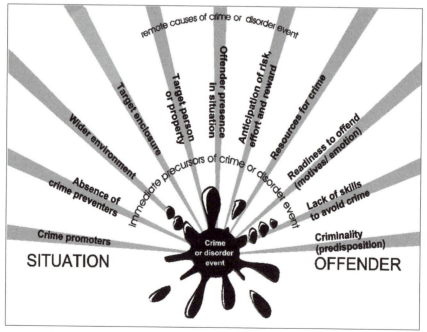

Figure 5.5 The conjunction of criminal opportunity

room, vehicle etc.); target person or property; offender presence in situation; application of risk, effort and reward (perceptions of the pay-offs and risks); resources for crime (the capacities and tools for committing the offence); readiness to offend (immediate states of mind such as motives/emotion, effects of drugs), lack of skills to avoid crime (for example for avoiding conflict or earning an honest living); and criminality (longer term personality/disposition), any of which can be understood both as immediate circumstances for the crime event or as resulting from conditions that are more distant in time or space. Ekblom's CCO is manifestly about crime and disorder rather than the other problems that police and partners might address, though it is likely also to be applicable to much low level antisocial behaviour. Though analysis is unlikely to be able to pin down and test hypotheses about the full array of near and distant causes of crime, it may be able to narrow down possibilities and focus on conditions that appear to be important and also be open to practical intervention.

Response

With strong scanning and analysis, thinking through promising, well-targeted responses should become more straightforward. Various tools are available to help inform decisions about responses.

What to focus on: further use of the problem analysis triangle – PAT 2

The problem-analysis triangle can be used not only for analysing problems but also for identifying potential points of intervention. Eck (2003) has developed a useful supplement to it to help think through responses, shown in Figure 5.6. What Eck's adaptation of PAT shows is that problem-solvers can think of six basic ways of dealing with problems:

1 Remove the location (for example by closing a crack house or troublesome club).

2 Remove the offender (for example through detection, disruption, treatment or incarceration).

3 Remove the target or victim (for example by creating turnstiles at stations rather than having vulnerable ticket collectors).

4 Add a handler (someone who knows the person liable to offend and can exert influence over them) to inhibit the offender (for example by teachers in schools where bullying may occur).

5 Add a manager to oversee the place (for example by introducing a car park attendant).

6 Add plausible guardianship to protect the victim or target (for example with lighting, CCTV or security guards).

Figure 5.6 PAT 2: finding solutions from the problem analysis triangle

Different specific problems will be most appropriately approached through different intervention points. Though all problems clearly must have location, offender and victim, so-called 'duck problems' (for example repeat victimisation) are those where suitable victims or targets seem to be the key, and here victim/target-focused preventive strategies may be most appropriate. 'Wolf problems' (for example organised crime) are those where likely offenders may be the key to the problem and offender-focused interventions may be needed. 'Den problems' (for example bars and city centres) are those where locations are the key.

How to change situations to reduce problems: situational crime prevention

One of the most developed menus of specific intervention possibilities has been developed by Ronald Clarke and his collaborators, and relates to situational crime prevention, which focuses on reducing opportunities, excuses and provocations for problem behaviour.

Table 5.7 lays out the most recently developed typology, showing 25 techniques (Cornish and Clarke 2003; Clarke and Eck 2003), listed under the five headings of risk increase, effort increase, reward decrease, provocation reduction, and excuse removal. These can be adapted to help think about specific problems. Martha Smith (2004) has used it specifically in relation to responses to the problems of crime against taxi drivers, as shown in Table 5.8. There is ample evidence that well targeted situational measures can reduce crime problems.

Designing out problems

Design and redesign responses to problems are closely associated with situational crime prevention. Places, products and systems can all create more or fewer opportunities for crime. Modifications to the layout of buses and housing estates, to the design of cars and mobile phones, and to the registration arrangements of motor vehicles, and checks on credit cards all comprise types of design response to specific problems (see, for example, Webb 2005; Tilley 2005b; Poyner 2006).

Problem neighbourhoods, crime and fear of crime: signal crimes, broken windows and informal social control

In some cases localised crime and anxiety about crime may be a function of behaviours that though intrinsically are not very serious in themselves create impressions of disorder or create what seems to be a permissive environment for crime and antisocial behaviour. There has been research on 'signal crimes' and their reduction, and older work on 'broken windows' and ways to fix them. In addition to both of these, suggestions have been made that increasing 'collective efficacy' may be a way of reducing crime in problematic neighbourhoods.

Signal crimes
There is a growing literature on signal crimes, which address problems that are of concern within neighbourhoods and give rise to feelings of insecurity, and in this way adversely affect residents' quality of life. They are not necessarily the most serious crimes, as ordinarily measured. Rather they are those that are noticed and which give rise to unease. Martin Innes (2004a, 2004b, 2005) has been at the forefront of these developments within the National Reassurance Policing Programme agenda (see Chapter 6). Identifying and removing what

Table 5.7 Twenty five techniques of situational prevention

Increase the effort	Increase the risks	Reduce the rewards	Reduce provocations	Remove excuses
1 *Target harden*	6 *Extend guardianship*	11 *Conceal targets*	16 *Reduce frustrations and stress*	21 *Set rules*
• Steering column locks and ignition immobilisers	• Go out in group at night	• Off-street parking	• Efficient queues	• Rental agreements
• Anti-robbery screens	• Leave signs of occupancy	• Gender-neutral phone directories	• Polite service	• Harassment codes
• Tamper-proof packaging	• Carry cell phone	• Unmarked armoured trucks	• Expanded seating	• Hotel registration
			• Soothing music/ muted lights	
2 *Control access to facilities*	7 *Assist natural surveillance*	12 *Remove targets*	17 *Avoid disputes*	22 *Post instructions*
• Entry phones	• Improved street	• Removable car radio	• Separate seating for rival	• 'No parking'
3 *Screen exists*	8 *Reduce anonymity*	13 *Identify property*	18 *Reduce temptation and arousal*	23 *Alert conscience*
• Ticket needed for exit	• Taxi driver IDs	• Property marking	• Controls on violent pornography	• Roadside speed display boards
• Export documents	• 'How's my driving?' decals	• Vehicle licensing and parts marking	• Enforce good behaviour on soccer field	• Signatures for customs declarations
• Electronic merchandise tags	• School uniforms	• Cattle branding	• Prohibit racial slurs	• 'Shoplifting is stealing'

4 *Deflect offenders*
- Street closures
- Separate bathrooms for women
- Disperse pubs

5 *Control tools/ weapons*
- 'Smart' guns
- Restrict spray paint sales to juveniles
- Toughened beer glasses

9 *Utilise place managers*
- CC-TV for double-deck buses
- Two clerks for convenience stores
- Reward vigilance

10 *Strengthen formal surveillance*
- Red light cameras
- Burglar alarms
- Security guards

14 *Disrupt markets*
- Monitor pawn shops
- Controls on classified ads
- License street vendors

15 *Deny benefits*
- Ink merchandise tags
- Graffiti cleaning
- Disabling stolen cell phones

19 *Neutralise peer pressure*
- 'Idiots drink and drive'
- Disperse trouble-makers at school

20 *Discourage imitation*
- Rapid repair of vandalism
- V-chips in TVs
- Censor details of modus operandi

24 *Assist compliance*
- Easy library checkout
- Public lavatories
- Litter receptacles

25 *Control drugs imitation and alcohol*
- Breathalysers in bars
- Server intervention programmes
- Alcohol-free events

Table 5.8 Situational techniques used by taxi drivers (from Smith 2004)

Increase the effort	Increase the risks	Reduce the rewards	Reduce provocations	Remove excuses
1 *Target harden* • Safety shields ■ Keep windows rolled up ■ Stay inside cab – unless escaping attack from within	6 *Extend guardianship* • Have GPS system & alarm ◀ Have radio, alarm or 'open mike' ◀ Keep dispatch informed ◀ Info. on 24-hr locations • Have CB radio, cell phone • Use buddy system • Carry an extra key	11 *Conceal targets* • Limit change to small bills ■ Never flash cash 'I just started,' 'It's been slow,' 'Just ticking over' ■ Keep cash in more than one place	16 *Reduce frustrations and stress* ◆ Have supervised ranks ◆ Have honest dispatch times ■ Make eye contact ■ Be courteous	21 *Set rules* ◆ Regulate the industry ◆ Provide explicit provisions about how fare disputes are to be handled
2 *Control access to facilities* ◆ Limit no. of passengers ◀ Pre-book all bar pick ups • Do not obstruct windows ■ Screen passengers ■ Use central door locks	7 *Assist natural surveillance* ◆ Move ranks to 24-hour stores or other locations • Do not obstruct windows ■ Use street lighting well ■ Travel main routes	12 *Remove targets* ◆ Use fare cards ■ Decal re: limited money ◀ Allow credit or debit cards ■ Use safe or drop off money ■ *Look for escape opportunity*	17 *Avoid disputes* ◆ Display driver photo & licence ◆ Require knowledge tests • Ask for money up front • Inform passenger of route	22 *Post instructions* ◆ Hand out taxi rules & regulation at key venues (e.g., airports) • List rules, regulations & fares in passenger area

3 Screen exits
- Ask 'rowdies' to get out
- Use central door locks
- *Park to prevent door opening prior to payment*
- *Prevent runner from exiting by grabbing*

4 Deflect offenders
- Limit seating options
- Get destination up front
- Avoid dark places
- Avoid alleys and dead ends

6 Control tools/weapons
- Don't carry a weapon
- Put all bags in the trunk

8 Reduce anonymity
- Keep passenger trip book
- ▲ Use Caller ID
- ▲ Have regular riders

9 Utilise place managers
- ◆ Supervise ranks
- Have security cameras
- Have second person ride up front with driver

10 Strengthen formal surveillance
- ◆ CCTV at ranks
- ◆ Trouble lights on cabs
- *Authorised police stops*
- ◆ Decoy police (as drivers)

13 Identify property
- Use cab-locator system (GPS)

14 Disrupt markets

15 Deny benefits
- ▲ Disable-vehicle capacity
- ▲ Have inside trunk release
- Notice culprit's description
- Have first-aid kit

18 Reduce temptation and arousal
- ◆ Exclude violent drivers (vet)
- ◆ Control the industry to reduce driver abuses
- *Do not threaten non-payers with violence*
- *Do not resist a robber*

19 Neutralise peer pressure
- Ask troublemakers in a group to get out

20 Discourage imitation
- Censor details of modus operandi in press releases & interviews
- Keep crime prevention tips during training 'in house'

23 Alert conscience
- Post notices re: community awareness and 'Cab safe' programs at ranks and in cabs

24 Assist compliance
- Use multiple payment systems
- Provide a sick bag

25 Control drugs and alcohol
- Increase passenger sobriety prior to pick-up
- Prohibit drug or alcohol consumption in cab

General source of control: • Driver, radio company/vehicle owner, or regulator (all three needed, in italics); ■ Driver (reactive tactics, in italics); ◆ Regulator, police, or city; and ▲ Radio company or vehicle owner.

are found in specific neighbourhoods to function as signal crimes and substituting instead 'control signals' comprises one technique for increasing public confidence. Members of the public and non-enforcement agencies clearly have a role to play in finding and removing signal crimes and in introducing control signals.

Broken windows

The broken windows approach (Wilson and Kelling 1982; Kelling and Coles 1996), though distinct from signal crimes, has some resemblance. 'Broken windows' suggests that areas on the cusp of spirals of decline may be thrown into them if early problems and signs of problems are not removed. The neglect of minor incivilities might lead people to believe that antisocial behaviour is either acceptable or will not be noticed. Increases in disorder may then escalate to the point where they become overwhelming.

Sloan-Hewitt and Kelling (1997) showed that quick removal and cleaning of graffiti-covered coaches in New York's underground subway system, combined with some targeted enforcement activity, led to a fairly rapid and sustained fall in the rate of re-emergence of graffiti. Offenders were denied the reward of seeing their 'works of art' on display.

Informal social control: creating collective efficacy

To deal with problem neighbourhoods in addition to the reduction of signal crimes and the removal signs of emerging disorder, the stimulus of informal social control has been mooted as a possibility, since communities that are otherwise alike have very varying levels of crime and disorder, reflecting different levels of 'collective efficacy' (Sampson et al. 1997). Because of the greater informal control effected on criminal behaviour within them, communities with relatively higher levels of collective efficacy, whatever their physical state, suffer less crime than those with lower levels collective efficacy. What is less clear is how increases in collective efficacy or effective informal social control can be activated in communities where it is already missing.

Criminal justice responses: policing and enforcement

So far mostly responses requiring action by non-enforcement agencies have been mentioned. There are also problem-solving responses by enforcement agencies that can sometimes usefully be considered.

Patrol and hotspots

A common technique used by the police and other members of the 'extended police family' (including community support officers, wardens, police specials, security guards, etc.) is visible patrol. Random patrol has a poor track record as a crime control measure (Clarke and Hough 1984; Bright 1969), though targeted patrol is one way that has been found useful to contain problems, at least in the short term (Jones and Tilley 2004).

Crackdowns and consolidation

Crackdowns (short-term intensive targeted enforcement activity) are also frequently attempted when problems become acute, and there is some evidence that they can push rates down (Sherman 1990). Crackdowns often have an effect that outlasts their application (*ibid.*). The repeated use of crackdowns, reapplied when crime rates have come to approach the previous level, may create longer term impacts, though the effects of long-term crackdowns tend to fade. Crackdown and consolidation strategies, where time-limited crackdowns to drive crime down are followed by longer-term consolidation strategies to effect changes in the environment or to activate informal social control, appear to be promising (Farrell *et al.* 2000; Tilley 2004b). Moving crackdowns round to maximise uncertainty over what will be targeted and levels of risk that will be encountered in committing an offence comprise one suggested use of limited enforcement resources to maximise their impact (Sherman 1990).

Dealing with problem individuals: warnings, ASBOs, ABCs and criminal prosecutions

In relation to individuals known to be sources of problems there are a variety of enforcement tools to try to control their behaviour. These include: use of restorative justice, for example family group conferences to shame and reintegrate those who offend; Antisocial Behaviour Orders (ASBOs) to restrict the behaviour of those causing nuisance; Dispersal Orders to prevent the congregation of individuals where they may engage collectively in threatening or antisocial behaviour; Parenting Orders to mobilise parents to take some responsibility for their children's antisocial behaviour; Civil Injunctions prohibiting specific behaviours; and Probation Orders to retain oversight and control of convicted offenders. In addition to these formal orders Acceptable Behaviour Contracts (ABCs) comprise agreements between a child and his or her parents and the police (and their partner organisations) that set out the boundaries of acceptable behaviours (Bullock and Jones 2004). They are like an ASBO but have no legal implications, though have been used as an early warning for an ASBO or other civil injunction.

In addition to civil actions, criminal prosecutions may themselves comprise interventions taken to address problems. Moreover, informal warnings, discussions with parents, and mobilisation of teachers may occur prior to individuals reaching the point where formal action is deemed necessary. These actions may successfully control the problem individual's behaviour informally. If not their use provides part of the background that can be used in the application of formal orders.

There is relatively little strong evidence-based guidance on ways of dealing long-term with those already heavily involved in criminal behaviour to deter or divert them from continued involvement in it. There is, though, quite robust evidence that most men (and it is men overwhelmingly who are prolific offenders) age out of crime by the time they are in their thirties.

Addressing problem facilitators

'Facilitators' (Clarke and Eck 2003, 2005) and 'resources for offending' (Ekblom and Tilley 2000) make crime more likely by increasing the capacity for it or need for it. Drugs, alcohol and stolen goods markets comprise three important examples.

Reducing alcohol and drug-related problems

Many problems may be linked with the market in illicit drugs: drug-dependent offenders may commit crime to pay for their drugs; drugs (and alcohol) may help provoke criminal behaviour or disinhibit individuals who become violent when provoked; and the illicit drugs market itself creates a forum for organised crime and opportunistic crime against dealers. Most is probably known about effective tools to deal with some forms of alcohol-related crime. High-rate random breath testing creates uncertainty of the (potentially very high) risk of being caught drinking and driving. It had a very marked and sustained effect in New South Wales (Homel 1988, 1990). Changed management of bars and the abandonment of cheap happy-hour drinking have had a marked effect on alcohol-related violence (Homel *et al.* 1997). The Tackling Alcohol-related Street Crime (TASC) project was a police-led multi-agency, multi-intervention scheme which successfully reduced alcohol-related crime and disorder in central Cardiff and Cardiff Bay. Key interventions included: focused dialogue between the police and members of the licensed trade, measures aimed at improving the quality and behaviour of door staff and targeted policing operations directed at crime and disorder hotspots. Longer-term cognitive behavioural programmes for repeat offenders, a training programme for bar staff, education programmes for schoolchildren and support for victims of alcohol-related assaults attending hospital were also developed (see Maguire and Nettleton 2003).

Disrupting the market in stolen goods
Many property crime problems in theory may be addressed by disrupting the market in stolen goods, which facilitates a range of property crimes by providing a means of converting stolen goods to utilities wanted by the offender. There is a strong literature on the stolen goods market, with equally strong arguments that intervening in it may be a promising way of addressing problems (Sutton *et al.* 2001). The experience to date in implementing efforts to disrupt stolen goods markets on the ground has been disappointing (Harris *et al.* 2003), but the basic theory still seems sound (Sutton 2005).

Publicity and pre-ignition

There is some evidence that situational measures put in place can have an effect before they become operational (Smith *et al.* 2002). The plan had originally been to refer to this phenomenon as 'pre-ignition' to stress how the effect was brought about, though in the event the term used was 'anticipatory benefit', to signify the nature of the effect. What is identified across many studies are the ways in which the impact is felt 'too soon' – before measures applied become operational. The too-soon effects may be a consequence of any of a variety of factors. The most interesting is probably the effect that may be brought about independently by publicity for a measure before it is actually in place. The publicity for the measure, the argument goes, alters the perceived opportunity for prospective offenders, who are thereby deterred from attempting it even if the measure has not yet been applied.

Planning strategies

Tilley and Laycock (2002) lay great store on the importance of clarity over the expected problem-solving mechanisms that will be activated in the specific context for the problem behaviours to produce changes in them. They are critical of efforts to address problems using standard methods that are not attuned to the ways in which they might alter the behaviours producing the problems. The COPS problem-oriented guides for police series provide detailed guidance on the identification and specification of problems, and on what measures might make sense in what circumstances to reduce the problem. At the time of writing so far 35 are available, as indicated in Table 5.9. Updates and further guides are planned.

Each guide reviews a wide range of evidence relating to the specific problem and responses to it, and includes a summary table showing each possible 'response', 'how it works' (its primary mechanism), 'works best if' (the context needed for the mechanisms to be activated) and 'considerations' (other matters to take account in including it as a response), indicating those for which there is some evidence of effectiveness and those for which there is evidence of limited effectiveness.

Getting measures implemented

In relation to responses it is one thing to identify what might reduce or remove a specific problem. It is another to get responses put

Table 5.9   COPS problem-specific guides (available at: www.popcenter.org/problems.htm)

Assaults in and around bars	Identity theft
Acquaintance rape of college students	Illicit sexual activity in public places
Bomb threats	Loud car stereos
Bullying in schools	Misuse and abuse of 911
Burglary of retail establishments	Panhandling
Burglary of single-family houses	Prescription fraud
Cheque and card fraud	Rave parties
Clandestine drug labs	Robbery at automated teller machines
Crimes against tourists	Robbery of taxi drivers
Cruising	School vandalism and break-ins
Disorder at budget motels	Shoplifting
Disorderly youth in public places	Speeding in residential areas
Drug dealing in open-air markets	Stalking
Drug dealing in privately owned apartment complexes	Street prostitution
False burglar alarms	Street racing
Financial crimes against the elderly	Thefts of and from cars in parking facilities
Graffiti	Under-age drinking
Gun violence among serious young offenders	

in place, and if they are implemented to have them implemented properly.

A key rationale for partnership problem solving is that the police have rather little direct control of most of the conditions that produce and maintain problems of crime and disorder (or indeed many of the other problems, such as missing persons and road traffic accidents, which come to their attention). It is clear that enforcement represents just one of a range of possible forms of response. In many cases third parties will need to be persuaded that they need to accept some responsibility for dealing with problems and will need to be told what they can and should do.

Goldstein (1997) has developed a hierarchy of levers for persuading others to accept ownership of problems. This is shown in Table 5.10. Goldstein's principle is in general that less leverage is preferable to more. This is sound for several reasons. First, as the hierarchy is climbed strategies become slower and more expensive. Second, as the hierarchy is climbed more political and constitutional objections can

Table 5.10 Goldstein's hierarchy of levers, as shown in Hough and Tilley (1998)

1 *Providing advice and information,* for example advice leaflets
2 *Straightforward informal requests,* for example asking burglary victims to increase their security
3 *Targeted confrontational requests,* for example telling a car park proprietor about offences taking places in their car park, what needs to be done to reduce the crime rate, and their responsibility to put those measures in place
4 *Engaging another existing service agency,* for example the fire service, local authority, etc. as appropriate
5 *Pressing for the creation of a new organisation to assume ownership,* for example a new community organisation
6 *Public shaming,* for example publishing names of businesses where customers are at high risk
7 *Withdrawing police services,* for example refusing to attend repeat crimes against businesses where suggestions for preventive methods have been ignored
8 *Charging a fee for services,* for example to attend alarm call-outs where there have been many false ones
9 *Legislation mandating adoption of a preventive strategy,* for example advocating the creation of byelaws against public drinking
10 *Bringing civil actions,* for example helping businesses take civil action against staff and customers who steal from them

be anticipated. Third, if the high-level strategy fails then many people will have been unnecessarily inconvenienced and their freedom of action pointlessly limited. Finally, heavy handedness is liable to be unpopular and to jeopardise the legitimacy of those jumping quickly to it. Scott (2005) gives many examples, often taken from entries to the Goldstein and Tilley Awards.

Assessment

Notoriously, assessment has been the weakest element of problem solving. This is partly because it is technically difficult. Difficulties are especially severe with relatively small-scale interventions where low numbers will make drawing firm conclusions difficult, especially in relation to areas where rates of problem behaviour fluctuate quite widely in the short term anyway. Moreover only partial records are often kept, and there are also frequent changes in tactics that are made in the light of experience. This makes pinpointing what was done when and what may have been active ingredients in effecting change impossible to establish with any real degree of objectivity. As important as technical details may be the fact that practitioners may often find assessment of what they did dull, pointless and potentially threatening once they believe the original problem has been resolved. Moreover, use of precious resources to look at what has already been done may often seem a waste – of little or no practical use. In view of the circumstances in which most problem solving is attempted the expectation that all work will be 'properly' assessed is quite unrealistic. Notwithstanding these obstacles there may be good reasons in some circumstances for 'quick and dirty' assessment. It may also sometimes be important to conduct a thorough systematic evaluation, where the scale and consistency of the problem-solving efforts allows it and where fresh lessons for future practice may be drawn.

The following sections sketch some standard considerations in conducing practical and informative evaluations of problem-oriented initiatives. More extended discussion can be found in Eck (2002, 2005), Clarke and Eck (2003) and Tilley (2002b).

Threats to the validity of findings

One of the chief challenges in evaluation is that of estimating what would have happened in the absence of the problem solving measures. This is the so called 'counterfactual'. If any observed change would have happened even without the measures put in place no effect has been created. The canny evaluator has to be aware of the potential ways they may be misled. Table 5.11 lists a standard set, drawn from Cook and Campbell (1979). These are threats to what is often referred to as 'internal validity', that is, the validity of any claim that the measure or measures put in place really were responsible for some supposed change.

Given the list in Table 5.11, it is clear that simple before and after measures risk misleading the evaluator. It is all too easy to fall prey to self-deception or bias, especially where local rates fluctuate quite widely and where the evaluator can pick from a range of plausible before and after periods and measurements. Here, it is relatively simple to weave a success story. This may not be undertaken cynically, but is a quite natural way of behaving when all measurements are to some degree dubious and there is a strong sense that the problem solving has been successful. Some of the threats listed in Table 5.11 show that evaluators may also miss positive effects, where comparisons are made with others whose actions are rendered different from what they would otherwise be by the compensatory treatment being provided for them.

Few evaluations of problem-oriented work have made much effort to rule out these threats to the internal validity of the findings reported. Doing so can be technically challenging.

Overcoming threats to internal validity

Double-blind experiments (where neither those receiving nor those administering the treatment know who belongs to the experimental or control group, with random allocation to each, alongside the use of placebos) are used to try to eliminate these threats to internal validity in medical trials. They are to a greater or lesser extent inoperable in crime prevention. Moreover, whilst placebos are used to eliminate the effects of perception and expectation in medicine, these mechanisms are at the very heart of social interventions, which almost always aim to change people's behaviour via their reasoning rather than mechanically via physical causes. In general, something other than randomised control trials is needed to adduce persuasive evidence to determine whether or not the response has been effective. What makes sense has been hotly disputed and the details of those debates lie beyond the scope of this book (see, for example, Farrington 1997 1998 versus Pawson and Tilley 1998a, 1998b).

If there has been the sort of detailed scanning, analysis and response development outlined in this chapter and as a result the

Table 5.11   Threats to internal validity

Threat	Explanation
History	Something happens to create change that would have happened anyway, without any intervention
Maturation	Treatment subjects mature in the change direction anyway, regardless of intervention
Testing	The measurement creates the change not the intervention measure itself
Instrumentation	The measurement methods change and create the impression of real change whilst there is none
Statistical regression	Treatment targets begin at an extreme position and tend naturally to regress towards the mean without any need for intervention
Selection	Those selected for treatment are atypical and especially susceptible to influence
Mortality	Drop-outs may be different from those staying the course, and the latter may change anyway
Interactions with selection	Selection biases may interact with other threats to internal validity, for example selection-maturation
Ambiguity about direction of causality	Apparent effects may be associated with treatments but it may be the effect causing the treatment
Diffusion or imitation of treatments	Those not treated or those areas not treated may adopt the intervention measure themselves
Compensatory equalisation of treatments	Those not treated may be given additional services to compensate for missing out on the treatment given to the target group
Compensatory rivalry by respondents receiving less desirable treatments	Those not treated may work especially hard to equal or outperform the treatment group or area
Resentful demoralisation of respondents receiving less desirable treatments	Those not receiving treatments may under-perform because they feel neglected and resentful

strategy is targeted at well defined problems operating with a fully articulated underlying theory, effectiveness assessment should be possible without serious risk of threats to internal validity. That is, it should be possible to predict fairly precise outcome patterns if the measures are operating in the expected way in relation to the specific targets. An example may help here. The Small Business and Crime Initiative (SBCI) addressed the problem of crime against small businesses in two areas of Leicester. Initial analysis found high rates of crime and in particular very high rates of repeat victimisation. The strategy adopted was to attempt in various ways to reduce repeat events at highly victimised premises. The evaluation used a census of businesses in the area before the initiative and two years later after it had been completed. The findings were that concentration (crimes per victim) had increased but prevalence (proportion of businesses victimised once or more) had fallen: quite the opposite of what would have been expected had the initiative worked as expected. Recorded crime data suggested that the areas where the initiative operated had outperformed surrounding areas in terms of crimes against businesses. The initiative had failed in terms of the specific way it was expected to reduce business crime. Even though business crime fell it fell in the 'wrong' way (Tilley and Hopkins 1998). In the event a later interpretation surmised that the publicity given to the initiative might have contributed to the overall fall as an 'anticipatory benefit', given that the fall began before the measures that were applied became operative (Smith *et al.* 2002).

Any evaluation needs to consider the plausibility of the potential threats to validity outlined in Table 5.11. The more precisely the theory predicts changes in the target group, and the more this differs from those in sub-groups not targeted, the less likely that the potential threats to validity are real. This would not be enough for the experimentalist committed to randomised control trials since it cannot rule out all the possible threats to internal validity. It can, though, contribute to a highly plausible evaluation.

Simple before and after comparisons of numbers of incidents of the specified kind may be valid where the change is rapid, where the change takes place at the expected time and place, where the change does not form part of a pre-existing trend, where there is no other plausible explanation for the change, and where stability and volume of problem numbers suggest that in the absence of the intervention larger than observed numbers of problem incidents could be expected. In other words big effects occurring at the right time and place, and serious and explicit attention to potential rival explanations for the changes, will provide fairly persuasive evidence.

Statistical tests can be used to estimate whether the change observed could be due to random variation or regression to the mean. However, it is beyond the scope and intention of this chapter to discuss such tests here.

Assessing process

Before the effectiveness of a response is determined it is critical to check whether it has been implemented and also to check what else may have been done at the same time in relation to the specific target problem. Inputs (what is invested in the response) and outputs (what is actually delivered on the ground) need to be determined in order to gauge what there is to assess. The level of input may also be used to estimate the costs of the intervention. Processes of quite detailed record keeping will be needed if it is going to be possible to link up what is put in place in the response with precise expected outcomes. It is often difficult to have this happen in practice (Forrest *et al.* 2005).

Taking account of displacement

One rather general theory of crime underlies one set of efforts to evaluate responses to crime problems. This is the 'hydraulic' model which holds that there is a fixed amount of crime representing the distribution of crime dispositions or the underlying criminality in a society, and that because of this any efforts to reduce a specific crime problem will lead only to a redistribution of crime. This is often referred to as the displacement hypothesis. Several forms of displacement have been identified (Reppetto 1976; Hakim and Rengert 1981, Barr and Pease 1990):

1 *Geographical.* The same crime type is committed but somewhere else.
2 *Target.* The same crime is committed but against someone, or something else.
3 *Technique.* The same crime is committed but by a different MO.
4 *Time.* The same crime is committed but at a different time.
5 *Crime.* A different crime is committed instead.
6 *Person.* The same crime is committed but by someone else.

It is of course possible in theory that several types of displacement may occur at the same time or that combinations of displacement may occur, for example to a different crime type at a different time and location.

Taking account of diffusion of benefits

A second hypothesis, mirroring that anticipating displacement, expects 'diffusion of benefits' (Clarke and Weisburd 1994; Smith *et al.* 2002). The theory behind diffusion of benefits is that offenders, far from being driven to crime by their dispositions or social conditions can be put off offending to the degree to which opportunities for it are circumscribed. Uncertainty over the scope of problem-solving measures means that offenders are discouraged from committing a wider range of offences than those operationally covered by the response measures put in place.

Estimating net effects

It is possible of course that some displacement and some diffusion of benefits may occur in relation to the same response measure/s. The net effect of a response to a crime problem is:

The direct preventive effect + diffusion of benefits − displacement

The challenge for the assessor is to find some way of testing the displacement and diffusion of benefits hypotheses. This is normally done by taking the more plausible forms of displacement and diffusion in the light of the specific problem and solution and interrogating available data to see if there is any evidence to corroborate or falsify the hypotheses. It is easy to state the displacement hypothesis in ways that defy test. If the hypothesis is that displacement can take place to any crime at any place and any time, then in effect the hypothesis becomes untestable − an article of faith. The hypothesis has to be made more specific to inform efforts at measurement. If the most plausible form of displacement cannot be discerned then it seems unlikely that less plausible forms will have taken place. Much the same argument would go for diffusion of benefits.

Geographical Information Systems are now available increasingly to police and partners and can be used to try to test hypotheses where geographical displacement/diffusion might be predicted (for an example analysis see Bowers, Johnson and Hirshfield 2003, 2004). Concentric zones can be created to compare patterns of change within the area in which the problem-solution or preventive measure is operational with those in potential displacement and diffusion zones.

The same crime type geographical displacement of crime and diffusion of benefits is often the most plausible and the most straightforward to measure. Other forms are more difficult to measure and decisions about those that are likely and methods of their measurement have to be made on a case-by-case basis.

Change measurement practicalities

Difficulties in making valid comparisons of before and after problem levels can be compounded by a range of measurement difficulties. More offences/problem behaviours may be reported if those experiencing them believe they will elicit a sympathetic or preventive response. Those recording incidents may subconsciously pay more attention to the correctness of the category into which they assign events and numbers may go down because the problem category is used more precisely. Equally they may go up as those recording incidents become more attuned to the need to take reports seriously. Though it is very difficult to rule out the effects of these measurement problems, the likelihood of each has to be considered separately and efforts made to see whether independent evidence can be really consequential. The more precisely the expected outcome is specified in advance in terms of place, time, sub-group to be affected the less likely that it will not be possible to find some comparison group amongst which the measurement problem would be expected but not the response effect. Given that such a group exists trends in it can be compared with the precisely expected trends in the sub-group where effects are anticipated.

Conclusion

This chapter has provided a Cook's tour of many of the resources that can be used in problem-oriented policing and partnership work but in the event are rarely used in practice. It has been written with a view to helping improve the implementation of future problem-oriented efforts. None of the resources should be difficult to use, and none is too complex to understand. They do, though, require a little effort and several will require access to data and some computing power.

Further details of most of the resources described here and of others besides are readily available from various websites. The best single source is www.popcenter.org, from which it is possible to download Clarke and Eck's steps guides for analysts (2003, 2005), as well as the problem-specific guides listed in Table 5.9. A growing number of additional guides relating to tools for analysis and frequently used types of response can also be downloaded from www.popcenter. org. Other websites that provide useful resources include www. crimereduction.gov.uk and www.homeoffice.gov.uk/rds, from which recent Home Office Development and Practice Reports as well as other practice-relevant research can be downloaded. For those interested in broadening their understanding of problem solving and crime reduction, the book series Crime Prevention Studies is a valuable resource, including much work relating specifically to problem-oriented policing and partnership.

Chapter 6

The changing context of British problem-oriented policing

It has been seen that problem-oriented policing represents a change (and hence a challenge) for the police service but in turn the implementation of problem-oriented policing has itself been influenced by other changes in policing. For instance, the institutional setting in which policing is conducted in the UK has changed significantly over recent years. Changes that affect policing will inevitably affect problem-oriented policing but some institutional changes have been much more directly relevant to the implementation of problem-oriented policing than others. These contextual changes have had various impacts: some have facilitated implementation (or at least have had the potential to), whilst some have created new challenges. Others again have made us think differently about problem-oriented policing, its impact, and about how it should be implemented in the UK. Key developments have included:

1 The public service modernisation agenda and Evidence-based Policy and Practice (EBPP).
2 The increasing emphasis on partnership in government in general and crime reduction in particular.
3 The development and implementation of intelligence-led policing and the National Intelligence Model.
4 The reassurance agenda and neighbourhood policing.
5 The extended police family and the mixed economy of policing.
6 Improvements in ICT, hotspotting and geographical information systems.

The public service modernisation agenda and Evidence-based Policy and Practice

The last few years of the twentieth century saw accelerating interest in evidence-based policy and practice (EBPP). There is nothing new about the idea that policy and practice should be informed by evidence (Nutley *et al.* 2003), but as mentioned in Chapter 1 of this volume the rise of EBPP has become associated with the New Labour government's modernisation agenda, and in particular its focus on the implementation of policies and practices based on evidence. Indeed, as Davies *et al.* (2000) note, the 'rise of *evidence-based policy* reached its apotheosis in 1997, when the Labour government was elected with the philosophy of "what matters is what works"' (Davies *et al.* 2000: 1). Davies *et al.* (2000) also refer to a severe dilution in confidence that the judgement of 'doctors, police officers, teachers and other professionals' can be trusted. Following this, 'there has arisen the important notion of *evidence-based practice* as a means of ensuring that what is being done is worthwhile and that it is being done in the best possible way' (Davies *et al.* 2000: 2). Indeed, the government is as concerned with effective practice as it is with effective policy making and so there has been a renewed focus on evidence informing practice (Solesbury 2001).

Evidence-based Policy and Practice

In principle, EBPP does exactly what it says on the tin: it is about utilising evidence to inform professional practice. Generally it has taken root differently in different areas of social policy but there is some agreement on its basic underpinnings (Nutley *et al.* 2002): there should be agreement about what counts as evidence in what circumstances; there should be a strategy of creating evidence in priority areas with concomitant systematic efforts to accumulate evidence in the form of robust bodies of knowledge; evidence should be disseminated to where it is needed; and strategies should be in place to ensure the integration of evidence into policy and encourage the utilisation of evidence in practice.

In reality, its application has been a bit less straightforward and there are issues still to grapple with (Nutley *et al.* 2002). First, the issue of what counts as 'evidence' is tricky and in practice can be considered to be very broad (Solesbury 2001). Indeed, evidence has been described by the Cabinet Office to include: 'expert knowledge, published research, existing statistics, stakeholder consultations, previous policy evaluations, the internet, outcomes from consultations, costings of policy options, outputs from economic and statistical knowledge'. This ambiguity is not evident in all areas of public policy. In health care especially, a hierarchy of evidence for assessing effectiveness has been developed with randomised control studies, or better yet systematic reviews of these, considered to be at the top of that hierarchy (Nutley *et al.* 2003). In the criminal justice field what counts as evidence is much more hotly contested: there is little experimentation and there are deep divisions between quantitative and qualitative research (Davies and Nutley 2002). Second, there have been considerable efforts (particularly in the field of health care) to implement EBPP but some disillusionment about its impact, especially on the integration of evidence into policy making and the utilisation of evidence in practice (Nutley *et al.* 2002). Third, there are large gaps and ambiguities in the knowledge base on which policy makers and practitioners can draw (Davies and Nutley 2002). Fourth, there is recognition that evidence is only one of many factors that influences policy making, as policy making is inherently political (Nutley *et al.* 2003).

Problem-oriented policing and EBPP

Problem-oriented policing is a form of evidence-based policing. First, as we have seen, there is plenty of evidence to show that where problem-oriented policing is properly implemented it reduces crime. In this sense it could be considered to be an evidence-based response to tackling crime problems effectively. Second, the evaluation of problem-oriented policing and partnership efforts can in part provide the knowledge base from which those seeking to implement evidence-based solutions can draw. Third, the language and processes of problem-oriented policing fit generally well with the language and philosophy of evidence-based policy and practice: the focus on effectiveness, reducing the impact of problems, focusing on those issues that concern the community, implementing what works, measuring outcomes and assessment, all fit well with the concerns of the problem-oriented agenda. However, they are not the same thing.

Partnership

Crime reduction beyond the police service

The past few years have seen growing emphasis in Britain on partnership to deal with those 'wicked issues' that, it is thought, cannot be adequately dealt with by specific single agencies acting as 'silos', but require instead co-operation and co-ordination across organisations. Health, economic regeneration and child protection comprise specific examples of issues that cannot be adequately addressed by any individual agency on its own. Government regional offices (nine in England and one for Wales) bring together civil servants from a range of government departments to facilitate co-ordination. Local Area Agreements and Local Strategic Partnerships have emerged to foster and oversee partnership working across a range of issues within local areas.

Consistent with this, as we shall see, is a rather longer history than most other substantive policy areas in partnership working, which has come to dominate crime reduction policy and practice (see Crawford 1998). It has become widely recognised that the police service cannot directly affect many of the causes of crime and so needs to draw on the services of other agencies to reduce crime (Bullock *et al.* 2000; Moss and Pease 1999). The general aim of working in partnership in the field of crime reduction is to share and mobilise resources in order to target them to best effect and to avoid unnecessary confusion, duplication and contradiction.

The 1998 Crime and Disorder Act represented perhaps the most significant development in British inter-agency crime reduction – putting inter-agency crime reduction planning on a statutory footing for the first time. Sections 5 and 6 of the Crime and Disorder Act 1998 state that the local authorities and the police, in co-operation with the probation service, health and police authorities were to produce a cogent three-year community safety strategy, the first of which was to be published on 1 April 1999. There have been subsequent strategies in 2002 and 2005. The strategies are supposed to be based on an audit of crime and disorder problems in the locality and consultation with the wider community. At the time of writing, a review (based on consultation with a range of interested parties) of the partnership provisions of the 1998 Crime and Disorder Act had just been published (Home Office 2006). This review makes a number of recommendations for the future governance and delivery of Crime and Disorder Reduction Partnerships; these are summarised briefly.

1 *Structures* The review proposes that the strategic functions of Crime and Disorder Reduction Partnerships (e.g. the assessment of priorities and oversight) are separated from the delivery functions (e.g. plans for action).

2 *Delivery* The review proposes that delivery should be based on the police National Intelligence Model (see subsequent sections in this chapter). Chief officers should provide strategic assessments on a six-monthly basis. Instead of triennial reporting there should be annual rolling three-year community safety plans underpinned by the six-monthly assessments and informed by consultation with the community. It also recommends that the provisions of the Crime and Disorder Act should be strengthened to make it easier to disclose depersonalised data.

3 *Governance and accountability* The review proposed that Crime and Disorder Reduction Partnerships should engage more fully with communities and report on what they are doing to improve community safety.

4 *Mainstreaming* The review proposes strengthening section 17 of the Crime and Disorder Act to account for antisocial behaviour.

5 *National standards* The review proposes that a set of national standards for partnership working should be put in place.

The vehicle for these changes is the 2006 Police and Justice Bill, which is likely to receive the royal assent in autumn 2006. At the time of writing, the implications for statutory partnership working in the field of crime prevention are, of course, unclear.

Inter-agency crime reduction and problem-oriented policing

There are very clear, broad overlaps between the stages of problem-oriented policing and the requirements of the 1998 Crime and Disorder Act. Whilst perhaps not explicitly so, the Crime and Disorder Act has effectively offered a broad forum for delivery of area-based problem-oriented policing in a partnership context at the local level. However, the impact that this has had in terms of the implementation of problem-oriented policing processes or on crime itself is far from clear. Early audits and strategies were certainly of variable quality (Phillips *et al.* 2000). It is not surprising that those responsible for developing crime and disorder strategies experienced problems seen more generally in implementing problem-oriented policing (see Chapter 2). Phillips *et al.* (2000) noted that partnerships pointed to limitations in data collection, including: agencies not providing data; difficulties in comparing data (different areas, time periods) and data quality problems. Similarly, over-broad categorisation of problems and a tendency to include non-specific plans for implementation were noted. HMIC (2000) reported similar findings: limited use of data, variable quality plans and weaknesses in evaluation. More recently, a National Audit Office (2004) report stated that there has been 'steady progress' in the performance of crime and disorder partnerships, although the report provides little evidence about what this actually means. The implications that the Crime and Disorder Act review and the 2006 Police and Justice Bill will have are unclear at the time of writing.

More generally, partnership working itself has been seen as an important aspect of problem-oriented policing. Indeed, Goldstein (1990) stressed the need for the police service to search for the *best response* to crime problems, which would not necessarily be police enforcement. He pointed especially to the need for officers to develop a range of alternatives to the criminal justice system for tackling problems and to recognise other ways of controlling behaviour. This might include (amongst other many things): drawing in other agencies; using mediation or negotiation; conveying information; mobilising community resources; changing the physical setting and increasing regulations (Goldstein 1990). However, working in partnership is not an end in itself. The aim of partnership working in crime reduction is typically to share resources, to use resources to best effect and to minimise duplication. The aim of problem-oriented policing is to develop appropriate responses to identified problems of community concern and thereby also reduce demands on the police service. The strong implication is that, *only where appropriate*, the police service should seek to draw in the resources of other agencies to tackle identified problems.

That said, problem-oriented policing, especially that on a large scale, seems to be facilitated by the establishment of multi-disciplinary or multi-agency teams (Read and Tilley 2000). Generally, though, it is recognised that whilst the police service has to get others on board in implementing problem-oriented policing that has not always happened (Hope 1994; Pollard 1996; Leigh *et al.* 1998).

Intelligence-led policing and the National Intelligence Model

Problem-oriented policing has an affinity with intelligence-based policing models, which are increasingly important in the UK. Whilst problem-oriented approaches to crime reduction focus on crime problems, intelligence-led policing tends to focus on individuals (or groups or networks of individuals) as the causes of crime (Ekblom

2003). The process is focused around the collection of information about offenders with the aim of developing enforcement-based responses to disrupt that offender's activities. The focus of intelligence-led policing is traditional law enforcement, but applied in a smarter manner (Ekblom 2003; Tilley 2003).

A key development in UK policing has been the formulation and implementation of the National Intelligence Model in all police services in England and Wales. The stated aim of the Model has been to 'help managers to plan and work in co-operation with partners to ensure the implementation of community policing; manage performance and risk and to account for budgets' (http/www.ncis.co.uk/nim. asp 2003). John and Maguire (2003) provide a detailed discussion of the background to the National Intelligence Model, which can be summarised as follows:

1 A range of reports showing the specialist and *ad hoc* nature of the use of intelligence in the police service and pointing to the need for a more central role of intelligence, which should *drive* police business.

2 A 1993 Audit Commission report which highlighted the grossly undeveloped nature of intelligence in the British police service.

3 A powerful lead from the former Chief Constable of Kent Constabulary (Sir David Philips).

4 Concern about the *ad hoc* development of capacity for the collection and use of intelligence in the police service, with huge differences between forces.

In practice, the National Intelligence Model provides a range of standardised products that aim to enable planning of objectives based on local priorities as identified by intelligence. These include key intelligence products and a number of standardised analytical, knowledge and system products. Because the intelligence products are supposed to be standardised, the model offers the potential for their aggregation to levels higher than a single police service area (see www.ncis.co.uk/nim.asp for more details). The National Intelligence Model provides, thus, a standardised approach to the collection, collation and use of information (Clarke and Eck 2003).

At the time of writing, the National Intelligence Model is very influential. It is widely endorsed, by the Association of Chief Police Officers, the Home Office and HM Inspectorate of Constabulary. The Policing White Paper (*Building Communities, Beating Crime* 2004) reinforces the message that the National Intelligence Model is the model through which all police services in England and Wales *should conduct their business*. All forces were required to implement it by April 2004 and indeed the White Paper and the National Policing Plan (2005–08) suggest that all forces had adopted minimum standards by that date. Therefore, this model has the potential to frame how policing is done in the future and clearly has implications for the implementation of problem-oriented policing in the UK.

In addition to specifying a range of intelligence processes and products, the National Intelligence Model identifies different 'levels' of policing: BCU and local; force and cross-border; national and international. Problems may manifest themselves at more than one level and intelligence is supposed to flow between them. Strategies and tactics to address these problems emerge from regular (quarterly to annual) 'Strategic Tasking and Co-ordinating Group' and (weekly, fortnightly or monthly) 'Tactical Tasking and Co-ordinating Group' meetings that ensure that attention is paid to intelligence and that action is taken as a result. Analysts play a key part in these meetings, collating and presenting intelligence about patterns of criminal activity and feeding back results of actions taken (see Cope 2003; John and Maguire 2003).

Implementation of the National Intelligence Model

Despite its importance, it is misleading to assume that the Model is being implemented in a straightforward manner. As we have argued, the implementation of any new programme in the police service is far from trouble-free. Early research has highlighted problems with putting the National Intelligence Model into practice (John and Maguire 2003; 2004a, 2004b).

1 John and Maguire found that leadership and commitment have been variable between and within police service areas, and that these are vital at all levels amongst the police service for the successful implementation of the Model.

2 They discovered problems with the tasking and co-ordinating groups themselves. These included limited input from partners and over-reliance on police-generated information, over-attention to performance indicators and conflicts between competing priorities (especially national versus local ones). Further problems were identified in the variable frequency of meetings, the seniority of the chair (which in turn could affect attendance) and in some cases

the conduct of meetings (which could sometimes ignore analytical evidence and/or come to resemble 'resource bidding' sessions).

3 John and Maguire noted problems with the intelligence products themselves. They identified variety in quality (and availability) of strategic assessments, and the lack of standardisation (and again variation in quality) of tactical assessments.

4 They found a lack of standardisation of practices and products between police service areas. This will be difficult to change, as forces and individual BCUs have already become accustomed to their own ways of doing things.

5 They identified problems retaining good-quality analytical staff because of low pay, the lack of a well developed career and promotion structure and competition for good analysts.

6 They uncovered problems with the ownership and understanding of the Model. There are knowledge gaps across rank-and-file officers (which might be to do with the technical language associated with the Model). Some resistance to the Model itself based both on ignorance and on dislike of its 'academic' structure and language was also noted.

The National Intelligence Model and problem-oriented policing

Despite these early implementation problems, the Model is important, and currently looking likely to stay, so what does it mean for British problem-oriented policing? There is still debate as to whether the National Intelligence Model and problem-oriented policing processes could and should be brought together. Certainly, there are similarities between problem-oriented policing and the National Intelligence Model: they are both concerned with reforming the police service, both focus on the key role that the systematic use of information should play in policing and both are concerned with reducing crime (Tilley 2003a). But there are differences too: problem-oriented approaches are potentially wider in scope than the National Intelligence Model. They are more focused on long-term systematic analysis; they are more likely to look at non-crime (as well as crime) problems and they are less likely to depend on police enforcement as the strategy for tackling problems (Tilley 2003).

That said, it has been argued that *in principle* the National Intelligence Model and problem-oriented approaches are complementary (Clarke and Eck 2003; John and Maguire 2003; McPherson and Kirby 2004).

And, as the National Intelligence Model is supposed to have wide scope, it could potentially incorporate rather wider practice than appears to be the case from some reports of it and from typical current applications (John and Maguire 2003). Indeed, in practice, there have already been local attempts to bring the two together. Lancashire Constabulary, which, as has been seen, is a relatively well developed problem-oriented force, was also a front runner in the implementation of the National Intelligence Model. Lancashire's approach has been to attempt to integrate the two: the working assumption there is that there are broad areas of overlap between the two models, as shown in Figure 6.1.

The policing White Paper (*Building Communities, Beating Crime* 2004) also suggests that the National Intelligence Model can be used in a partnership context and suggests (without details of where and how) that this is happening in some areas. The police reform website (www.policereform.gov.uk/implementation/natintellmodel.html)

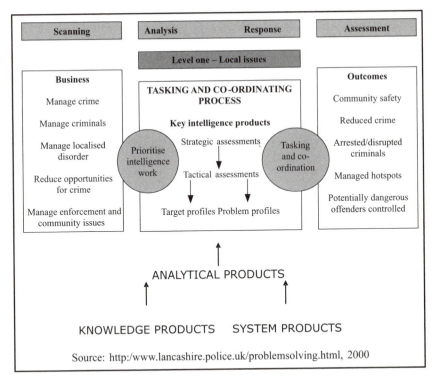

Figure 6.1 Integration of NIM and POP

also states that there should be strong links between the Model and partnership working. It suggests moreover that partners should provide information and be encouraged to assist in the development of tactical solutions. However, the site also makes it clear that the Model is 'primarily a business model for use in allocating *police* resources'. And that 'it must be recognised that much of the information and intelligence produced by the model at a tactical level is of a restricted or confidential nature ... Whilst attendance of partners at the Tasking and Co-ordinating Groups may be possible at a strategic level, it may not always be possible or practicable at a tactical level'. As we have seen, the review of the 1998 Crime and Disorder Act (Home Office 2006) also makes reference to plans to adapt the National Intelligence Model to a partnership environment and to require (by means of national standards) its use by all those discharging the strategic or operational functions of community safety (Home Office 2006). However, it would seem that whilst the recommendation is to apply *similar processes* it is to apply them separately from the police model. Indeed, the review notes that some of the processes of the National Intelligence Model may not be appropriate to a partnership setting (Home Office 2006).

Certainly, early research has suggested that the processes of the National Intelligence Model are dominated by the police service's view of what constitutes a problem (linked to police performance indicators): the use of police data and the development of police responses. Whilst there may be some evidence of Crime and Disorder Reduction Partnership involvement in the Model's processes and in multi-agency Tasking and Co-ordinating Groups, this would appear to be piecemeal and *ad hoc*. Further, as the quotes above suggest, there would appear to be some confusion about the role that partnership *should* be playing in the implementation of the Model. At the time of writing, whilst there might be the potential for problem-oriented policing approaches to be integrated with National Intelligence Model processes in principle, its routine realisation would appear to be some way off in practice.

Community policing, neighbourhood policing and reassurance policing

As an ideal and as practice community policing is widely espoused (especially in the US) and encompasses a range of police and non-police activity. Authors have struggled to define exactly what community policing is but it is generally associated with efforts to improve relations between the police and community. It also embraces the notion that the community is a key partner in addressing crime problems. Community policing commonly comprises in part a solution to a perceived problem: that of a poor relationship between the public and the police. This rationale for community policing contrasts with problem-oriented approaches which see the starting point of interventions to be the identification of problems that cause harm to a community, rather than police relationships with the community as ends in themselves (Tilley 2003). Moreover, for problem-oriented policing, whether the community acts as a key partner in addressing a crime problem facing the community cannot be a foregone conclusion. For some – indeed, perhaps many – problems, community involvement of some sort may comprise an ingredient in the response, but this will not necessarily always be so.

Distilling the key components of community policing has proved difficult but they include: consultation with communities, decentralisation of police resources to local-level, problem-oriented policing, and the establishment of local policing teams (often at ward level). Thus, rather than acting in a problem-oriented approach, community-policing models may incorporate some problem-solving, despite the fact that they have been deemed identical by some commentators (see Tilley 2003).

Neighbourhood policing, as it has developed in the UK, is probably best viewed as a form of community policing. It starts from the premise that policing needs to better address the needs of the community. It incorporates elements of problem-oriented policing and is based (typically) at local (normally beat) level. Despite its recent rise to greater prominence in police policy making and practice (see the 2004 White Paper *Building Communities, Beating Crime* and the 2005–08 National Policing Plan), the ideal and implementation of neighbourhood policing are far from new in the UK. It was developed as a response, at least in part, to the recommendations of the 1981 Scarman Report on the Brixton riots (Irving and Dixon 2002). The aim initially was (as in US community policing) to create an effective relationship between the police and communities. It has also been to widen the range of methods to reduce time spent responding to calls, to improve the intelligence base about effective policing responses and to engage the public and other agencies in policing. Early efforts to implement neighbourhood policing were conducted in Surrey and the London Metropolitan Police Service. It was called 'neighbourhood policing' seemingly to distinguish it from 'community policing' which had already been implemented in the Devon and Cornwall police service (Irving and Dixon 2002).

More recently there has been a major central government drive to implement neighbourhood policing in all police services in England and Wales. First, there is the National Reassurance Policing Programme, which consisted of the implementation of a community policing approach in 16 pilot ward-based sites, research and evaluation. The National Reassurance Policing Programme builds on the signal crimes perspective developed by Dr Martin Innes and colleagues at the University of Surrey and previous community policing models such as the Chicago Alternative Policing Strategy (see Skogan *et al*. 2004). Interventions can be summarised as: the presence of visible, accessible and locally known authority figures (generally police officers and Police Community Support Officers); community involvement in the process of identifying problems; targeted policing and problem-oriented policing activity (Tuffin *et al*. 2006).

Second, a new legislative framework for policing focuses strongly on the implementation of neighbourhood policing. The 2004 White Paper (*Building Communities, Beating Crime*) and the National Policing Plan (2005–08) make much of 'citizen focus policing' and 'community policing'. The Policing Plan is focused on using the National Intelligence Model to allocate resources and on providing a citizen focus to policing. Citizen focus would involve the implementation of neighbourhood policing teams, more effective engagement between the police and public and giving more say to the public over what they can expect from policing. It also involves public service agreements to measure public satisfaction and policing plans to include actions to improve citizen focus and quality of service commitments. Improved accessibility and a more representative police service are also considered to be important.

The White Paper provides more details about what the development of neighbourhood policing means in practice. It more explicitly links neighbourhood policing with the National Intelligence Model, problem-orientation and achieving greater responsiveness to local demands. The White Paper also more explicitly links neighbourhood policing with a clear crime reduction focus which differentiates it to some extent from community policing more generally (Tuffin *et al*. 2006). It suggests specifically that neighbourhood policing should include a dedicated area-based resource, an emphasis on local problem-oriented policing, community engagement, public involvement in shaping priorities and a mechanism to hold police and partners to account.

The more recent Home Office publication *Neighbourhood Policing: Your Police, Your Community, Our Commitment* (2005) distils the key aspects of neighbourhood policing into the following elements:

1 Dedicated teams of police officers, community support officers, specials and volunteers for particular areas.
2 More police and community support officers.
3 Feedback to the public about police performance locally.
4 Public say in setting priorities.
5 Information for local people about who the local police officers are and how to contact them.

Little detailed information is provided about how any of this will be done in any of these documents. Seemingly, the intention was not to be prescriptive about how neighbourhood policing is to be implemented locally. The National Centre for Policing Excellence (2005) guidance is intended to provide more information about how neighbourhood policing should be done in practice. Amongst other things, the guidance says neighbourhood policing should include: deployment based on the National Intelligence Model, involvement of the community in addressing problems, the development of an effective engagement, communication and feedback strategy, and rigorous performance management. In particular, the guidance makes a great deal of the way neighbourhood policing should be driven by thorough analysis and integrated into the National Intelligence Model processes, and especially that it should be driven through multi-agency co-ordination and tasking. Indeed, the guidance argues that integration with the National Intelligence Model is fundamental to the success of neighbourhood policing.

Neighbourhood policing in practice

So what is happening in practice? We have already seen that, actually, the concepts of neighbourhood policing are far from new. There is a long history of implementation of community policing in the US and some efforts to implement neighbourhood policing in the UK have been made and evaluated. Drawing on their 1989 review of the early implementation of neighbourhood policing in Surrey and London, the Police Foundation argued that whilst senior police officers claimed that neighbourhood policing had been implemented, not much had actually changed on the ground (Irving and Dixon 2002). Irving and Dixon (2002) went on to observe that despite the spread of the ideal of neighbourhood policing across the UK over the next few years there remained a gulf between the rhetoric of neighbourhood policing and actual change on the ground.

That said, more recently the evaluation of the National Reassurance Policing Programme concludes that there was an overall positive effect on (amongst other things) self-reported victimisation, perceptions of the crime rate and antisocial behaviour problems, as well as public confidence in the police, presence of visible police patrol, familiarity and engagement and awareness of police activity (Tuffin *et al.* 2006). As was set out earlier in this chapter, problem orientation was a key element of the programme. Tuffin *et al.* (2006) conclude that those sites that showed significant change in public perceptions of juvenile nuisance also appeared to have implemented problem-oriented policing well and shared the following characteristics: community involvement in identifying and defining the problem; a very detailed specification of at least two elements of the problem analysis triangle (see Chapter 5); and the use of multiple sources of information to specify the nature of the problem.

More generally, a review of the implementation of neighbourhood policing following the 2004 White Paper showed that there were a variety of approaches to the implementation of neighbourhood policing, including some variation across forces (Quinton 2005). The variation across forces has mainly been due to differences in targeting resources, the need to adapt the approach to local conditions and in some cases to choices made by the BCU commander. This report focused mainly on the establishment of dedicated teams. Quinton's review had less to say about how police services have risen to the challenge of involving the public in setting priorities and feeding back information about performance and locally based problem-oriented policing. There is, however, evidence from other efforts to improve community involvement in policing. Consultation with communities can be done in a number of ways. Focus groups, citizens' panels, surveys and the media are all used by the police service and partners to communicate with the public. Perhaps the most common way, however, is through police/community meetings. Recommended in the Scarman Report (1981) as a means of improving the relationship between the police service and the public, community consultative groups are widely established in the police service. However, there have been problems of low attendance and concern about how representative of the public these groups actually are. The Crime and Disorder Act 1998 similarly called for consultation with the community, including 'hard to reach' groups, and this too spurred activity in this area. Studies have suggested that there has in fact been extensive consultation with voluntary and statutory bodies as part of the development of crime and disorder audits and strategies but the extent of consultation with individuals within the community is less clear (Hester 2000; Newburn and Jones 2001). The evaluation of the National Reassurance Policing Programme (Tuffin *et al*. 2006) suggested that more traditional forms of engagement (such as public meetings or beat surgeries) were not enough to effect change in the public's perception of the police service. Those areas that successfully improved public perceptions conducted wider engagement activity aimed at reaching a broad section of the population, for example door knocking, outreach workers, large-scale public surveys and media activity.

Commentators have stressed the need for community involvement in problem definition and in the development of police and other crime reduction responses (e.g. Goldstein 1979, 1990). Some research suggests that this had not happened in practice (Skogan 1988; Hope 1994). The public's voice in crime reduction activity may in fact be somewhat limited in a practical sense (Capowich and Roehl 1994). The public may not wish to take responsibility for crime control and when it does it may not be well directed (Gilling 1996). Gilling suggested that there might be disagreements between the police and the public about what constitutes a problem and what can be done about it (Gilling 1996). However, more recently, Tuffin *et al*.'s (2006) study of the impact of the implementation of the National Reassurance Programme showed an overall positive programme effect on: the proportion of people who felt that their local police were very or fairly effective at working with the local community; the proportion of people who reported that they knew what the police planned to do in an area; and the proportion of people who knew how to get their views across to the police locally (Tuffin *et al*. 2006).

As well as noting generally low levels of community involvement in crime reduction activities, research has highlighted *differential* participation in community-based crime prevention initiatives. People who get involved have tended to be better-off, long-term residents who own their own homes and have children (Skogan 1988). In low-crime-rate, affluent areas people are prepared to work together to keep out a threat that is perceived to come from elsewhere. In poor, high-crime-rate areas people are suspicious of each other, because the threat of crime is perceived to come from within the area in which they are living. There may also be suspicion of the police and thus unwillingness to work with them. Such suspicion may undermine community crime prevention efforts. That said, attendance rates at police/community meetings in beat meetings in Chicago have been shown to be highest in poor, high-crime communities (Skogan *et al.* 2000). High levels of attendance here seemed to be related to need. The authors themselves point out that this is fairly unusual and that the Chicago project has been particuarly successful in sustaining attendance in areas where it is needed most. Key to sustaining actual participation in the meetings appear to be community factors and personal contacts between the police and community.

However, Skogan *et al.* (2000) also noted that poor and internally divided beats experienced greater difficulty translating aspirations of problem-oriented policing into reality than did better-off homogeneous areas, even though attendance at the meetings was higher. They argued that there was still a real risk that a problem-oriented policing approach might principally assist those who need it least.

In a Development and Practice report intended to inform greater community involvement in problem-solving, Forrest *et al.* (2005) reviewed the limited amount of documented recent experience in Britain. They note the scarcity of community involvement through the whole problem-solving process, and many of the practical difficulties of achieving involvement, especially in the fractured high-crime neighbourhoods where needs are greatest.

Neighbourhood policing and problem-oriented policing

Rather than comprising a problem-oriented policing approach *per se*, neighbourhood policing models encompass, along with other things, problem-oriented policing processes. Resonating with American models of community policing, there have been efforts to implement neighbourhood policing in the UK over the last twenty-five years. It has now become a cornerstone of policing policy and without a doubt there has been a diffusion of the ideal of neighbourhood policing across the UK. Despite the stated role of problem-oriented policing in neighbourhood policing models, the nature and extent of problem-oriented policing conducted by neighbourhood policing teams is far from clear and the potential for it in practice remains to be seen, although early indicators are promising (Tuffin *et al.* 2006). The extent to which the National Intelligence Model will play a role in the tasking of neighbourhood policing teams also remains to be seen and work in this area is on going. This presumably could in principle constitute a link between neighbourhood and wider problem-oriented policing, though the previous section of this chapter has already highlighted the problematic and hitherto uncertain connection that exists in most places between the National Intelligence Model and problem-oriented policing.

The mixed economy of policing and the extended policing family

The police can no longer plausibly be deemed to include only those attached to an organisation made up of paid sworn police personnel and special constables (volunteer part-time officers who have full police powers). In recent years these officers have been joined by a range of new visible presences including Police Community Support Officers, Neighbourhood Wardens, private security guards and private individuals (Crawford and Lister 2004). Though by now numbers will have increased, Crawford (2003) provided estimates of the numbers employed in the mixed economy of policing in 2001–02, as shown in Table 6.1.

Neighbourhood and other street wardens have been funded by the Office of the Deputy Prime Minister and the Home Office and employed by local councils. Neighbourhood wardens have provided a uniformed, semi-official presence in residential areas and the general aim is to improve quality of life, promote community safety and assist with environmental improvements. Street wardens are basically the same as neighbourhood wardens but may have a more general emphasis on improving the physical appearance of an area.

Table 6.1 Numbers involved in the mixed economy of policing

Body	Number
Professional police	131,548
Civilian staff	58,909
Special constables	11,598
Community Support Officers	1,281
Traffic wardens	2,233
Neighbourhood wardens	1,454
British Transport Police	2,073
Private security guards	125,000

Source: Crawford (2003).

More recently the Home Office has made considerable funds available to police services to employ Police Community Support Officers (sometimes called Community Support Officers). Community Support Officers were introduced as part of the 2002 Police Reform Act. Cooper *et al.* (2006) state that at the time of their study of these officers there were 6,000 employed in England and Wales and there is a government commitment for police services to employ 24,000 by 2008. The main thrust of the Community Support Officer role is to provide a visible and accessible uniformed presence and to engage with the public and as such they spend the majority of their time patrolling on foot and dealing with low-level antisocial behaviour (Cooper *et al.* 2006).

As well as wardens and Community Support Officers a uniformed presence is provided by traffic wardens and a range of private security personnel that are deployed in a range of settings such as pubs and clubs, shopping centres and car parks and sometimes in estates and streets. Crawford (2003) noted the difficulties in estimating the size of the private security industry and offered the (probably) conservative estimate of 125,000 employees provided in Table 6.1. It is however, quite clear that the numbers employed have been increasing. Drawing on Johnson (1992), Crawford (2003) described the main functions of the security industry as follows: the provision of staffed services (uniformed presence); the provision of security equipment (CCTV, bolts and locks, etc.); and investigative services (bailiffs, debt collectors, private detectives).

Additionally, some voluntary groups such as Neighbourhood Watch provide a visible police presence. However, as pointed out by Crawford (2003), in practice patrols by Neighbourhood Watch or other civilian groups have never taken off in the UK to any great extent.

It is very clear, then, that the provision of visible policing today is no longer the preserve of the sworn police officer and provision is more fragmented and tiered than ever before (Crawford and Lister 2004). What are the implications of this? Crawford and Lister (2004) suggest that there are advantages in this mixed economy of visible patrol. In particular it responds to the public's increasing demand for a police presence. Crawford and Lister's (2004) study of initiatives that aimed to provide increased public reassurance through visible police patrol in Yorkshire and Humberside pointed to difficulties co-ordinating and organising the division of labour in the mixed economy of provision. They suggested that developments have been *ad hoc* and driven by local markets and that the boundaries between the local markets were unclear. They conclude that the result was diverse approaches which led to differences in the levels of visibility. The diversity, they argued, was caused by: differences in the *aim* of patrol; the approach of senior officers; differences in how local authorities have responded to the public demand for visible police presence; and accordingly how local authorities have applied for grants to fund wardens, Community Support Officers, etc. Whilst Community Support Officers appeared to be highly valued by the public and other police officers, Cooper *et al*. (2006) also noted variation between areas in the role and activity of Community Support Officers.

The emergence of a mixed economy of policing clearly raises issues of co-operation in problem solving *within* the overall policing function to add to the issues of co-operation in problem solving for partnerships *across* policing and non-policing agencies. It is rather too early yet to know how this will work through in practice - whether the problems of organisation and co-ordination highlighted by Crawford and Lister are teething troubles or whether they will prove to be stubborn. There is the potential to engage with a wider range of issues, with a wider range of personnel. The risk is that in a rush to meet public needs for visibility the focus on outcome effectiveness in dealing with real problems underlying the demand for more presence on the streets is lost.

Hotspotting and the role of Geographical Information Systems

The potential for analysis of crime patterns has expanded dramatically since the 1980s. Twenty years ago some police services were still dependent on paper records, and analysis involved painstaking transfers of data from paper to computers. Today all police services have computerised records and many software packages have been developed to enable specific analyses of various sorts easily to be undertaken. Other agencies likewise are keeping records on crime and disorder-related incidents. For example there are now national standard computerised records of reported fly-tipping, brought together in 'Flycapture'. Generic data analysis packages, such as Excel, SPSS and MapInfo are also used in analyses of individual data sets or to bring varying data sets together. Census data are provided for small areas that can be built on in analysing patterns. Computing hardware continues to become cheaper and more powerful. The potential is there for much greater analysis of national and local crime and disorder problems. Amongst the most important developments have been those related to Geographical Information Systems (GIS) and spatial analysis of patterns of crime and disorder.

Crime mapping

It is clear that crime is not randomly distributed (Bottoms and Wiles 1997). Some people and some places are at higher risk than others are and historically there has been much interest in the relationship between crime and place (Brantingham and Brantingham 1995; Tilley and Laycock 2002). That crime risk is geographically concentrated has opened up the possibility of deploying resources on this basis to areas where they are most needed. Geographical Information Systems provide a means of capturing, displaying, managing and analysing data that is spatially referenced. Crime data can be layered with maps representing other information (which might include land use, population data, health data, etc.) to represent the areas where crimes occur (Chainey and Ratcliffe 2005). Crime data are suited to GIS analysis because much crime is inherently geographically based (Chainey and Ratcliffe 2005).

Crime mapping and the use of geographical information systems has in fact become very big business in policing and crime reduction planning (Bryne and Pease 2003) and there is now a proliferation of software available to support spatial analysis (Cope 2003). The growth in crime mapping has been fuelled by improvements in technology and the availability of electronic crime records (Boba 2005; Chainey and Ratcliffe 2005). However, its growth is also associated with the increasing importance attached to the situational or 'proximal' causes of crime when understanding the geography of crime (Boba 2005).

Crime mapping is not, however, just about the identification of crime hotspots and the deployment of resources. GIS can play an important role in a range of activities. As well as identifying crime hotspots for the deployment of police officers and targeting crime reduction interventions, Chainey and Ratcliffe (2005) noted the following potential uses for GIS:

1 Recording and mapping police activity, crime reduction projects and calls for service/incidents.
2 Supporting of briefing of operational officers by showing where crime has recently occurred and predicting where it may occur in the future.
3 Helping to understand the distribution of crime and to explore the mechanisms and dynamics of criminal activity through analysis with other data.

4 Monitoring initiatives.
5 Using the maps visually to show crime statistics to the public and initiatives that are being implemented.

Whilst the use of mapping software and geographical information to identify and display hotspots is widespread and the role potentially wide-ranging, it should be noted that the process is not unproblematic. First, early problems with the use of GIS included organisational and management problems, information sharing obstacles, technical problems and geo-coding problems: these problems have not been unique to the police service and they have not gone away (Chainey and Ratcliffe 2005). Second, the maps are only as good as the data they are based on and systems are still heavily reliant on police data, with which there are inherent difficulties (Cope 2003). Third, merely mapping crime does not necessarily explain it: it simply represents it and explanations of data patterns are essential if they are to be used properly (Cope 2003). Fourth, it is not always clear whether geographical hotspots are stable across time or are merely time-limited blips (Byrne and Pease 2003). Fifth, hotspots for preventive or patrol attention are not always identified on evidence-based grounds; local politicians, for example, may have a vested interest in identifying local hotspots as a basis to lobby for extra resources for their area (Byrne and Pease 2003). Lastly, most current methods of hotspotting are inherently retrospective: they show what happened in the past rather than predict what will happen in the future (Cope 2003). Despite these problems Geographical Information Systems and hotspotting are clearly being widely used to support policing and crime reduction planning in the UK.

Crime mapping and problem-oriented policing

Clearly, being able to identify and analyse geographically based crime hotspots is an important element of the problem-oriented policing processes. There are connections between crime mapping and problem-oriented approaches to crime reduction in relation to analysis of data and evaluation of initiatives. Indeed, the 1996 Audit Commission Report (*Streetwise*) highlighted the need for police officers to identify and analyse hotspots in developing solutions to problems as a means of reducing demand on the police service (Audit Commission 1996). How are geographical information systems being used to support problem-oriented policing? There is very limited evidence regarding this issue. The Home Office conducted a survey of Police and Crime and Disorder Reduction Partnership employees who were involved in crime analysis between November 2004 and April 2005. The questionnaire focused on how respondents use Geographical Information Systems in their crime analysis work. The survey was circulated to all principal analysts in police forces (for circulation to analysts in their force) and to members of regional analyst forums which include police and Crime and Disorder Reduction Partnership analysts. In total there were 171 responses (90 from police forces, 75 from Crime and Disorder Reduction Partnerships and six from other organisations). Respondents were asked to: assess their understanding of the concept of problem-oriented policing for crime reduction planning; describe their involvement in problem-oriented policing work; indicate why problem-oriented policing was not part of their role if this was the case; and, describe how GIS is used to support their problem-oriented policing work. The results are shown in Tables 6.2 to 6.5.

The results of the survey show that just under three in five respondents (57%) felt that their understanding of the concepts of problem-oriented policing was good or very good. However, almost a quarter of respondents felt that their understanding of the concepts was basic, very basic or that they were unfamiliar with the concepts. Fifty-four per cent of respondents felt that problem-oriented policing was a fairly important or very important part of their current role although one-fifth (21%) stated that it was not part of their role or not an important part. Where respondents stated that problem-oriented policing was not part of their role they were asked to state why not. (This was only 32 respondents.) Of these, seven respondents said that someone else was responsible for problem-oriented policing work and 12 said that all their time was spent doing something else. A number of respondents pointed to lack of knowledge or specialism as a reason for not being involved in problem-oriented policing work. Seven respondents stated that they did not have sufficient knowledge

Table 6.2 Understanding of the concept of problem-oriented policing for crime reduction (%; $n = 152$)

Very good	17
Good	40
Moderate	25
Basic	13
Very basic	4
Unfamiliar with the concept	2
Total	101

Table 6.3 Involvement in problem-oriented policing for crime and disorder reduction in your current role (%; *n* = 152)

A very important part of my job	25
A fairly important part of my job	30
Of moderate importance	24
Not an important part of my job	16
Not part of my job	5
Total	100

Table 6.4 Why problem-oriented policing was not part of the analyst's role (% agreeing; *n* = 32)

All of my time is taken up with other forms of crime analysis (e.g. producing maps for performance management or tasking and co-ordinating purposes)	38
I am not a crime and disorder specialist – the main focus of my work is in another area	25
Someone else is responsible for problem-oriented policing work	22
I do not have sufficient knowledge of problem-oriented policing techniques or criminological theory	22
I do not have access to sufficient data to understand the problems	19

Note Answered by 32 respondents who indicated that problem-oriented policing was 'not an important part of my job' or 'not part of my job'.

Table 6.5 Use of Geographical Information Systems to support problem-oriented policing (%; *n* = 147)

To identify that a crime and disorder problem exists	85
To improve understanding of the problem (e.g. exact geographic location and patterns, social demographic context of problem)	84
To help evaluate the impact of action taken to reduce the problem	51
To help establish the possible causes of the crime and disorder problem	49
To help design a crime and disorder reduction measure to tackle the problem	39
I don't use GIS in my problem-oriented policing work	1

Note Answered by all respondents except those who indicated that problem-oriented policing was 'not part of my job'.

to do this kind of work, six said that they did not have access to the data to do it and eight stated that they were not a crime and disorder specialist. Lastly, respondents were asked to discuss the role that Geographical Information Systems play in their problem-oriented policing work. More than eight in ten (85%) stated that Geographical Information Systems were used to help to identify crime and disorder problems and a similar proportion (84%) said that they used Geographical Information Systems to improve understanding of that problem. However the use of Geographical Information Systems falls substantially when it comes to helping to establish the cause of the problem (50%) and just 40 per cent used them to help design interventions to tackle the problems. Fifty per cent stated that they used it to evaluate interventions.

As has been argued, Geographical Information Systems have great potential to facilitate crime reduction planning and there are links between crime mapping and problem-oriented policing. If crime mapping and Geographical Information Systems, in particular, were used more widely to support the implementation of a version of the National Intelligence Model that centred on problem solving and did not build-in a tendency towards enforcement as a natural response to problems, GIS could fruitfully be woven into problem-oriented processes and practices. However, it is probably fair to say that at the moment, in terms of supporting problem-oriented policing, Geographical Information Systems are being used only in a limited way. They would seem to be used primarily to identify the *size* of a problem and the *location* of that problem. It is typically not being used to understand the proximal causes of crime problems and to develop responses to them. Even though it would appear to be an obvious additional use of GIS, it would also seem that geographical information systems are not being used regularly to evaluate the impact of crime reduction interventions. A future issue is clearly how to make greater *proactive* use of the mapping software available for understanding immediate causes of and developing responses to problems, rather than using it merely to identify and describe crime problems. We have already noted in this chapter that the utility of mapping software would seem to be at its highest when it is used to predict future crime patterns, rather than just describe past crime problems. There are now moves towards this. Kate Bowers and Shane Johnson at the Jill Dando Institute of Crime Science at University College London have developed prospective mapping techniques which have been shown to be more effective in predicting future burglary hotspots than previous methods (Bowers *et al.* 2004). This works through using recent historic crime data to generate forecasts which can be displayed using a Geographic Information System and superimposed on an Ordnance Survey map of the policing area. The challenge here would appear to be whether the maps can be recreated in an operational setting, effective preventative interventions developed and implemented and crime reduced. Currently the Government Office for the East Midlands is collaborating with the Jill Dando Institute and the Home Office to test the implementation of and crime reduction outcomes associated with the predictive maps.

Conclusion

This chapter has highlighted a number of key developments in UK policing and crime reduction planning which are shaping the context for the implementation of problem-oriented policing. First, there are affinities between problem-oriented policing, the government's broad modernisation agenda and moves to evidence-based policy and practice. Especially, problem-oriented policing could be considered a form of evidence-based practice and evaluations from problem-oriented policing could inform EBPP. More generally, the languages and processes of the two are similar; they both have a focus on effectiveness, reducing the problems that concern communities and seeking to implement the most appropriate responses. Second, there are general overlaps in the development of inter-agency crime reduction in the UK. Problem-oriented policing is about searching for the best responses rather than presuming that a police response alone will always be the most effective. Hence drawing on the resources of other agencies is an important element of the approach. The Crime and Disorder Act 1998 offered the potential for broad-based problem-oriented methodology in partnership to be built into statutory crime reduction planning. There are clear continuities between processes of problem-oriented policing and the 1998 Act. However, the analytical stages of the development of audits and strategies have exhibited similar problems to the analysis stages of problem solving. Moreover, the assessment stages in problem-oriented policing and in the Crime and Disorder Act audit and review cycle have both been weak. Third, intelligence-led approaches in general and the National Intelligence Model in particular have become increasingly important in UK policing. In principle, at least, there are overlaps between the Model and problem-oriented policing, but in practice the Model may still be too limited in scope to be considered as a means through which problem-oriented approaches could be delivered. Fourth, neighbourhood policing models have become a major feature of policing policy. The language of neighbourhood policing is all about local problem-oriented policing and the deployment of local resources via the National Intelligence Model. At present the implementation of neighbourhood policing would appear to vary between (and within) police services. What will happen in practice as it is fully rolled out is unclear, but it is unlikely to provide a panacea for community-involved problem solving, especially given the difficulties encountered in effectively engaging local residents in the most fractured high-crime areas. Fifth, the emergence of a mixed economy of policing raises issues of co-operation in problem solving *within* the overall policing function to add to the issues of co-operation in problem solving for partnerships *across* policing and non-policing agencies. Sixth, mapping crime and Geographical Information Systems have become important and their application is widespread. Used properly, they may inform area-based problem-oriented policing, but in practice they are probably underused and largely limited to managing the deployment of police officers to crime hotspots.

Key challenges remain. Is the National Intelligence Model capable of perceiving and tackling problems more widely than experience suggests so far? Can and will the police service engage partners in National Intelligence Model tasking? How will neighbourhood policing resources be deployed and can and does this fit with problem-oriented policing and especially National Intelligence Model tasking? To what extent can the police use crime mapping and Geographical Information Systems to make inferences about the causes of crime and predict the risk of victimisation and develop responses on this basis? This volume has so far pointed to the fragility of problem-oriented policing. The risk is that it could be thrown off course rather than strengthened by new developments in policing. Fashions change in policing, and there is a risk that problem-oriented policing will not have the capacity to resist this. Generally, we have seen a lack of explicit commitment to problem-oriented policing as an overarching basis of policing into which other developments must fit (with the possible exception of Lancashire, see Chapter 3). The potential of problem-oriented policing is far from achieved and difficulties of implementation raised in Chapter 2 will remain.

Chapter 7

Conclusion:
Problem-oriented policing
and Evidence Based Policy
and Practice

We have argued that problem-oriented policing and partnership working comprises an effort to deliver Evidence-Based Policy and Practice (EBPP) in relation to crime reduction and order maintenance, as well as a wide range of other issues that fall within the remit of the police, such as children going missing and road traffic accidents. As shown in Chapters 1 and 2, the theory and practice of problem-oriented policing (and more recently partnership) now go back more than a quarter of a century. Chapters 3 and 4 looked in some detail at what can reasonably be considered some of the best contemporary problem-oriented efforts in Britain. Chapter 5 outlined a range of resources that have been devised to enable improvements in evidence-based problem-oriented work. Chapter 6 discussed the changing contexts for developing and delivering evidence-based problem-oriented policing. This chapter considers what has been learned from the experience of problem-oriented policing and partnership about the scope for, obstacles to and methodology appropriate to EBPP in the police service.

The part played by evidence in problem-oriented policing and partnership

Where the problem-oriented model of policing and partnership is fully implemented evidence plays a part throughout the process. It is used to identify problems, to analyse them, to select responses and to assess the effects (Goldstein 1990), making full use of the types of tools and techniques described in Chapter 5. Problem-oriented policing and partnership aspire to identify families of similar issues or incidents that call for attention by police and partnerships. These comprise the specific problems to be targeted. They transcend the particulars of individual incidents, but fall short of broad categories that may be too heterogeneous for analysis and coherent response development (Goldstein 1977; Clarke 1998). They are, in this sense, 'middle range' problems. It is these that have been found to be open to solution through the assembly of evidence, analysis and informed strategy development. The results should have sufficient generality to be applied in other places where presenting issues have salient similarities.

Problem-oriented policing is not confined to identifying those measures that do (always) work and those that do not (ever) do so. Indeed, the origins of problem-oriented policing are rooted in findings that standard responses cannot be depended on. Rather, problem-oriented policing is concerned with middle-range problems that can be dealt with effectively by identifying 'pinch points' (by which is meant relatively modifiable necessary conditions for problem behaviours, as against their frequently intractable 'root causes') and targeting measures at them.

The main focus of full problem-oriented work is on those knotty problems for which habitual responses have proved inadequate. The results should inform responses to similar problems in the future. They might also lead to wider implementation of measures to deal with problems that are found more broadly than those specific examples focused on in a particular project. Individual findings can be synthesised into guides to help police and their partners to decide what factors to look at when addressing a new issue and which kinds of response might most sensibly be tried in the circumstances. This work of synthesis is found in the growing library of guides published by the US Department of Justice and available through the Center for Problem-oriented Policing, which is described in Chapter 5. Problem-oriented policing and partnership initiatives building on these guides, if conducted fully, can then feed back into a growing understanding of problems and ways to address them. The in-built provisions for revising the Department of Justice guides aim to do just this.

What is created, at least in theory, is a cumulative understanding of middle-range problems and ways to address them. However, the nature of the problems focused on by police and their partners varies by place and changes over time: offenders innovate, new tools for crime become available, new targets for crime emerge, new forms of transport come to be provided, and patterns of everyday life change, opening up new crime opportunities and closing off old ones. With the emergence of cyberspace there is a fundamental change in the nature of the locations in which some crimes occur (see Ekblom 1997; Newman and Clarke 2003). The substance of crime and disorder is quite fluid. Those attempting to understand problems and to respond to them effectively cannot always depend on past practice that has been found to work, but may cease to be relevant. They need to be able to intelligently apply tested theories to changing problem patterns, which are identified and analysed as they emerge. Since crime and disorder problems (and other issues addressed by the police) are subject to change whilst progress may be made there is unlikely to be an end-point where we have a complete catalogue of problems and ways to deal with them. Fresh problems will call for fresh problem-oriented efforts, making use of principles from past efforts but building on them.

The analysis of entries to the Tilley Award reported in Chapter 4 showed that full implementation of problem-oriented policing principles is relatively rare, even in what are deemed to be amongst the best examples of problem-oriented work in the UK. In particular high-quality evaluations are unusual, though other parts of the SARA process were also often found wanting. The findings of this review echo those of other exercises that have scrutinised what is being delivered as problem-oriented policing and partnership both in the UK (Read and Tilley 2000; HMIC 2000) and the US (Scott 2000; Clarke 1998). Moreover, the current exercise found no improvement in the general standard of problem-oriented efforts over the years from which award entries were selected.

There is a growing view amongst scholars involved in trying to help develop problem-oriented policing that it would better be conceived of as a specialist activity undertaken by dedicated officers in relation to a small number of problems at any point in time, rather than as a model whose principles would pervade all that is done within a police organisation or agency (see Knutsson 2003).

In 2003 Herman Goldstein, the original architect of problem-oriented policing, concluded, alongside other commentators, that 'the vast percentages of efforts to date, even when they contained some of the elements of the original concept, were nevertheless superficial' (Goldstein 2003: 15). His proposal was for a centrally directed and managed five year programme in the United States in which each year:

1 Ten individuals be given special three to six month training in the knowledge and skills of problem analysis.

2 Ten committed police executives, in exchange for a trained analyst, commit their agency to take one to three problems for detailed study, analysis and implementation of a new response that would also be evaluated.

3 These executives would commit to a seminar where they would explore 'in depth the elements of problem-oriented policing, the partnership to which they were committing themselves, and, in specific terms, what would be expected of them' (Goldstein 2003: 39–40).

Goldstein also suggested an 'outreach program – to mayors, city managers, judges, prosecutors, advocacy groups, business interests and others – using the results of the project ...'. This comprises Goldstein's response to the evident failure to produce significant sustained evidence-based problem-oriented policing as originally envisaged in his 1979 article and 1990 book.

More generally, in many police services we have witnessed a move away from the language of 'problem-orientation' to that of 'problem solving'. Often, as noted in Chapter 1, this is supposed to be a matter of taste rather than substance – a preference not to adopt an American term as the ideas behind it are appropriated and adapted to a British context. Likewise the references to problem-oriented (or solving) *partnership* represent more an effort to reflect the responsibilities set out in the 1998 Crime and Disorder Act than a basic breach with the original thinking.

Whatever the intention in the move from talk of 'problem-orientation' to talk of 'problem solving', the latter does capture more closely what this and previous overviews of efforts purporting to be problem-oriented have found generally to have been delivered. 'Problem solving', as characterised in Chapter 1, in comparison with 'problem-orientation', is less ambitious in terms of its analytical depth and evaluative rigour. But it does comprise a significant, and in our view very welcome, move away from exclusively responsive ways of dealing with crime incidents and other types of incident that come within the remit of the police and their partners.

We attempt to capture the range of what is being delivered in practice in Figure 7.1. The horizontal axis shows a continuum from systematically following the painstaking and iterative SARA process fully as required in 'problem-orientation' on the left, to *ad hoc* 'problem

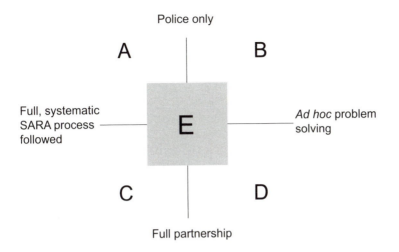

Police only

A | B

Full, systematic
SARA process ——— E ——— *Ad hoc* problem
followed   solving

C | D

Full partnership

Figure 7.1 Problem-orientation, policing, partnership and problem solving

solving' on the right, where there may be attention only to a single issue at a single place with little if any attention to what is entailed in following the SARA process. On the vertical axis, at the top we have work that involves the police alone and at the bottom police working fully and on equal terms with partners. The extremes are 'ideal types' and rarely found in practice. The shaded area around the intersection of the two axes (E) encompasses what seems most often to be delivered in the name of problem-orientation and problem solving. This describes a significant shift from police-only unreflective or rule-bound responses to individual incidents, even though it falls short of the vision of problem-orientation provided by Goldstein. The volume of work at A and C is very small. There may be some NIM work at B and partnership work at D which involve the application of relatively standard methods to relatively standard issues with little more than standardised analyses tracking emerging issues in local areas. However, operating in the E zone, whilst not strictly consonant with all the principles of problem-oriented policing, may comprise a practicable way of delivering fairly wide-scale improved policing and partnership work in the field. Although it may be more or less 'evidence-attentive', drawing on some evidence of local problems and some of the results of previous problem solving efforts, it seldom includes either the rigorous evaluation or the systematic analysis which is called for in evidence-based problem-oriented endeavours. It is certainly closer to what happens on the ground in the name of 'problem solving' or 'problem-orientation' than either the traditional responses to crime or the strict requirements of problem-oriented pieces of work. The forces described in Chapter 3 have conducted some work at A and C, where the principles of problem-oriented policing have been followed with some rigour. But they have also put increasing volumes of their work in the E zone.

It is important not to forget the many concrete benefits found to have been delivered from work that falls short of the problem-oriented ideal. Whilst few of the projects described in Chapter 4 lived up to the full requirements of problem-orientation (almost all fell somewhere within the E zone), for as many as a third of them the evidence of benefits produced was found convincing by the authors of this volume. There may be something to be said for Goldstein's proposals for ways of increasing the supply of genuinely problem-oriented policing (and partnership) activity. Yet this should in no way be taken to disparage what has been achieved where what has been delivered falls short of the problem-oriented ideal, but nevertheless comprises improved preventive attention to recurrent problems and to evidence in deciding what to do about them.

We will return to the issues raised here towards the end of this chapter. Meanwhile, we turn to explanations for the limitations of what in practice has been delivered in the name of problem-orientation. What has fostered interest in and delivery of problem-oriented policing EBPP, and what has led to recurrent disappointments in what has been delivered on the ground? A range of political, technical, personnel, organisational and accountability, and cultural factors all seem to play a part.

Political factors

We saw in Chapter 6 that EBPP has been tied up with the 'modernisation agenda' in Britain. 'Modernisation' has included, among other things, performance management, local responsiveness, a move in principle to government steering (setting priorities and targets) and local agency rowing (deciding what to do to get there), joined-up working and the promise of devolved authority for those who perform well (earned autonomy), in addition to an emphasis on EBPP and the improved effectiveness, efficiency and value for money that are expected to follow suit.

The principles of problem-oriented policing and partnership sit well with much of this. Local responsiveness, joined-up working, and local 'rowing', for example, as well as EBPP all have affinities with problem-oriented policing and partnership.

Some aspects of the modernisation agenda, however, fit less well. We have already raised in Chapter 3 concern about the potential impact of the performance management regime, with its emphasis on national targets, on the implementation of problem-oriented policing. National targets were seen to have the potential to eclipse attention to local community problems and priorities. That said, the review of problem-oriented initiatives (see Chapter 4) found that a very wide range of issues had been addressed. It was far from the case that nothing beyond government priorities was addressed, and there are numerous examples, including vandalism, bullying, airport safety, business crime, begging and even nuisance caused by hazardous horses! So, though the performance targets may partly shape decisions about problems to address, it is not to the exclusion of all else. Moreover, the developments in neighbourhood policing, as described in Chapter 6, represent an effort to make sure that there continues to be systematic attention to local priorities as well as national ones, although it is more likely that this will facilitate problem solving than problem-orientation.

Hough has noted that in the interests of speeding up the achievement of national targets, the government has been tempted into rowing as well as steering (Hough 2004: 242). To the extent to which this has happened, it again fits uneasily with problem-oriented policing and partnership, and compromises the use of evidence to identify problems and work out what to do about them as they manifest themselves in their local contexts.

There are, of course, unavoidable normative issues at stake in deciding what problems to prioritise using scarce resources, and what methods to use in addressing them. Decisions about how much attention to pay to different crime and nuisance types, about which variety of response to put in place, and about balancing conflicting interests in local neighbourhoods clearly include normative dimensions. The empirical evidence assembled in problem-oriented policing work cannot resolve these normative questions. Moreover, the nature of the evidence available often itself reflects previous normative judgements, for example about what to record, and the analysis of the evidence will also inevitably partly reflect normative assumptions about what matters. Yet carefully and critically interrogated evidence is able to furnish information relating to the rates and distributions of problems that can feed into the normative judgements which partnerships, agency policy makers and practitioners make about their priorities. It can also suggest means that might plausibly reduce or remove problems on the basis of evidence even though the selection of means again involves normative considerations that cannot be determined through evidence alone. Moreover empirical evidence can help identify conflicting interests that need to be considered in deciding what to do in local areas. Central government's priorities over ends and means represent its judgements about these normative issues. The funding arrangements for policing, where the Home Office pays for 51 per cent of the costs, may explain why local attention to government priorities is generally deemed to be quite proper within police services.

Technical factors

Previous chapters have noted that developments in IT have made data available in a form that allows them to be analysed. Hardware has become progressively cheaper and more powerful. Software, including GIS systems in particular, has become more sophisticated and user-friendly. But this volume makes it is very clear that there remain difficulties. The weaknesses in recording, accessing and using data have been described. Key data on the details of crime and disorder incidents and other calls for police and partnership attention, which lie at the heart of problem-oriented policing and partnership, have been found to be poorly kept, at least for analytical purposes, wherever and whenever problem-oriented work has been attempted. Moreover, it has proved difficult to pool data in some cases, where agencies have been reluctant to release information at a level of detail needed for many forms of analysis, often on grounds that it might breach the provisions of the Data Protection or Human Rights Acts but sometimes because the data are not available in a manner that makes them easily accessible. Finally data that are germane to many issues are in short supply. For example, many forms of antisocial behaviour, such as noise, litter and graffiti, often concern residents but are not recorded routinely and hence patterns are not open to systematic analysis without special data collection exercises.

Personnel factors

The implementation of problem-oriented policing and partnership depends on a supply of personnel with the skills and personal attributes that will enable the work to be done. It also depends on the appropriate selection and tasking of those personnel. The supply of some types of staff is especially important for facilitating the implementation of problem-oriented policing. In particular, analysts comprise an expert cadre that should have the specialist skills to inform problem-oriented work. Goldstein (2003) estimated that one per 500 sworn officers might be needed. With the advent of the National Intelligence Model, there is now about one per 100 sworn officers in London's Metropolitan Police Service. Numbers have grown enormously in the last few years, and the credentials of those employed have improved. As well as technical skills, Clarke (1998) suggest, these individuals also need an education in environmental criminology to give them the theoretical grounding to enable them to make sense of data, to make meaningful inferences from their analyses and to develop the responses that will have an impact on identified problems. Analysts with these abilities are in short supply. Efforts, however, are being made to change this.

Clarke and Eck have produced guidance documents respectively for analysts in the UK and the US to help them fulfil their potential (Clarke and Eck 2003, 2005). More relevant training is being provided: in the UK for example at the Jill Dando Institute of Crime Science based at University College London. It may, though, be that in addition to the provision of these formal resources face-to-face facilitation will be required to pass on the tacit skills that seem to be necessary to produce high-quality work (Tilley 2006).

It is not enough that analysts with the necessary skills are available in principle. Those individuals must also be selected and tasked in ways that foster problem-orientation, and this depends in part on the attributes and abilities of policy makers and practitioners.

Whilst there are relatively large numbers of crime analysts employed in the UK, in practice they are not for the most part focused strictly speaking on problem-oriented policing. Rather they tend to serve the National Intelligence Model, tracking short-term patterns of crime and criminality. In this way they inform targeted enforcement and deployment decisions and some of the problem solving that takes place through tactical tasking and co-ordinating processes. They may also contribute to 'strategic' tasking and co-ordination, looking at longer-term trends and setting broad directions. But this does not constitute problem-oriented work. Thus, though there is a growing supply of specialist staff that might contribute to problem-oriented policing and partnership EBPP, this may form only a very small part of what they have done in many police services. They mostly inform the smarter application of traditional policing methods of enforcement and patrol. We would argue that this is no small achievement in itself, but falls short of problem-oriented policing.

The attributes of police officers (and those with whom they work in partnership) are also important to undertaking problem-oriented work, which will include making appropriate use of analysts and the research on which analysis is based. The entries to the Tilley Award analysed in Chapter 4, for example, do not suggest that there is a high level of research literacy. Police officers are more oriented to reacting immediately to problems than to drawing on literature about how to tackle problems and keeping up to date with new research about what is effective in reducing crime (cf. Holdaway 1983, Young 1991). Indeed, they often do need to make decisions quickly, notably when dealing with emergencies. In these circumstances there is no time to go away, read through reports, sift evidence and then respond. The practical 'can do' approach to emergencies is not enough, however, in problem-oriented work, which requires evidence-based responses to recurrent problems. Whilst the Tilley Award entries reviewed in Chapter 4 reveal an appetite for problem solving they do not provide much evidence that there is orientation to research that lies at the heart of the evidence-based problem-oriented project. The increasingly educated police staff being employed and the broadening of the agenda of the National Intelligence Model may provide a more secure personnel basis for evidence-based problem-oriented policing in the future. Moreover developments in dedicated, university-based education for police and community safety officers may produce personnel who are more capable of leading work of this kind, provided the courses are designed with it in mind.

Organisational and accountability factors

Organisational issues have also been highlighted as having an impact on the implementation of evidence-based problem-oriented policing. Internally, police services are disciplined, hierarchical organisations with formal lines of accountability that operate within a legal framework. Externally, they are held to account by politicians, the inspectorate, the mass media and the police authority as well as the local community. The primary role of the police is seen by many, both within the police service and outside, to be about enforcement of the law (the 'thin blue line') and response to emergencies. Although in practice police officers have to use discretion on the streets (Reiner 1992: 107), the formalised accounting systems in the police service, based typically on outputs such as numbers of arrests, do not fit well with the flexibility and creativity required for problem-oriented work.

Moreover, the formal lines of accountability within policing have not been very tolerant of failure where discretion has been used. This does not sit well with an evidence-based approach to dealing with problems where informed experimentation is required and where the value of the work rests on honest reports of research findings. Police officers say of their initiatives that they are 'doomed to succeed', by which they mean that the results of any assessment are a foregone conclusion (cf. HMIC 1998, 2000). There are, of course, police officers and police organisations that are experimental, self-critical and open. Chapter 3 gave an account of two such British police services and some of the officers within them. They are, though, exceptional and this may explain the fragility of problem-oriented policing.

Partnerships by definition involve those from different community or organisational constituencies coming together to decide what to prioritise and what to do. Whilst this brings the obvious benefits of access to diverse data sources, the potential for multi-stranded and co-ordinated strategies, and thinking that transcends the boundaries of specialist agencies, it also creates space for problems of collusion, special pleading, fudging, organisational back scratching, power broking, delay and the dilution of any acceptance of responsibility. The more rational, evidence-based considerations called for in problem-oriented partnership work are easily overwhelmed (see Byrne and Pease 2003).

Both policing and partnership activities have been taking place in the context of programme-related funding regimes that necessarily reflect the priorities of funding bodies. The fragility and the requirements of those funding regimes rarely serve well the open-ended needs of evidence-based problem oriented policing and partnership. Indeed, the experience of the British Crime Reduction Programme (1999-2002), which was intended to facilitate problem-oriented work, reveals the difficulties. Pressure for quick wins, short-term bidding windows and the requirement that pre-specified plans should ordinarily be followed all undermined the delivery of fully problem-oriented evidence-based work by police services and partnerships (Homel *et al.* 2004; Hough 2004; Maguire 2004; Laycock and Webb 2003; Hope 2004; Tilley 2004a).

Cultural factors

Evidence-based problem-oriented policing and partnership may seem a rather academic exercise to many police officers. Many of the reference points for analysis and action lie outside policing. They lie in research, using the sorts of tools, techniques and knowledge base referred to in Chapter 5. Done properly, adopting a problem-oriented approach can appear slow and rather ponderous compared with the time scales required in responding to incidents. Preparation before response just takes time (Kelling 2005).

Problem-oriented policing and partnership work also requires that problems should not be construed only in terms of honest folk and villains. It often looks to proximal causes that relate not to individuals or groups of individuals but to product designs, organisational practices, service delivery patterns, security levels and environmental design (Ekblom 1994). These factors have been considered by police services, but mostly by specialist crime prevention officers, crime reduction officers, architectural liaison officers and, to some degree, community beat officers. These specialists have not enjoyed high status within the police service and their influence has been rather limited (see Weatheritt 1986; Grimshaw *et al.* 1989). They have been marginal to the main focus of policing, though recent emphases on neighbourhood policing may reflect some change here (Byrne and Pease 2003).

There is not a strong research tradition within policing in the UK. There is much more research that is *about* policing than there is research that is *in* or explicitly *for* policing. Most policing is rooted in custom and common sense. Police officers tend to take their lead from other police officers. EBPP is not well established. Those seeking to implement problem-oriented policing face steep challenges within police services. That the challenges are not insuperable is evidenced by some of the work described in Chapters 3 and 4, though the relative scarcity of it and the limitations in what has been achieved even in the best that we know of reflects in part these obstacles.

Bringing together problem solving and problem-orientation: a realistic agenda

The discussion in this chapter so far argues that, although there has been quite a lot of problem solving, problem-orientation, properly speaking, is rare. Whilst evidence is used in problem solving, it is not used as systematically, critically or widely as is called for in problem-oriented work. Moreover we have identified a variety of factors that make problem-orientation difficult, even though they are not so overwhelming that they leave no space for problem solving.

Given the strong case for problem-oriented policing as evidence-based practice, and given the limitations identified, what is realistically possible? Figure 7.2 presents a framework suggesting how threads of routine practice, problem solving and problem orientation might be brought together to inform improvements in policing and partnership work.

The horizontal distribution of the boxes in Figure 7.2 follows the same pattern used in Figure 7.1. Some of the letters in parentheses (A, B, C, D and E) are also drawn from Figure 7.1. The rest of the letters (F, G and H) describe relevant activities not captured in Figure 7.1. F includes the kinds of activities undertaken to synthesise findings in the US Department of Government Problem-oriented Guides for Police Series discussed in Chapter 5, though there are other examples also (see, for example, the Home Office toolkits at www.crimereduction. gov.uk and also Tilley *et al.* 2004). G and H refer to problem-oriented projects and the policies and practices that follow from them, which transcend local conditions. As Goldstein and others have recognised the same problem may be tackled in different ways at different levels of its manifestation. For example, there may be assaults at a particular Accident and Emergency (A&E) hospital unit, or fuel drive-offs at a particular petrol station, or car thefts at a particular car park, or children missing from a particular children's home, or overnight thefts from curtain-sided lorries at a particular motorway service area, and the respective problems might be addressed in

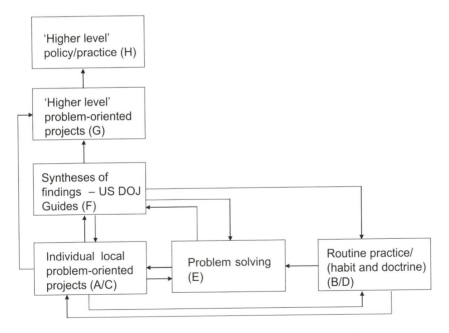

Figure 7.2 Networked problem solving and problem-orientation

their individual locations in the light of the specific conditions there. However, the problem of assaults at A&E units, of fuel drive-offs, of car park car thefts, of children missing from children's homes, and of overnight thefts from curtain-sided lorries may be more general. National-level problem-oriented projects would identify their scope and possible pinch points that would extend beyond any individual manifestation of the problem. So, for instance, influencing car park proprietors to accept some responsibility for the crime in their lots and to incorporate attention to it in the design and management of their facilities comprises a higher-level intervention than one that related only to a particular individual car park. Moreover problems of car theft might be taken more broadly still, where the design of cars themselves is the focus of higher-level projects rather than only the specific locations where they take place (see Webb 2005).

At the bottom right-hand corner of Figure 7.2, box B/D represents the routine practices of police and partners as they respond to events. The experience of these events feeds into most problem solving (shown at E), which attempts to target activity because of recurrent, emerging or increasing demands. The National Intelligence Model does just this for current priority issues, generally with a view to delivering standard enforcement or patrol responses, but sometimes taking a wider view. The projects reviewed in Chapter 4 fell largely in the E zone though with more effort at analysis, longer-term attention and somewhat fuller assessment than is possible in National Intelligence Model work, which tends to focus on shorter-term patterns and priorities.

Box A/C describes problem-oriented projects, encompassing the sort of work envisaged by Goldstein. They often emerge out of the everyday work of the police (and, where relevant, other agencies). They might also grow out of problem solving work either because it has developed what seem promising directions for work or because they have failed to deal with an issue which then calls for the more sustained and systematic treatment required of problem-orientation. Some of these transitions were identified in Chapter 4 where we refer to repeat entries to the Tilley Award in which early problem solving gradually gives way to problem-orientation. The work in A/C may feed back both into more informed routine responses to issues (box B/D) and into problem solving (the E zone).

Box F includes works of evidence synthesis, drawing on work of the problem-oriented projects included in box A/C but also some initiatives in box E, to provide overviews of what seems to work in what circumstances in relation to specific local issues. In a book on EBPP, Pawson (2006) argues strongly that across policy domains relatively weak research – which would include much that is undertaken in the E zone – can still play a useful part in syntheses aimed at showing what we know now for the purpose of policy and practice development, and this is reflected in the efforts of synthesis undertaken at F. Where findings are strong and consistent, they might feed back into what is sometimes referred to by the police as 'doctrine' in relation to responses to emerging incidents. They also have a crucial role to play in informing local problem solving, indicating how better decisions can be arrived at over forms of intervention in relation to the specific problem. Where significant gaps are found, then syntheses may also suggest needs for further problem-oriented efforts at box A/C.

Box G describes the work referred to a few paragraphs earlier where significant recurrent problems which reveal themselves in different local areas are analysed with a view to finding interventions that can be applied at a 'higher' level. The focus for that work is likely to come from local problem solving and problem-oriented projects, which suggests that similar issues may repeatedly be surfacing because of some generic condition. In Britain the Home Office has in the past generally taken the lead in this type of work, for example in relation to pre-payment gas and electricity meters that were often broken into during burglaries on council estates (Hill 1986), in relation to types of car that were frequently targeted in crime (Houghton 1992) and in relation to repeat domestic violence (Hanmer *et al.* 1999). Box H describes the 'higher-level' policy and practice lessons that follow from the problem-oriented projects in box G. Here there have been substantial efforts to develop EBPP.

Being realistic: how the linkages work now

Much work of the police alongside some of that of their partners unavoidably falls within box B/D. There are imperatives to respond to emergencies as they occur. Quite a lot of police and partnership work happens within the E zone, which stretches from work that does little more than respond to identified short-term patterns of problem behaviour in ways that are never documented (much within the National Intelligence Model) to broad-based but weakly evaluated strategies to address systematically identified long-term problems, which are written up as entries for awards even if the work done falls some way short of what is required according to the canons of problem-orientation. Activity in the E zone is to varying degrees evidence-attentive, but falls some way short of full EBPP.

The review reported in Chapter 4 confirms other findings that truly problem-oriented work is a rarity. There is relatively little in box A/C, which describes rigorous EPBB.

On both sides of the Atlantic, there have been fairly intensive efforts to draw together evidence both from box A/C and the E zone to distil and feed back what has been learned about ways of addressing specific problem (box F). This offers a strong contribution to improved evidence-based practice both in problem solving and in routine responses to incidents.

Higher-level problem-oriented work (boxes G and H) occurs, but does so only sporadically when problems become so widespread that they can no longer be ignored at a national level by government or those incurring losses. Examples have included credit card fraud, burglary involving loss from cash pre-payment meters and robbery involving the loss of mobile phones.

Building on the realistic agenda

The traffic between the boxes shown in Figure 7.2 is largely a matter of luck. There are some systematic efforts in the National Intelligence Model to go from box B/D to parts of the E zone. But beyond that what is done is to a large degree fortuitous. Moreover the relative volume of what is done within each box is largely left to the tastes of those with access to or control over it. The result is that little is done within A/C since it competes with the more immediately pressing front-line work of the police and their partners. The syntheses conducted in the US are funded by the Department of Justice with specific grants, and depend on the energy and commitment of the individuals leading the work. The Home Office-funded syntheses in Britain are undertaken also on an *ad hoc* basis. Higher-level problem-oriented activity is a function of policy priorities, often driven by crises when particular crime or disorder types come to be seen to be unacceptably high. The Street Crime Initiative, addressing snatch thefts and personal robbery, is the most conspicuous example, though even here what was done fell short of problem-orientation, and the assessments of what was delivered were weak (Tilley *et al.* 2004; HMIC 2003).

There is, we think, scope for improvements in the linkages (and balance) between the evidence-based activities shown in Figure 7.2, which would lead to improvements in practice and policy based on evidence.

We concur with Goldstein's judgement that there is insufficient genuinely problem-oriented work and see merit in his suggestions for some form of targeted special funding in the US to support it, though as he suggests money alone is not likely to be sufficient, a point borne out by the disappointments of the British Crime Reduction Programme (Bullock and Tilley 2003). We would also suggest that every individual force in the UK, given their relatively large size compared with most American counterparts, should be able to take the lead with some major problem-oriented projects that would promise findings of national relevance. We would suggest establishing mixed discipline teams, including an analyst, to take a specific problem and work it through in the detail required over the longish time scales (perhaps up to two years) that would be required. We also see benefits in drawing in suitably qualified and interested academics to work alongside the teams, rather as David Kennedy and his colleagues worked with Boston in the Boston Gun project (Braga *et al.* 2001), as Ken Pease and his colleagues did in the Huddersfield repeat victimisation project (Anderson *et al.* 1995; Chenery *et al.* 1997) and as Jalna Hanmer and her colleagues did with the Killingbeck domestic violence project in West Yorkshire (Hanmer *et al.* 1999), to enhance analysis and provide greater technical rigour and independence in assessment than would otherwise be possible.

The emerging National Policing Improvement Agency (NPIA) may come to be the a possible organisation within the UK to oversee and facilitate the traffic between the boxes in Figure 7.2. This could include identification and encouragement of local problem-oriented work where and when it is needed, brokerage between the different types of activities identified, transmission of robust lessons to practice sites where they can be acted on, some quality control over work that is ostensibly problem-oriented, and the development of national problem-oriented projects where it seems likely that high-level responses might be formulated. In some cases, of course, funding may be required but this is far from all that is needed to improve on the rather haphazard operation of the linkages and balances between activities shown in Figure 7.2. We think making these improvements may comprise a way not only of stimulating improvements in problem-oriented policing, but also of enhancing what is delivered by the police and their partners more generally in their problem solving activities.

Pursuing joined-up problem solving and problem-oriented work of differing kinds and at different levels along the lines sketched out here, would be made easier if the capacity for problem-oriented work of police services were increased and if there were improvements in the volume and quality of work within the E zone. There may be lessons here from the experiences on Lancashire and Hampshire that were discussed in Chapter 3. Increasing local capacity for developing and delivering evidence-based problem-oriented and problem solving work will require, as implied earlier, better education and training for police officers, analysts and partners; improvement in data quality; and greater data exchange within and between agencies. It will also call for more consistent leadership within police services, improved coaching in problem solving, release from performance measures that inhibit longer-term problem solving by steering attention to short-term trends, and the formulation of rewards for work that addresses problems systematically. It could be that the NPIA will be in a position to not only to help manage and oversee the linkages between the elements shown in Figure 7.2, but also to help engineer conditions in which problem solving can thrive.

There are some similarities between the obstacles Walter *et al.* (2004) find in relation to research use in social care and those identified in this book in delivering evidence-based problem-oriented policing. Walter *et al.* map out a 'whole systems approach' to trying to foster research use in social care, as we have tried to map sets of relationships that need to be involved in delivering improved policing using problem-oriented policing. Whilst the conceptions are different these exercises agree on the need to conceive the process holistically.

Methodological questions for problem solving in problem-oriented policing and EBPP

There are important questions relating to methodology, the forms of knowledge to be developed and the way findings can best be used for problem-oriented policing and partnership.

The problem for problem solvers in drawing on evidence from problem-oriented work is that the same presenting problem can have different sources in different places and at different times. The rationale for problem-specification was that problems need to be broken down so that relevantly similar attributes of sets of incidents can be identified, and decisions about interventions then made. For the problem solver a decision needs to be made as to whether the problem being addressed in any local setting is similar in relevant respects to that which has successfully been addressed earlier. It is unlikely that it will ever be identical. The user of research therefore needs to develop sufficient understanding of that which took place earlier to make an educated judgement about how and to what extent it can be drawn on in a new situation. They also need to assemble relevant local evidence.

If problem solvers are to make use of results from problem-oriented policing, then those producing the results need to ensure that the findings are presented in ways that maximise scope for appropriate use by those who wish to draw on them. This requires that the key elements of the specified problem be laid out alongside the identified points of intervention and the evidence about how and to what extent they had intended and unintended effects. Without a grasp of the context in which problems occur and responses are developed, there are serious risks that efforts to apply past findings will fail (Tilley 1993; Hughes and Edwards 2005). Summary reviews of previous pieces of problem-oriented work need to highlight what circumstances specific problems have or have not responded to interventions in ways that most easily allow problem solvers to draw on them for a similar problem-situation. This is what is done in the (box F) COPS problem-specific guides discussed earlier.

Within problem-oriented policing and partnership an action research methodology is needed. Both to improve prospects of achieving intended outcomes and to help produce transferable findings the researcher (who might be a police or local authority analyst) has to be closely involved with the action, in developing analysis of the problem, in working through the implications of findings, in tracking the implementation of responses, in gauging what effects are being had, in informing and following adjustments to the response and in assessing the outcomes. There are clearly risks to objectivity here. In problem-oriented policing and partnership the researcher is a core part of the process, and whilst this may improve the chances of success and enable more close-grained accounts of what was done, it also undermines the independence that external researchers would have. There is a trade-off between the benefits of involvement and detachment. Problem-oriented policing and partnership requires involvement but may miss the benefits of detachment.

Because of the dangers of self-deception and of pressure to produce organisationally acceptable findings (remember the 'doomed to succeed' scenario) that are associated with researcher/evaluator involvement in the development of a project, there is a particular need in problem-oriented policing and partnership work to be transparent about data sources and methods, to consider the threats to internal validity noted in Chapter 5 and to acknowledge uncertainties.

Moreover, because the purpose of assessment is to inform future action, it is necessary to go beyond issues of internal validity, explicitly to try to spell out the theory behind the interventions and the implications of findings for it, for it is well specified theory that can be drawn on by problem solvers and successor problem-oriented policing initiatives. Just as we argued that the problems for problem-oriented work should be 'middle-range' (neither confined to the specifics of a case, nor broadly defined categories such as 'crime'), so too the theory needs to be middle-range (again neither specific to the presenting case nor universal generalisations), see Merton (1968). Theory that is usable by problem solvers needs to spell out:

1 The specific class of problems to which the problem-oriented piece of work relates.

2 The nature of the conditions understood to generate the problem that the measures introduced were designed to change.

3 What it was about those conditions that was targeted by the intervention.

4 The mechanisms through which the intervention was expected to work.

5 The particular pattern of outcomes that are therefore expected.

The assessment in problem-oriented work comprises a test of the theory and a description of any lessons learned about the implementation of the measures included in the intervention. If they are to contribute to evidence-based problem solving, evaluations need to aim at 'external validity' that is applicability to the (middle-range) problem class addressed by the problem-oriented endeavour (cf. Eck 2002, 2005; Pawson and Tilley 1997).

Conclusion: implications of the experience of problem-oriented policing and partnership for EBPP

The past 25 years of efforts to put in place problem-oriented policing and partnership work suggest the following:

1 The nature of the substantive area of policy and practice is important for the kind of evidence needed, the methods of its acquisition and its use. The issues facing policing and partnership change substantially by place and time. Off-the-peg solutions to standard problems will not be available. Evidence collection,

presentation and use need to reflect this. Hence action research, middle-range theory and syntheses of findings informing decisions about the details of specific problems to be addressed will be needed rather than some equivalent to clinical trials for standard treatments to standard conditions.

2 Problem-oriented policing and partnership work is facilitated by an infrastructure of data, computing power and specialist staff. Though data, computing power and technically skilled analysts are in greater supply now than they ever have been in the past, and hence there is more potential for problem-oriented work, they are not sufficient to make evidence-based problem-oriented policing and partnership work on their own.

3 Problem-oriented policing and partnership also depend on organisations and the staff within them, to encourage problem-oriented work and ring-fence time to develop and deliver evidence-based efforts to deal with long-term problems, and accept that many efforts will fail. These conditions have been found to be precarious.

4 Organisations that might take part in evidence-based problem-oriented policing and partnership, including in particular police agencies, operate in a political and administrative context. Here they are subject to a variety of external pressures, notably from government departments, local and national politicians, inspectorates, the police authority, the local authority, local communities and the mass media. This circumscribes the degree to which evidence can drive activity and hence the scope for problem-oriented policing and partnership work.

5 Value judgements are critical in determining what issues to address in problem-oriented policing and partnership and in determining acceptable forms of response. The evidence used in problem-oriented work can feed into those judgements but it cannot resolve them. As a result of informed analysis problem-oriented policing will often, however, identify potential ways of dealing with issues that avoid some of the ethical problems that come with the use of routine enforcement methods to try to curtail unwanted behaviour.

6 The daily work of policing and responding to emerging issues of crime and disorder in local neighbourhoods may sensibly include routine problem solving, drawing on common sense, the

findings of problem-oriented endeavours and everyday agency and community resources. It may also use some of the tools developed to conduct problem-oriented work, for example the problem-analysis triangle. This, though, is rather different from problem-oriented policing and partnership work which takes more time, skill and resources (of the kind described in point 3) than will ordinarily be available in routine work. As Goldstein himself put it rather starkly, 'examples of full implementation of the concept, as originally conceived, are rare' (Goldstein 2003: 13). Experience suggests that it is neither reasonable nor realistic to expect the formality of problem-oriented work to filter through all everyday policing and partnership activities.

7 Experience of efforts to implement problem-oriented policing over the past quarter of a century show that problem-oriented policing and partnership as an evidence-based approach to dealing with problems is more taxing than had been anticipated. In the hurly-burly of real police work, real partnership work, real data, real organisational complexity, real political influence, and real efforts at local accountability, aspirations to wide-scale implementation of the pure model may be utopian. Instead reflective and relatively systematic problem solving as a general method of dealing with the troublesome issues that confront police and partners may be a more practicable possibility. What might be added, however, are protected corners of problem-oriented work, with adequate ring-fenced resources, where evidence-based problem-oriented work can be conducted to feed into the knowledge base of problem solving policing and partnership endeavours, where what is already known will not suffice.

8 There are important, but so far largely chance relationships between incident-response, problem solving, problem-oriented endeavours, reviews of ways of dealing with classes of problem, and varying levels at which any given problem can be addressed. There is scope for improving the connections between them more successfully to mobilise effective evidence-based policy and practice.

9 The past quarter century has seen huge improvements in policing and local problem solving, with better use of evidence, more attention to recurrent problems, a wider set of responses and more interest in outcomes (Weisburd and Eck 2004). Whilst this cannot all be credited to problem-oriented policing and

partnership work, problem-oriented work has certainly made a significant contribution. If this book as a whole and the final chapter in particular have expressed notes of caution about and some disappointment in relation to the early ambitious vision and hopes of problem-oriented policing, this does not in any way reflect a sense that problem-oriented work lacks value. Far from it. If policing and partnership are to develop as evidence-based enterprises problem-oriented work is essential. This book has comprised an effort to find out what can realistically be achieved by focusing on the best that has been delivered.

10 At least some of the experience of problem-oriented policing and problem solving may be relevant to efforts to introduce EBPP to other substantive areas of activity. The best efforts at problem-oriented work in Britain and the US have produced very substantial benefits. There have been, for example, fewer deaths from gang violence in the US and from motor-cycle accidents in the UK and fewer facial disfigurements from late-night fights involving glassing as a result of problem-oriented work. This type of work is worthy of emulation.

References

Anderson, D., Chenery, S. and Pease, K. (1995) *Biting Back: Tackling Repeat Burglary and Car Crime*. Crime Detection and Prevention Series 58. London: Home Office.

Audit Commission (1996) *Streetwise: Effective Street Patrol*. London: HMSO.

Barr, R. and Pease, K. (1990) 'Crime Placement, Displacement and Deflection', in N. Morris and M. Tonry (eds) *Crime and Justice: A Review of Research*, XII, Chicago: University of Chicago Press.

Barton, M. (1999) *POP on a Beer Mat*. Lancashire: Lancashire Constabulary.

Bazemore, G. and Cole, A. (1994) 'Police in the Laboratory of the Neighbourhood: Evaluating Problem-oriented Strategies in a Medium-sized City', *American Journal of the Police*, 13 (3): 119–47.

Bennett, T. and Kemp, C. (1994) *An Evaluation of Sector-based Problem-oriented Policing in Thames Valley Police Force Area*. Home Office Research and Planning Unit (unpublished).

Bittner, E. (1990) 'Some Reflections of Staffing Problem Oriented Policing', *American Journal of the Police*, 9 (3): 189–97.

Blagg, H., Pearson, G., Sampson, A., Smith, D. and Stubbs, P. (1988) 'Interagency Co-operation: Reality and Rhetoric', in T. Hope and M. Shaw (eds) *Communities and Crime Reduction*. London: HMSO.

Boba, R. (2005) *Crime Analyis and Crime Mapping*. London: Sage Publications.

Bottoms, A. and Wiles, P. (1997) 'Environmental Criminology', in M. Maguire, R. Morgan and R. Reiner (eds) *The Handbook of Criminology*. Oxford: Oxford University Press.

Bowers, K. J. and Johnson, S. D. (2005) 'Domestic Burglary Repeats and Space-time Clusters: The Dimensions of Risk', *European Journal of Criminology*, 2 (1): 67–92.

Bowers, K. J., Johnson, S. D. and Hirschfield, A. F. G. (2003) *Pushing Back the Boundaries: New Techniques for Assessing the Impact of Burglary Schemes.* Home Office Online Report 24/03. London: Home Office.

Bowers, K., Johnson, S. and Hirshfield, A. (2004) 'Closing off Opportunities for Crime: an Evaluation of Alley-gating', *European Journal of Criminal Policy and Research*, 10: 285–308.

Bowers, K. J., Johnson, S. D. and Pease, K. (2004) 'Prospective Hot-spotting: The Future of Crime Mapping?' *British Journal of Criminology*, 44 (5): 641–58.

Bowers, K. J., Johnson, S.D. and Pease, K. (2005) 'Victimisation Risk, Housing Type and Area: The Ecological Fallacy lives!' *Crime Prevention and Community Safety*, 7 (1): 7–18.

Braga, A. (2002) *Problem-oriented Policing and Crime Prevention.* New York: Criminal Justice Press.

Braga, A,. Kennedy, D., Waring, E. and Piehl, A. (2001) 'Problem-oriented Policing, Deterrence and Youth Violence: An Evaluation of Boston's Operation Ceasefire', *Journal of Research in Crime and Delinquency*, 38: 195–225.

Brand, S. and Price, R. (2000) *The Social and Economic Costs of Crime.* Home Office Research Study 217. London: Home Office.

Brantingham, P. L. and Brantingham, P. J. (1993) 'Environment, Routine and Situation: Toward a Pattern Theory of Crime', in R. V. Clarke and M. Felson (eds) *Routine Activity and Rational Choice.* New Brunswick NJ: Transaction Books.

Brantingham, P. L. and Brantingham, P. J. (1995) 'Location Quotients and Crime Hot Spots in the City', in C. R. Block, M. Dabdoub and S. Fregly (eds) *Crime Analysis through Computer Mapping.* Washington DC: Police Executive Research Forum.

Brantingham, P. L. and Brantingham, P. J. (1997) 'Mapping Crime for Analytic Purposes: Location Quotients, Counts and Rates', in. D. Weisburd and T. McEwen (eds) *Crime Mapping and Crime Prevention.* Crime Prevention Studies 8. Monsey NY: Criminal Justice Press.

Bridgeman, C. and Hobbs, L. (1997) *Preventing Repeat Victimisation: The Police Officer's Guide.* Police Research Series. London: Home Office.

Bright, J. (1969) *The Beat Patrol Experiment.* Home Office Research and Development Branch (unpublished).

Bright, J. (1997) *Turning the Tide.* London: Demos.

Brown, M. and Sutton, A. (1997) 'Problem-oriented Policing and Organisational Form: Lessons from a Victoria Experiment', *Current Issues in Criminal Justice*, 9: 1: 21–33.

Buerger, M. E. (1994) 'The Problems of Problem Solving: Resistance, Interdependencies and Conflicting Interests', *American Journal of Police*, 13 (3): 1–36.

Bullock, K. Moss, K. and Smith, J. (2000) *Anticipating the Impact of Section 17 of the Crime and Disorder Act 1998.* Home Office Briefing Note 11/00. London: Home Office.

Bullock, K., Farrell, G. and Tilley, N. (2002) *Funding and Implementing Crime Reduction Projects*. Online Report 13. London: Home Office.

Bullock, K. and Jones, B. (2004) *Acceptable Behaviour Contracts Addressing Antisocial Behaviour in the London Borough of Islington*. Home Office Online Report 02/04. London: Home Office.

Bullock, K. and Tilley, N. (2003a) 'The Role of Research and Analysis: Lessons from the Crime Reduction Programme', in J. Knutsson (ed.) *Crime Prevention Studies XV*. Monsey NY: Criminal Justice Press and Cullompton: Willan Publishing.

Bullock, K. and Tilley, N. (eds) (2003b) *Crime Reduction and Problem Oriented Policing*. Cullompton: Willan Publishing.

Byrne, S. and Pease, K. (2003) 'Crime Reduction and Community Safety', in T. Newburn (ed.) *Handbook of Policing*. Cullompton: Willan Publishing.

Cabinet Office (2002) *Reforming our Public Services: Principles into Practice*. London: Office of Public Services Reform.

Capowich, G. and Roehl, J. (1994) 'Problem-oriented Policing: Actions and Effectiveness in San Diego', in D. Rosenbaum (ed.) *The Challenge of Community Policing*. London: Sage Publications.

Capowich, G. E., Roehl, J. E. and Andrews, C. M. (1995) *Final Report to the National Institute of Justice Evaluating Problem Oriented Policing: Processes and outcomes in Tulsa and San Diego*. Alexandria VA: Institute for Social Analysis.

Chainey, S. P. and Ratcliffe, J. H (2005) *GIS and Crime Mapping*. London: Wiley.

Chan, J. (1996) 'Changing Police Culture', *British Journal of Criminology* 36, (1): 109–34.

Chan, J. (1997) *Changing Police Culture: Policing in a Multicultural Society*. Cambridge: Cambridge University Press.

Chenery, S., Holt, J. and Pease, K. (1997) *Biting Back II: Reducing Repeat Victimisation in Huddersfield*. Crime Detection and Prevention Paper 82. London: Home Office.

Clarke, R. (1995) 'Situational Crime Prevention', in M. Tonry and F. David (eds) 'Building a Safer Society: Strategic Approaches to Crime Prevention', *Crime and Justice: A Review of Research XIX*. Chicago: University of Chicago Press.

Clarke, R. (1997) *Situational Crime Prevention: Successful Case Studies*. NY: Harrow and Heston.

Clarke, R. (1998) 'Defining Police Strategies', in T. Shelley. and A. Grant (eds) *Problem Oriented Policing: Crime-specific Problems, Critical Issues and Making POP Work*. Washington DC: Police Executive Research Forum.

Clarke, R. and Eck, J (2003) *Become a Problem Solving Analyst*. Cullompton: Willan Publishing.

Clarke, R. and Eck, J. (2005) *Crime Analysis for Problem-solvers in 60 Small Steps*. Washington DC: US Department of Justice Office of Community Oriented Policing Services.

Clarke, R. and Goldstein, H. (2002) 'Reducing Theft at Construction Sites: Lessons from a Problem-oriented Project', in N. Tilley (ed.) *Analysis for Crime Prevention*. Crime Prevention Studies, XIII. Monsey NY: Criminal Justice Press and Cullompton: Willan Publishing.

Clarke, R. V. and Hough, M. (1984) *Crime and Police Effectiveness*. Home Office Research Study 79. London: HMSO.

Clarke, R. and Weisburd, D. (1994) 'Diffusion of Crime Control Benefits: Observations on the Reverse of Displacement', in R. Clarke (ed.) *Crime Prevention Studies*, II. Monsey NY: Criminal Justice Press.

Cohen, D. (2001) *Problem Oriented Partnerships: Including the Community for Change*. Washington DC: US Department of Justice Office for Community Oriented Policing Studies.

Cohen, L. and Felson, M. (1979) 'Social Change and Crime Rate Trends: A Routine Activities Approach', *American Sociological Review*, 44: 588–608.

Cook, T. and Campbell, D. (1979) *Quasi-experimentation: Design and Analysis Issues for Field Settings*. Boston MA: Houghton Mifflin.

Cooper, C., Anscombe J., Avenell, J., McLean, F. and Morris, J. (2006) *A National Evaluation of Community Support Officers*. Home Office Research Study 297. London: Home Office.

Cope, N. (2003) 'Crime Analysis: Principles and Practice', in T. Newburn (ed.) *The Handbook of Policing*. Cullompton: Willan Publishing.

Cordner, G. (1998) 'Problem Oriented Policing vs Zero Tolerance', in T. Shelley and A. Grant (eds) *Problem Oriented Policing: Crime-specific Problems, Critical Issues and Making POP Work*. Washington DC: Police Executive Research Forum.

Cornish, D. (1994) 'The Procedural Analysis of Offending and Its Relevance for Situational Prevention', in R. Clarke (ed.) *Crime Prevention Studies, III*. Monsey NY: Criminal Justice Press.

Cornish, D. and Clarke, R. (eds) (1986) *The Reasoning Criminal: Rational Choice Perspectives on Offending*. New York: Springer.

Cornish, D. and Clarke, R (2003) 'Opportunities, Precipitators and Criminal Decisions: A Reply to Wortley's Critique of Situational Crime Prevention', in M. Smith and D. Cornish (eds) *Theory and Practice on Situational Crime Prevention*. Crime Prevention Studies XVI. Monsey NY: Criminal Justice Press.

Crawford, A. (1997) *The Local Governance of Crime: Appeals to Community and Partnerships*. Oxford: Clarendon Press.

Crawford, A. (1998) *Crime Prevention and Community Safety*. London: Longman.

Crawford, A. (2003) 'The Pattern of Policing in the UK: Policing beyond the Police', in T. Newburn (ed.) *The Handbook of Policing*. Cullompton: Willan Publishing.

Crawford, A. and Jones, M. (1995) 'Community Crime Prevention: Some Reflections on the work of Pearson and Colleagues', *British Journal of Criminology*, 35: 17–33.

Crawford, A. and Lister, S. (2004) *A Study of Visible Security Patrols in Residential Areas*. York: Joseph Rowntree Foundation.

Davies, H. T. O., Nutley, S. M. and Smith, P. C. (eds) (2000) *What Works? Evidence-based Policy and Practice in Public Services*. Bristol: Policy Press.

Davies, H. and Nutley, S. (2002) *Evidence Based Policy and Practice: Moving from Rhetoric to Reality*. Research Unit for Research Utilisation Discussion Paper 2. St Andrews: University of St Andrews.

De Paris, R. (1997) 'Situational Leadership: Problem Solving Leadership for Problem Solving Policing', *Police Chief*, 64: 74–86.

De Paris, R. (1998) 'Organisational Leadership and Change Management', *Police Chief*, 65: 68–76.

Eck, J. (2001) 'Improving problem analysis'. Problem Oriented Crime and Disorder Partnership conference, 5–7 September.

Eck, J. (2002) 'Learning from Experience in Problem-oriented Policing and Situational Crime Prevention: The Positive Functions of Weak Evaluations and the Negative Functions of Strong Ones', in N. Tilley (ed.) *Evaluation for Crime Prevention*. Crime Prevention Studies, XIV. Monsey NY: Criminal Justice Press.

Eck, J. (2003) 'Police Problems: The Complexity of Problem Theory, Research and Evaluation', in J. Knuttson (ed.) *Problem-oriented Policing: From Innovation to Mainstream* Crime Prevention Studies, XV. Monsey NY: Criminal Justice Press and Cullompton: Willan Publishing.

Eck, J. (2005) 'Evaluation for Lesson Learning', in N. Tilley (ed.) *Handbook of Crime Prevention and Community Safety*. Cullompton: Willan Publishing.

Eck, J. and Clarke, R. (2003) 'Classifying Common Police Problems: A Routine Activity Approach', in M. Smith and D. Cornish (eds) *Theory and Practice on Situational Crime Prevention.* Crime Prevention Studies XVI. Monsey NY: Criminal Justice Press.

Eck, J. and Maguire, E. (2000) 'Have Changes in Policing Reduced Violent Crime? An Assessment of the Evidence', in A. Blumstein and J. Wallman (eds) *The Crime Drop in America*. Cambridge: Cambridge University Press.

Eck, J. and Rosenbaum, D. (1994) 'The New Police Order: Effectiveness, Equity and Efficiency', in D. Rosenbaum (ed.) *Community Policing: Testing its Promises* Newbury Park CA: Sage Publications.

Eck, J. and Spelman, W. (1987) *Solving Problems: Problem Oriented Policing in Newport News*. Washington DC: Police Executive Research Forum.

Edmonton Police Service (1996) *Community Policing in Edmonton*, fourth edition. Edmonton Alta: Community and Organisational Support Section, Edmonton Police Service.

Ekblom, P. (1994) 'Proximal Circumstances: A Mechanism-based Classification of Crime Prevention', in R. Clarke (ed.) *Crime Prevention Studies, II*, Monsey NY: Criminal Justice Press.

Ekblom, P. (1997) 'Gearing up against Crime: A Dynamic Framework to Help Designers Keep up with the Adaptive Criminal in a Changing World', *International Journal of Risk, Security and Crime Prevention*, 214: 249–65.

Ekblom, P. (2002a) 'From the Source to the Mainstream is Uphill: The Challenge of Transferring Knowledge of Crime Prevention through Replication, Innovation and Anticipation', in N. Tilley (ed.) *Analysis for Crime Prevention*. Crime Prevention Studies. Vol 13. Monsey NY: Criminal Justice Press. Cullompton: Willan Publishing.

Ekblom, P. (2002b) 'Towards a European Knowledge Base'. Paper on 5Is presented at EU Crime Prevention Network conference on Exchange of Good Practices, Aalborg, Denmark, October. Available at www.crimprev. dk/eucpn/docs/EUCPN-AalborgReport200210.doc

Ekblom, P. (2003) *5Is: A Practical Tool for Transfer and Sharing of Crime Prevention Knowledge – Introduction and Illustrative Guide*, www.crimereduction.gov. uk/learningzone/5isintro.htm

Ekblom, P. and Tilley, N. (2000) 'Going Equipped: Criminology, Situational Crime Prevention and the Resourceful Offender', *British Journal of Criminology*, 40 (3): 376–98.

Farrell, G., Chenery, S. and Pease, K. (2000) *Consolidating Police Crackdowns: Findings from an Anti-burglary Project*. Police Research Series Paper 113. London: Home Office.

Farrell, G., Edmunds, A., Hobbs, L. and Laycock, G. (2000) *RV Snapshot: UK Policing and Repeat Victimisation*. Crime Reduction Research Series Paper 5. London: Home Office.

Farrington, D. (1997) 'Evaluating a Community Crime Prevention Program', *Evaluation*, 3: 157–73.

Farrington, D. (1998) 'Evaluating Communities that Care: Realistic Scientific Considerations', *Evaluation*, 4: 204–10.

Felson, M. (1987) 'Routine Activities and Crime Prevention in the Developing Metropolis', *Criminology*, 25: 911–31.

Felson, M. (2002) *Crime and Everyday Life*. London: Sage Publications.

Fielding, N. (1994) 'The Organisational and Occupational Troubles of Community', *Policing and Society*, 4 (4): 305–22.

Fielding, N. (1995) *Community Policing*. Oxford: Clarendon Press.

Forrest, S., Myhill, A. and Tilley, N. (2005) *Practical Lessons for Involving the Community in Crime and Disorder Problem-solving*. Development and Practice Report 43. London: Home Office.

Forrester, D., Chatterton, M., and Pease, K. with the assistance of Robin Brown (1988) *The Kirkholt Burglary Prevention Project, Rochdale*. Crime Prevention Unit Paper 13. London: Home Office.

Forrester, D., Frenz, S., O'Connell, M. and Pease, K. (1990) *The Kirkholt Burglary Prevention Project: Phase II*. Crime Prevention Unit Paper 23. London: Home Office.

Foster, J. (2002) 'People Pieces: The Neglected but Essential Elements of Community Crime Prevention', in G. and A. Edwards (eds) *Crime Control and Community: The New Politics of Public Safety*. Cullompton: Willan Publishing.

Garland, D. (1996) 'The Limits of the Sovereign State: Strategies of Crime Control in Contemporary Society', *British Journal of Sociology*, 36 (4): 445–71.

Gilling, D. (1996) 'Problems with the Problem Oriented Approach', in R. Homel (ed.) *The Politics and Practice of Situational Crime Prevention*, Crime Prevention Studies V. Monsey NY: Criminal Justice Press and Cullompton: Willan Publishing.

Gilling, D. (2005) 'Partnership and Crime Prevention', in N. Tilley (ed.) *The Handbook of Crime Prevention and Community Safety*. Cullompton: Willan Publishing.

Goldblatt, P. and Lewis, C. (eds) (1998) *Reducing Offending: An Assessment of Research Evidence on Ways of Dealing with Offending Behaviour*. Home Office Research Study 187. London: Home Office.

Goldstein, H. (1977) *Policing a Free Society*. Cambridge MA: Ballinger.

Goldstein, H. (1979) 'Improving Policing: a Problem-oriented Approach', *Crime and Delinquency*, April, 236–58.

Goldstein, H. (1990) *Problem-oriented Policing*. New York: McGraw-Hill.

Goldstein, H. (1997) 'The Pattern of Emerging Tactics for Shifting Ownership of Prevention Strategies in the Current Wave of Change in Policing: Their Implications for both Environmental Criminology and the Police'. Paper presented at the sixth Annual Seminar on Environmental Criminology and Crime Analysis, National Police Academy, Oslo.

Goldstein, H. (2003) 'On Further Developing Problem-oriented Policing: The Most Critical Need, the Major Developments and a Proposal', in J. Knutsson (ed.) *Crime Prevention Studies, XV*. Monsey NY: Criminal Justice Press and Cullompton: Willan Publishing.

Goldstein, H. and Susmilch, C. (1981) *The Problem-oriented Approach to Improving the Police Service: A Description of the Project and an Elaboration of the Concept*, vol. 1 of the Project on Development of a Problem-oriented Approach to Improving the Police Service. Madison WI: University of Madison Law School (photocopy).

Goldstein, J. (1960) 'Police Discretion Not to Invoke the Criminal Process Low Visibility Decisions', *Administration of Justice*, 69: 543–94.

Green, J. (1981) 'Organisational Change in Law Enforcement', *Journal of Criminal Justice*, 9: 79–91.

Green, J. (1998) 'The Importance of Place in the Control of Crime', in T. Shelley and A. Grant (eds) *Problem Oriented Policing: Crime-specific Problems, Critical Issues and Making POP Work*. Washington DC: Police Executive Research Forum.

Green, J., Bergman, W. and McLaughlin, E. (1994) 'Implementing Community Policing: Cultural and Structural Change in Police Organisation', in D. Rosenbaum (ed.) *The Challenge of Community Policing*. London: Sage Publications.

Green Mazerolle, L. and Terrill, W. (1997) 'Problem-oriented Policing in Public Housing: Identifying the Distribution of Problem Places', *Policing: An International Journal of Police Strategies and Management*, 20 (2): 235–55.

Grimshaw, P., Harvey, L. and Pease, K. (1989) 'Crime Prevention Delivery: the Work of Police Crime Prevention Officers', in R. Morgan and D. Smith (eds) *Coming to Terms with Policing*. London: Routledge.

Hakim, S. and Rengert, G. (1981) *Crime Spillover*. Beverley Hills CA: Sage Publications.

Hanmer, J. (2003) 'Mainstreaming Solutions to Major Problems: Reducing Repeat Domestic Violence, in West Yorkshire', in K. Bullock and N. Tilley (eds) *Crime Reduction and Problem Oriented Policing*. Cullompton: Willan Publishing.

Hanmer, J., Griffiths, S. and Jerwood, D. (1999) *Arresting Evidence: Domestic Violence and Repeat Victimisation*. Policing Research Series Paper 104. Home Office: London.

Harper, G., Williamson, I., See, L. and Clarke, G. (2002) *Family Origins: Developing Groups of Crime and Disorder Reduction Partnerships and Basic Command Units for Comparative Purposes*. Online Report 07/02. London: Home Office.

Harper, G., Williamson, I., See, L., Emmerson, K. and Clarke, G. (2001) *Family Ties: Developing Basic Command Unit Families for Comparative Purposes*. Home Office Briefing Note 04/01. London: Home Office.

Harris, C., Hale, C. and Uglow, S. (2003) 'Theory into Practice: Implementing a Market Reduction Approach to Property Crime', in K. Bullock and N. Tilley (eds) *Crime Reduction and Problem Oriented Policing*. Cullompton: Willan Publishing.

Her Majesty's Inspectorate of Constabulary (1998) *Beating Crime*. London: Home Office.

Her Majesty's Inspectorate of Constabulary (2000) *Calling Time on Crime*. London: Home Office.

Her Majesty's Inspectorate of Constabulary (2003) *Streets Ahead: A Joint Inspection of the Street Crime Initiative*. London: Home Office.

Hester, R. (2000) *Crime and Disorder Partnerships: Voluntary and Community Sector Involvement*. Home Office Briefing Note 10/00. London: Home Office.

Hill, N. (1986) *Pre-payment Meters: A Target for Burglary*. Crime Prevention Unit Paper 6. London: Home Office.

Hirschfield, A. (2005) 'Analysis for Intervention', in N. Tilley (ed.) *The Handbook of Crime Prevention and Community Safety*. Cullompton: Willan Publishing.

Hirschfield, A. and Bowers, K. (2000) 'Targeting Resources for Crime Prevention', in S. Ballintyne., K. Pease. and V. McLaren (eds) *Secure Foundations: Key Issues in Crime Prevention, Crime Reduction and Community Safety*. London: IPPR.

Hoare, M., Stewart, G. and Purcell, C. (1984) *The Problem Oriented Approach: Four Pilot Studies*. Metropolitan Police Management Services Department Report No. 30/84. London: Metropolitan Police Service.

Hobbs, L. (2004) The Tilley Award for Excellence in Problem-oriented Policing: Update on Winning Projects 1999–2003. Home Office (unpublished).

Holdaway, S. (1983) *Inside the British Police*. Oxford: Blackwell.

Home Office, Department of Education and Science, Department of Environment, Department of Health and Social Security and the Welsh Office (1984) *Crime Prevention*. Circular 8/1984 London: Home Office.

Home Office, Department of Education and Science, Department of the Environment, Department of Health, Department of Social Security, Department of Trade and Industry, Department of Transport and the Welsh Office (1990) *Crime Prevention: The Success of the Partnership Approach*. Home Office Circular 44/1990. London: Home Office.

Home Office (1990) *Partnerships in Crime Prevention*. London: Home Office.

Home Office (1991) *Safer Communities: The Local Delivery of Crime Prevention through the Partnership Approach*. London: Home Office.

Home Office (1993) *A Practical Guide to Crime Prevention for Local Partnerships*. London: Home Office.

Home Office (1998) *The Crime and Disorder Act*. London: HMSO

Home Office (2004a) *National Policing Plan, 2005–2008: Safer, Stronger Communities*. London: Home Office.

Home Office (2004b) White Paper 2004, *Building Communities, Beating Crime: A Better Police Service for the 21st Century.* London: Home Office.

Home Office (2005) *Your Police, Your Community, Our Commitment.* London: Home Office.

Home Office (2006a) *Review of the Partnership Provisions of the Crime and Disorder Act 1998: A Report of Findings*. London: Home Office.

Home Office (2006b) *Police and Justice Bill*. London: Home Office.

Homel, P., Nutley, S., Webb., B. and Tilley, N. (2004) *Investing to Deliver: Reviewing the Implementation of the UK Crime Reduction Programme*. Home Office Research Study 281. London: Home Office.

Homel, R. (1988) *Policing and Punishing the Drinking Driver: A Study of General and Specific Deterrence*. New York: Springer.

Homel, R. (1990) 'Random Breath Testing and Random Stopping Programs in Australia', in R. J. Wilson and R. E. Mann (eds) *Drinking and Driving: Advances in Research and Prevention.* New York: Guilford Press.

Homel, R., Hauritz., M., McIlwain, G., Wortley, R. and Carvolth, R. (1997) 'Preventing Drunkenness and Violence around Nightclubs in a Tourist Resort', in R. Clarke (ed.) *Situational Crime Prevention: Successful Case Studies*, second edition. New York: Harrow & Heston.

Hope, T. (1985) *Implementing Crime Prevention Measures*. Home Office Research Series 86. London: Home Office.

Hope, T. (1988) 'Community Crime Prevention', in T. Hope. and M. Shaw (eds) *Communities and Crime Reduction*. London: HMSO.

Hope, T. (1994) 'Problem-oriented Policing and Drug Market Locations: Three Case Studies', in R. Clarke (ed.) *Crime Prevention Studies*, II. Monsey NY: Criminal Justice Press and Cullompton: Willan Publishing.

Hope, T. (2004) 'Pretend it Works: Evidence and Governance in the Evaluation of the Reducing Burglary Initiative', *Criminal Justice*, 4: 287–308.

Hope, T. and Murphy, J. (1983) 'Problems of Implementing Crime Prevention: The Experience of a Demonstration Project', *Howard Journal*, 22: 38–50.

Hough, M. and Mayhew, P. (1985) *Taking Account of Crime: Findings from the 1984 British Crime Survey*. Home Office Research Study No. 85. London: HMSO.

Hough, M. (2004) 'Modernisation, Scientific Rationalism and the Crime Reduction Programme', *Criminal Justice* 4: 239–53.

Hough, M. and Tilley, N. (1998a) *Getting the Grease to the Squeak*. Crime Detection and Prevention Series 85. London: Home Office.

Hough, M. and Tilley, N. (1998b) *Auditing Crime and Disorder: Guidance for Local Partnerships*. Crime Detection and Prevention Series 91. London: Home Office.

Houghton, G. (1992) *Car Theft in England and Wales: The Home Office Car Theft Index*. Crime Prevention Unit Paper 33. London: Home Office.

Hughes, G. and Edwards, A. (2005) 'Crime Prevention in Context', in N. Tilley (ed.) *Handbook of Crime Prevention and Community Safety*. Cullompton: Willan Publishing.

Innes, M. (2004a) 'Signal Crimes and Signal Disorders: Notes on Deviance and Communicative Action', *British Journal of Sociology*, 55: 335–55.

Innes, M. (2004b) 'Reinventing Tradition? Reassurance, Neighbourhood Security and Policing', *Criminal Justice*, 4: 151–71.

Innes, M. (2005) 'What's Your Problem? Signal Crimes and Citizen-focused Policing', *Criminology and Public Policy*, 4: 187–200.

Irving, B., Bird, C., Hibberd, B. and Willmore, J. (1989) *Neighbourhood Policing: The Natural History of a Policing Experiment*. London: Police Foundation.

Irving, B., Bourne, D. and Collins J. (2001) *Crime Tracking: Developing a Community Safety Intelligence System for the West Ham and Plaistow New Deal Programme*. London: Police Foundation.

Irving, B. and Dixon, B. (2002) *Hotspotting*. London: Police Foundation.

John, T. and Maguire, M. (2003) 'Rolling out the National Intelligence Model: Key Challenges', in K. Bullock and N. Tilley (eds) *Crime Reduction and Problem Oriented Policing*. Cullompton: Willan Publishing.

John, T. and Maguire, M., with the assistance of Quinn, A., Rix, A. and Raybould, S. (2004a) *The National Intelligence Model: Early Implementation in Three Police Force Areas*. Working Paper Series Paper 50. Cardiff: University of Cardiff.

John, T. and Maguire, M. (2004b) *The National Intelligence Model: Key Lessons from Early Research*. Online Research Paper 30/04. London: Home Office.

Johnson, L. (1992) *The Rebirth of Private Policing*. London: Routledge.

Johnson, S. D. and Bowers, K. J. (2004) 'The Burglary as Clue to the Future: the Beginnings of Prospective Hot-spotting', *European Journal of Criminology*, 1 (2): 237–55.

Jones, B. (2003) 'Doing Problem Solving across Borders in Low Crime Areas', in K. Bullock and N. Tilley (eds) *Crime Reduction and Problem-oriented Policing.* Cullompton: Willan Publishing.

Jones, B. and Tilley, N. (2004) *The Impact of High Visibility Patrols on Personal Robbery.* Findings 201. London: Home Office.

Kansas City Police Department (1974) *Directed Patrol: A Concept in Community-specific, Crime-specific, and Service-specific Policing.* Kansas City MO: Kansas City Police Department.

Kansas City Police Department (1980) *Response Time Analysis* II – Part One, *Crime Analysis.* Washington DC: US Government Printing Office.

Kelling, G. (2005) 'Community Crime Control: Activating Formal and Informal Social Control', in N. Tilley (ed.) *Handbook of Crime Prevention and Community Safety.* Cullompton: Willan Publishing.

Kelling, G. and Coles, C. (1996) *Fixing Broken Windows.* New York: Free Press.

Kelling, G., Pate, T., Dieckman, D. and Brown, C. (1974) *The Kansas City Preventative Patrol Experiment.* Washington DC: Police Foundation.

Kirby, K. and Reed, D. (2004) *Developing a Problem-oriented Organisation.* London: Association of Chief Police Officers.

Kirby, S. (no date) *The Implementation of Problem Oriented Policing in Lancashire* (unpublished manuscript).

Kirwin, S. and Bibi, N. (2006*) Police Service Strength England and Wales, 30 September 2006.* Home Office Statistical Bulletin 01/06. London: Home Office.

Kock, B. (1998) *The Politics of Crime Prevention.* Aldershot: Ashgate.

Knutsson, J. (2003) (ed.) *Problem-oriented Policing: From Innovation to Mainstream.* Crime Prevention Studies, XV. Monsey NY: Criminal Justice Press and Cullompton: Willan Publishing.

Lamm Weisel, D. (2003) 'The Sequence of Analysis in Solving Problems', in J. Knutsson (ed.) *Problem-oriented Policing: From Innovation to Mainstream.* Crime Prevention Studies, XV. Monsey NY: Criminal Justice Press.

Lancashire Police Authority (2004) *Annual Policing Plan 2004-2005.* Preston: Lancashire Police Authority.

Laycock, G. (2005) 'Deciding What to Do', in N. Tilley (ed.) *Handbook of Crime Prevention and Community Safety.* Cullompton: Willan Publishing.

Laycock, G. and Webb, B. (2003) 'Conclusion: The Role of the Centre', in K. Bullock and N. Tilley (eds) *Crime Reduction and Problem-Oriented Policing.* Cullompton: Willan Publishing.

Leigh, A., Mundy, G. and Tuffin, R. (1999) *Best Value Policing: Making Preparations.* Police Research Series 116. London: Home Office.

Leigh, A., Read, T. and Tilley, N. (1996) *Problem-oriented Policing: Brit POP.* Crime Prevention and Detection 75. London: Home Office.

Leigh, A., Read, T. and Tilley, N. (1998) *Brit Pop II: Problem-oriented Policing in Practice.* Police Research Series 93. London: Home Office.

Liddle, M. and Gelsthope, L. (1994a) *Interagency Crime Prevention: Organising Local Delivery*. Crime Prevention and Detection Unit Paper 52. London: Home Office.

Liddle, M. and Gelsthorpe, L. (1994b) *Crime Prevention and Interagency Co-operation*. Crime Prevention Unit Paper 53. London: Home Office.

Maguire, M. (1998) 'Problem Oriented Policing, Intelligence Led Policing and Partnership', *Criminal Justice Matters*, 32: 21–2.

Maguire, M. (2004) 'The Crime Reduction Programme in England and Wales: Reflections on the Vision and the Reality', *Criminal Justice*, 4: 213–37.

Maguire, M. and John, T. (1995) *Intelligence Surveillance and Informants: Integrated Approaches*. Crime Detection and Prevention Series 64. London: Home Office.

Maguire, M. and Nettleton, H. (2003) *Tackling Alcohol Related Violence*. Home Office Research Series 265. London: Home Office.

Mcpherson, I. and Kirby, S. (2004) *Integrating the National Intelligence Model with a Problem Solving Approach*. London: Association of Chief Police Officers.

Macpherson, W. (1999) *The Stephen Lawrence Inquiry: Report of an Inquiry by Sir William Macpherson of Cluny*. Command Paper 4262–1. London: HMSO.

Merton, R. (1968) *Social Theory and Social Structure*. New York: Free Press.

Metcalf, B. (2001) 'The Strategic Integration of Problem-oriented Policing and Performance Management: A Viable Partnership?' *Policing and Society*, 11: 209–34.

Morgan, R. (1995) *Making Consultation Work: A Handbook for Those Involved in Police Community Consultation Arrangements*. London: Police Foundation.

Morgan, R. and Maggs, C. (1984) *Following Scarman: A Survey of Formal Police/Community Consultation Arrangements in Provincial Authorities in England and Wales*. Bath: University of Bath.

Morgan, R. and Maggs, C. (1985) *Setting the PACE: Police Community Consultation Arrangements in England and Wales*. Social Policy Paper 4. Bath: University of Bath.

Morris, P. and Heal, K. (1981) *Crime Control and the Police*. Home Office Research Study 67. London: Home Office.

Moss, K. and Pease, K. 1(999) 'Crime and Disorder Act 1998, Section 17: A Wolf in Sheep's Clothing', *Crime Prevention and Community Safety*, 1 (4): 15–19.

National Audit Office (2004) *Reducing Crime: The Home Office Working with Crime and Disorder Reduction Partnerships*. London: National Audit Office.

National Centre for Policing Excellence (2005) *Practice Advice on Professionalising the Business of Neighbourhood Policing*. Bramshill: CENTREX.

National Criminal Intelligence Service (NCIS) (2000) *The National Intelligence Model*. London : NCIS.

National Institute of Justice (2001) *Reducing Gun Violence: The Boston Gun Project Operation Ceasefire*. Washington DC: National Institute of Justice.

Newburn, T. and Jones, T. (2001) *Widening Access: Improving Police Relationships with Hard to Reach Groups. Police Research Series* 138. London: Home Office.

Newburn, T. and Jones, T. (2002) *Consultation by Crime and Disorder Partnerships*. Home Office Briefing Note 148. London: Home Office.

Newman, G. and Clarke, R. (2003) *Superhighway Robbery*. Cullompton: Willan Publishing.

Norris, G. (1999) *POP: Putting Policy into Practice: Lancashire Police/POP Workshop and Questionnaire Analysis*. District Audit (unpublished).

Nutley, S., Walter, I. and Davies, H. (2002) *From Knowing to Doing: A Framework for Understanding the Evidence-into-Practice Agenda*. Research Unit for Research Utilisation Discussion Paper 1. St Andrews: University of St Andrews.

Nutley, S., Walter, I. and Davies, H. T. O. (2003) 'From Knowing to Doing: A Framework for Understanding the Evidence-into-Practice Agenda', *Evaluation*, 9: 125–48.

Pawson, R. (2006) *Evidence-based Policy: A Realist Perspective*. London: Sage Publications.

Pawson, R. and Tilley, N. (1994) 'What Works in Evaluation Research?' *British Journal of Criminology*, 34: 291–306.

Pawson, R. and Tilley, N. (1997) *Realistic Evaluation*. London: Sage Publications.

Pawson, R. and Tilley, N. (1998a) 'Caring Communities, Paradigm Polemics, Design Debates', *Evaluation*, 4: 73–90.

Pawson, R. and Tilley, N. (1998b) 'Cook-book Methods and Disastrous Recipes: A Rejoinder to Farrington', *Evaluation*, 4: 211–13.

Pearson, G., Blagg, H., Smith, D., Sampson, A. and Stubbs, P. (1992) 'Crime, Community and Conflict: The Multi-agency Approach', in D. Downes (ed.) *Unravelling Criminal Justice*. London: Macmillan.

Phillips, C., Considine, M. and Lewis, R. (2000) *A Review of Audits and Strategies Produced by Crime and Disorder Partnerships in 1999*. Home Office Briefing Note 8/00. London: Home Office.

Phillips, C., Jacobson, J., Prime, R., Carter, M. and Considine, M. (2002) *Crime and Disorder Reduction Partnerships: Round One Progress*. Police Research Paper 151. London: Home Office.

Pollard, C. (1996) 'Problems Solved', *Police Review*, 19: 19–20.

Poyner, B. (1986) 'A Model for Action', in K. Heal and G. Laycock (eds) *Situational Crime Prevention: From Theory into Practice*. London: HMSO.

Poyner, B. (2006) *Crime-free Housing in the Twenty-first Century*. London: UCL Jill Dando Institute of Crime Science.

Quinton, P. (2005) Approaches to Neighbourhood Policing: Summary Findings from Phase One of the Neighbourhood Policing Study (unpublished).

Ratcliffe, J. H. (2004) 'The Hotspot Matrix: A Framework for the Spatio-temporal Targeting of Crime Reduction', *Police Practice and Research*, 5 (1): 5–23.

Ratcliffe, J. and Chainey, S. (2005) *GIS and Crime Mapping*. London: Wiley.

Ratcliffe, J. and McCullagh, M. (2001) 'Chasing Ghosts? Police Perceptions of High Crime Areas', *British Journal of Criminology*, 41: 330–41.

Read, T. and Oldfield, D. (1995) *Local Crime Analysis*. Crime Detection and Prevention Series 65. London: Home Office.

Read, T., Tilley, N., White, J., Wilson, M. and Leigh, A. (1999) 'Repeat Calls for Service and Problem-oriented Policing', *Studies on Crime and Crime Prevention*, 8: 265–79.

Read, T. and Tilley, N. (2000) *Not Rocket Science? Problem Solving and Crime Reduction*. Crime Reduction Research Series 6. London: Home Office.

Reiner, R. (1992) *The Politics of the Police*. Hemel Hempstead: Harvester Wheatsheaf.

Reiner, R. (2000) *Politics of the Police*, third edition. Oxford: Oxford University Press.

Reppetto, T. (1976) 'Crime Prevention and the Displacement Phenomenon', *Crime and Delinqency* 22: 166–77.

Roman J. and Farrell, G. (2002) *Cost-benefit Analysis for Crime Prevention: Opportunity Costs, Routine Savings, and Crime Externalities*, Crime Prevention Studies 14. New York: Criminal Justice Press and Cullompton: Willan Publishing.

Ruess-Ianni, E. and Ianni, F. (1983) 'Street Cops and Management Cops: the Two Cultures of Policing', in M. Punch (ed.) *Control in the Police Organization*. Cambridge MA: MIT Press.

Sampson, A., Smith, D., Pearson, G., Blagg, H. and Stubbs, P. (1991) 'Gender Issues in Interagency Relations: Police, Probation and Social Services', in P. Abbott and C. Wallace (eds) *Gender, Power and Sexuality*. Basingstoke: Macmillan.

Sampson, A., Stubbs, P., Smith, D., Pearson, G. and Blagg, H. (1988) 'Crime, Localities and the Multi-agency Approach', *British Journal of Criminology* 28: 478–93.

Sampson, R. and Scott, M. (2000) *Tackling Crime and other Public-safety Problems: Case Studies in Problem-solving*. Washington DC: US Department of Justice, Office of Community-oriented Policing Services.

Sampson, R. J., Raudenbusch, S. W. and Earls, F. (1997) 'Neighborhoods and Violent Crime: A Multilevel Study of Collective Efficacy', *Science*, 277: 918–24.

Scarman, Lord (1981) *The Brixton Disorders, 10–12 April 1981*, Cmnd 8427. London: HMSO.

Scott, M. (2000) *Problem-oriented Policing: Reflections on the First Twenty Years*. Washington DC: Office of Community Oriented Policing Services, US Department of Justice.

Scott, M. (2005) 'Shifting and Sharing Police Responsibility to Address Public Safety Problems', in N. Tilley (ed.) *Handbook of Crime Prevention and Community Safety*. Cullompton: Willan Publishing.

Shapland, J., Wiles, P. and Wilcox, P. (1994) *Targeted Crime Reduction for Local Areas: Principles and Methods*. London: Home Office.

Sheldon, G., Hall, R., Carlton, M., Alvanides, S. and Mostratos, N. (2002) *Maintaining Basic Command Units and Crime and Disorder Partnership Families for Comparative Purposes*. Online Report 06/02. London: Home Office.

Sherman, L. (1990) 'Police Crackdowns: Initial and Residual Deterrence', in M. Tonry and N. Morris (eds) *Crime and Justice: A Review of Research*, XII. Chicago: University of Chicago Press.

Sherman, L. (1992) 'Attacking Crime: Police and Crime Control', in M. Tonry and N. Morris (eds) *Modern Policing, Crime and Justice: A Review of Research*, XV. Chicago: University of Chicago Press.

Sherman, L. and Eck, J. (2002) 'Policing for Crime Prevention', in L. Sherman, D. Farrington, B. Welsh and L. Mackenzie. (eds) *Evidence-based Crime Prevention*. London: Routledge.

Sherman, L., Gottfredson, D., MacKenzie, D., Eck, J., Reuter, P. and Bushway, S. (1998) *Preventing Crime: What Works, What Doesn't, What's Promising*. Report to US Congress prepared by the National Institute of Justice.

Skogan, W. (1988) 'Community Organizations and Crime', in M. Tonry and N. Morris (eds) *Crime and Justice: A Review of the Research*. Chicago: University of Chicago Press.

Skogan, W. and Hartnett, S. (1997) *Community Policing, Chicago Style*. New York: Oxford University Press.

Skogan, W., Harnett, S., DuBois, J., Comey, J., Kaiser, M. and Lovig, J. (2000) *Problem-oriented Policing in Practice: Implementing Community Policing in Chicago*. Washington DC: US Department of Justice.

Skogan, W., Harnett, S., DuBois, J., Comey, J., Twedt-Ball, K. and Gudell, E. (2000) *Public Involvement: Community Policing in Chicago*. Washington DC: US Department of Justice.

Skogan, W., Steiner, L., Benitez, C., Bennis, J., Borchers, S., DuBois, J., Gondocs, R., Hartnett, S., So Young, K. and Rosenbaum, S. (2004) *CAPS at Ten: Community Policing in Chicago*. Chicago: Illinois Criminal Justice Information Authority.

Sloan-Hewitt, M. and Kelling, G. (1997) 'Subway Graffiti in New York City: "Gettin' up" vs "Meanin' it and Cleanin' it"', in R. Clarke (ed.) *Situational Crime Prevention: Successful Case Studies*. New York: Harrow & Heston.

Smith, M. (2004) 'Routine Precautions used by Taxi-drivers: A Situational Crime Prevention Approach', paper presented at the American Society of Criminology meeting, Nashville TN.

Smith, M., Clarke, R. and Pease, K. (2002) 'Anticipatory Benefits in Crime Prevention', in N. Tilley (ed.) *Analysis for Crime Prevention*. Crime Prevention Studies 13. Monsey NY: Criminal Justice Press and Cullompton: Willan Publishing.

Solesbury, W. (2001) *Evidence Based Policy: Whence it Came and Where it's Going*. ESRC UK Centre for Evidence Based Policy and Practice Working Paper 1. London: ESRC UK Centre for Evidence Based Policy and Practice.

Stockdale, J. and Whitehead, C. (2003) 'Assessing Cost Effectiveness', in K. Bullock and N. Tilley (eds) *Crime Reduction and Problem Oriented Policing*. Cullompton: Willan Publishing.

Stockdale, J., Whitehead, C. and Gresham, P. (1999) *Applying Economic Evaluation to Policing Activity*. Police Research Series 103. London: Home Office.

Sutton, M. (1998) *Handling Stolen Goods: A Market Reduction Approach*. Home Office Research Study 178. London: Home Office.

Sutton, M. (2005) 'Complicity, Trading Dynamics and Prevalence in Stolen Goods Markets', in N. Tilley (ed.) *Handbook of Crime Prevention and Community Safety*. Cullompton: Willan Publishing.

Sutton, M., Schneider, J. and Hetherington, S. (2001) *Tackling Theft with the Market Reduction Approach*. Crime Reduction Research Series 8. London: Home Office.

Tilley, N. (1993) *After Kirkholt: Theory, Method and Results of Replication Evaluations*. Crime Prevention Unit Series 47. London: Home Office.

Tilley, N. (1999) 'The Relationship between Crime Prevention and Problem-oriented Policing', in C. Solé Brito and T. Allan (eds) *Problem-oriented Policing: Crime-specific Problems, Critical Issues and Making POP Work*, II. Washington DC: Police Executive Research Forum.

Tilley, N. (ed.) (2002a) *Analysis for Crime Prevention*. Crime Prevention Studies 13. Cullompton: Willan Publishing.

Tilley, N. (ed.) (2002b) *Evaluation for Crime Prevention*. Crime Prevention Studies 14, Cullompton: Willan Publishing.

Tilley, N. (2003a) *Problem-oriented Policing, Intelligence-led Policing and the National Intelligence Model*. London: UCL.

Tilley, N. (2003b) 'Community Policing, Problem-oriented Policing and Intelligence-led Policing', in T. Newburn (ed.) *Handbook of Policing*. Cullompton: Willan Publishing.

Tilley, N. (2004a) 'Applying Theory-driven Evaluation to the British Crime Reduction Programme: The Theories of the Programme and of its Evaluations', *Criminal Justice*, 4: 255–76.

Tilley, N. (2004b) 'Using Crackdowns Constructively in Crime Reduction', in R. Hopkins Burke (ed.) *Hard Cop, Soft Cop*. Cullompton: Willan Publishing.

Tilley, N. (2005a) 'Driving Down Crime at Motorway Service Areas', in M. Smith and N. Tilley (eds) *Crime Science: New Approaches to Preventing and Detecting Crime*. Cullompton: Willan Publishing.

Tilley, N. (2005b) 'Crime Prevention and System Design', in N. Tilley (ed.) *Handbook of Crime Prevention and Community Safety*. Cullompton: Willan Publishing.

Tilley, N. (2006) 'Knowing and Doing', in J. Knuttson and R. Clarke (eds) *Putting Theory to Work: Implementing Situational Crime Prevention and Problem-oriented Policing.* Crime Prevention Studies 20. Monsey NY: Criminal Justice Press and Cullompton: Willan Publishing.

Tilley, N. and Hopkins, M. (1998) *Business as Usual: An Evaluation of the Small Business Crime Initiative.* Police Research Series 91. London: Home Office.

Tilley, N. and Jones, B. (2004) *The Impact of High Visibility Patrol on Personal Robbery Hot Spots.* Research Findings 201. London: Home Office.

Tilley, N. and Laycock, G. (2002) *Working out What to Do: Evidence-based Crime Reduction.* Crime Reduction Research Series 11. London: Home Office.

Tilley, N., Pease, K., Hough, M. and Brown, R. (1999) *Burglary Prevention: Early Lessons from the Crime Reduction Programme.* Crime Reduction Research Series 1. London: Home Office.

Tilley, N., Smith, J., Finer. S., Erol, R., Charles, C. and Dobby, J. (2004) *Problem-solving Street Crime: Practical Lessons from the Street Crime Initiative.* London: Home Office.

Townsley, M., Homel, R. and Chaseling, J. (2003) 'Infectious Burglaries: A Test of the Near Repeat Hypothesis', *British Journal of Criminology*, 43: 615–33.

Townsley, M., Johnson., S. and Pease, K. (2002) 'Problem-orientation, Problem Solving and Organisational Change', in J. Knuttson (ed.) *Crime Prevention Studies* XV. Monsey NY: Criminal Justice Press and Cullompton: Willan Publishing.

Townsley, M. and Pease, K. (2002) 'How Efficiently can We Target Prolific Offenders?', *International Journal of Police Science and Management*, 4 (4): 323–31.

Townsley, M. and Pease, K. (2003) 'Two go Wild in Knowsley: Mainstreaming Evidence-led Crime Reduction', in K. Bullock and N. Tilley (eds) *Crime Reduction and Problem Oriented Policing.* Cullompton: Willan Publishing.

Tuffin, R., Morris, J. and Poole, A. (2006) *An Evaluation of the National Reassurance Policing Programme.* Home Office Research Study 296. London: Home Office.

Waddington, T. (1999) 'Police (Canteen) Subculture: An Appreciation', *British Journal of Criminology,* 39 (2): 286–309.

Walter, I., Nutley, S. and Davis, H. (2005) 'What Works to Promote Evidence-based Practice? A Cross-sector Review', *Evidence and Policy,* 1 (3): 335–63.

Walter, I., Nutley, S., Percy-Smith., J., McNeish., D. and Frost, S. (2004) *Improving the Use of Research in Social Care Practice.* Knowledge Review 7. Bristol: Policy Press and Social Care Institute for Excellence.

Weatheritt, M. (1986) *Innovations in Policing.* London: Croom Helm.

Webb, B. (2005) 'Preventing Vehicle Crime', in N. Tilley (ed.) *Handbook of Crime Prevention and Community Safety.* Cullompton: Willan Publishing.

Weick, K. E. (1984) 'Small Wins: Redefining the Scale of Social Problems', *American Psychologist,* 39 (1): 40–9.

Weisburg, W. (1994) 'Evaluating Community Policing: Role Tensions between Practitioners and Evaluators', in D. Rosenbaum (ed.) *The Challenge of Community Policing*. London: Sage Publications.

Weisburd, D., and Eck, J. (2004) 'What Can Police do to Reduce Crime, Disorder, and Fear?' *Annals of the American Academy of Political and Social Science*, 593: 42–65.

Wilkinson, D. and Rosenbaum, D. (1994) 'The Effects of Organisational Structure on Community Policing: A Comparison of Two Cities', in D. Rosenbaum (ed.) *The Challenge of Community Policing*. London: Sage Publications.

Wilson, C. (2000) *COP Knowledge: Police Power and Cultural Narrative in Twentieth Century America*. Chicago: University of Chicago Press.

Wilson, J. and Kelling, G. (1982) 'Broken Windows: The Police and Community Safety', *Atlantic Monthly*, March, 29–38.

Young, M. (1991) *An Inside Job: Policing and Police Culture in Britain*. Oxford: Clarendon Press.

Website references

http:/www.lancashire.police.uk/problemsolving.html, 2000
http/www.ncis.co.uk/nim.asp, 2003
www.lancashire.police.uk/problemsolving.html, 2000
http://www.crimereduction.gov.uk/toolkits
hhttp://www.popcenter.org

Index